Resources
Nolo.com

Legal Forms, Books, & Software
Hundreds of do-it-yourself products—all written in plain English, approved, and updated by our in-house legal editors.

Legal Articles
Get informed with thousands of free articles on everyday legal topics. Our articles are accurate, up to date, and reader friendly.

Find a Lawyer
Want to talk to a lawyer? Use Nolo to find a lawyer who can help you with your case.

 **The Trusted Name**
(but don't take our word for it)

"In Nolo you can trust."
THE NEW YORK TIMES

"Nolo is always there in a jam as the nation's premier publi.
of do-it-yourself legal books."
NEWSWEEK

"Nolo publications... guide people simply through the how,
when, where and why of the law."
THE WASHINGTON POST

"[Nolo's]... material is developed by experienced attorneys
have a knack for making complicated material accessible.
LIBRARY JOURNAL

"When it comes to self-help legal stuff, nobody does a bette
than Nolo..."
USA TODAY

"The most prominent U.S. publisher of self-help legal aia
TIME MAGAZINE

"Nolo is a pioneer in both consumer and business self-he
books and software."
LOS ANGELES TIMES

20th Edition

Legal Research

How to Find & Understand the Law

Attorney Cara O'Neill and Jessica Gillespie, M.S.L.I.S.

TWENTIETH EDITION	AUGUST 2024
Editor	CARA O'NEILL
Cover Design	SUSAN PUTNEY
Book Design	SUSAN PUTNEY
Proofreading	JOCELYN TRUITT
Index	RICHARD GENOVA
Printing	SHERIDAN

ISSN: 1539-4115 (print)
ISSN: 2377-7214 (online)
ISBN: 978-1-4133-3192-9 (pbk)
ISBN: 978-1-4133-3193-6 (ebook)

Please note

We know that accurate, plain-English legal information can help you solve many of your own legal problems. But this text is not a substitute for personalized advice from a knowledgeable lawyer. If you want the help of a trained professional—and we'll always point out situations in which we think that's a good idea—consult an attorney licensed to practice in your state.

MH Sub I, LLC dba Nolo, 909 N. Pacific Coast Hwy, 11th Fl, El Segundo, CA 90245

Acknowledgments

This book wouldn't be possible without the original author, Stephen R. Elias. Until his death in late 2011, Stephen R. Elias was a practicing attorney, president of the National Bankruptcy Law Project, and the author or coauthor of many Nolo books, including *Bankruptcy for Small Business Owners*, *Special Needs Trusts: Protect Your Child's Financial Future*, *How to File for Chapter 7 Bankruptcy*, and *Chapter 13 Bankruptcy*. Steve was also one of the original authors of Nolo's bestselling *WillMaker* software. He held a law degree from Hastings College of the Law and practiced in California, New York, and Vermont before joining Nolo in 1980.

Over the years, other wonderful people have also contributed to this book in different ways, particularly Susan Levinkind, an original coauthor, Alayna Schroeder, a subsequent author, and many of the researchers and editors of Nolo.

About the Authors

Cara O'Neill is a legal editor and writer at Nolo specializing in bankruptcy and small claims litigation. She has practiced law for more than 25 years in civil and criminal litigation, bankruptcy, and administrative law. Before joining Nolo, she served as an administrative law judge, took dozens of cases to jury verdict, appeared before the California appellate court, and taught undergraduate and graduate law courses. She earned her law degree in 1994 from the University of the Pacific, McGeorge School of Law, where she served as a law journal editor and graduated as a member of the Order of the Barristers—an honor society recognizing excellence in courtroom advocacy. Cara authors several Nolo book titles, including *How to File for Chapter 7 Bankruptcy*, *Chapter 13 Bankruptcy*, *The New Bankruptcy*, and *Everybody's Guide to Small Claims Court*. She coauthors *The Foreclosure Survival Guide*, *Solve Your Money Troubles*, and *Credit Repair*, and edits several more.

Jessica Gillespie is a legal editor and Nolo's Research Director. Jessica received a B.A. from the University of Virginia, an M.S. in Library and Information Science from Long Island University, an M.A. in U.S. History from North Carolina State University, and did doctoral work at the University of Tennessee. In addition to managing the Nolo Editorial team's research needs, she writes and edits articles on estate planning and personal injury and is a cocreator of many of Nolo's online legal forms, including those used in online LLC and corporation formation services. When Jessica began her legal research career in the library of a large law firm, she was given a copy of Nolo's *Legal Research* to get her bearings. With book in tow, she gained valuable hands-on experience in tracking down what we usually just call "the law." Now, more than 20 years later, she finds herself beyond honored to be coauthoring the very book that kickstarted her career, and, despite all that's changed in the world of legal research since the book was first published, she's confident that it still sets the standard for learning how to find and understand the law.

Table of Contents

Your Legal Research Companion

I f you're new to legal research, you might be apprehensive about finding, understanding, and applying the law. Whether you're in a law library or at a computer, it's common to feel like you'll never find what you need. After all, there are many different research resources and places to look.

Fortunately, legal research isn't as difficult as it might seem, and with the help of this book, you'll soon be finding the law that applies to your case. Not only will we help you navigate the legal research process, but we will also help you understand what you're looking at once you find it. For instance, here are some of the things this book covers:

- where to find legal resources
- how to phrase your legal "issue" or problem like a lawyer
- where to find legal resources like statutes, regulations, and cases
- when a "secondary source" can help with complicated legal principles, and
- how to ensure you're using current law.

Also, you can feel comfortable using this book to improve your legal research skills or when representing yourself in court. The techniques we explain are the same as those used by lawyers, law students, paralegals, and other legal professionals. When it comes to finding what you need, if it's out there, we'll help you locate it.

Understanding the Basics of the Law

Trying to research the law can be a daunting task. But it doesn't have to be complicated. Anyone can develop solid legal research skills and learn to find current, relevant law. Because a legal foundation starts with understanding how the law works, we cover the following topics in this initial chapter:

- what "the law" is
- the differences between case law, statutory law, and administrative law
- when state and federal law apply, and
- the structure of the courts.

Understanding these basics will help you quickly and efficiently find the answers needed to resolve private disputes, work with legal professionals, advance a career, and more.

What Is the Law?

Most of us don't spend much time thinking about what "the law" means. No one needs to see a written law to know that stealing or destroying someone else's property is a crime. And we know we can be held responsible by our legal system. So, the law doesn't play much of a part in our daily lives until we get a traffic ticket, are denied a government service, buy or sell a house, or dispute a bill. However, when a legal issue arises, knowing how to maneuver within the legal system is essential, and understanding where particular types of law come from can help pinpoint the law that applies to a specific problem. So that's where we'll start.

Sources of Law

You won't find the law in a single set of books. Instead, many different types of laws exist, with most published in their own multivolume sets. Here are the general categories you can expect to encounter:

- **The U.S. Constitution.** This high-level, comparatively short document explains how our legal system is structured. It outlines the responsibilities of the three branches of government and the federal government's power. The Constitution explicitly gives the remaining power—any power not retained by the federal government—to the states. The amendments guarantee citizens' fundamental rights that the government can't take, such as the right to speak freely against the government, practice religion, and own guns.
- **Federal statutes.** As explained below, Congress frequently passes new laws. These written laws or "statutes" are assigned a number and kept in code books in numerical order.
- **Federal cases.** Federal courts decide court lawsuits and publish the decisions (usually appellate decisions) when the decision clarifies how to interpret previous court rulings or federal statutes. How to apply case law or statutes to a factual situation isn't always clear or even anticipated. Comparing the facts in a published case to your situation or reading how a judge applied a statute helps predict how a judge might rule.
- **Federal administrative regulations.** The legislature can't write all the statutes needed to regulate society—there simply isn't enough time. Instead, the legislature shifts specific law-making authority to government agencies through an "enabling statute." For instance, the U.S. Congress created the Equal Employment Opportunity Commission, the Internal Revenue Service, and the Environmental Protection Agency. The agencies are responsible for issuing "regulations" using the authority granted by the enabling statute. Regulations are part of federal administrative law.

CAUTION
Sovereign Native American tribes have their own courts and laws. These essentially function outside the system we describe here and are beyond the scope of this book.

- **State constitutions.** Like the federal government, each state has a constitution that describes the state's legal structure.
- **State statutes.** Like Congress, the state legislature passes statutes. The state's statutory law is in code books or published online on the state legislature's website. While federal laws apply everywhere, these laws apply only within the state.
- **State cases.** State courts decide cases about state law. The written opinions appear in case law reporters according to date.
- **State administrative regulations.** State legislatures create agencies to regulate particular areas of law. The agencies write and enforce regulations (the state's administrative law).
- **Local ordinances.** Local governments pass ordinances that become municipal codes, police codes, building codes, planning codes, health codes, and so forth.

Your legal research will probably touch on only two or three of these legal sources in most cases. For example, suppose you want to sue your mechanic because your brakes failed after being worked on, and you were injured. In that case, you'd turn to state statutory and case law. You wouldn't need to look at the federal constitution or local ordinances. We'll explain more about these sources of law below.

TIP
You can skip the rest of the chapter and return later. Most people learn about an area of law by reading a "secondary source," a fancy term for a book that explains the law—not from cases and statutes. At least, not initially. The following chapters explain why secondary sources are more accessible and how to find them. If you understand state and federal constitutional law, statutory law, case law, and administrative law well enough, you can probably skim or skip the rest of this chapter unless you'd like to dive deeper into how each type of law comes about.

Constitutions

Both state constitutions and the federal constitution are the founding documents that form the basis of authority for all other forms of law—that is, they tell each government branch what power they have to create or veto new laws. As explained below, a constitution gives legislatures and judges the power to make law, but that law can't conflict with the mandates of the constitution.

Statutes: Legislative-Made Law

Most of us think of the law as the acts passed by our federal and state legislatures. We might understand, for example, that Congress has decided the income tax rate or that our state legislators have determined that it's illegal to discriminate against someone in the workplace based on sexual orientation.

A statute comes into being when the legislature passes a bill. The text is written down, given an identification number, and arranged in numerical order in a code book (or "codified"). Changes are also incorporated into the code books when the legislature amends existing statutes.

Both federal and state statutes are usually organized by subject matter. For example, the California Family Code includes divorce, legal separation, and child custody laws, and most state criminal laws will be in a Criminal or Penal Code. Business, Fish and Game, Education, Civil Procedure, Corporations, and Tax are other standard statutory code titles. This organizational system makes finding relevant materials much easier when it's time for legal research. We'll discuss how to use and understand statutes in greater detail in Chapter 5.

Common Law: Judicial Interpretation

While statutes are essential to our law, we don't always agree on what statutes or constitutions mean. We need courts to provide guidance and to explain how to apply them in particular situations. As a result, interpreting these laws is primarily a responsibility of our court system.

The law created in the judicial system is called "case law," and it's an essential part in our legal system. You'll know case law when you see it because the opinion will be lengthy and have a title at the top, such as "*Smith v. Smith.*" The case opinion will include the lawsuit's facts and the applicable statutory or case law. The opinion will also have the court's decision and reasoning. Judicial opinions form what is known as "common law" or "case law." It's a judge's view of what the statute or previous opinion means when applied to the case's particular facts.

For example, suppose a child custody statute says that a judge should consider the "best interests" of the child when deciding custody. However, the statute doesn't say whether living primarily with the mother or sharing equal time with both parents is in the child's best interests. A judge will look at case law to see how previous judges handled factual situations similar to the one before the judge. For instance, suppose case law says that parents should share time equally as long as neither parent can prove neglect. If there is no evidence of neglect, the judge will award 50/50 custody. The case law helped the judge determine what "best interests" meant before applying it to the facts involved in the current lawsuit.

Common law is developed over time as opinions build on one another (most jurisdictions require judges to follow the logic of certain earlier opinions—more below). So you won't find common law written down in one place, like a statute that sets forth a clear rule.

Also, not all opinions are published. When an opinion provides new legal guidance or a factual situation that hasn't been addressed before, the case is selected for publication in books called "reports" or "reporters." The reporters contain all the case opinions that must be followed as "law." Federal and state courts have separate sets of reporters that organize opinions, or "cases," by date.

Because common law is part of the law, judges must consider what judges before them have said on the same issue. In other words, court opinions serve as authority or "precedent" that other judges must consider when deciding similar cases. The reasoning in previous cases that a judge must follow is called "binding" authority.

But courts are arranged in a hierarchical system. Every judge isn't required to consider every other judge's opinion each time a similar issue comes up—just the opinions of the courts above them in the same jurisdiction. As a result, you'll need to know which judicial opinions to review when researching a legal issue. We'll explain how to do that in Chapter 7.

What If a Judge Was Wrong?

The system of judicial precedent works well when judges correctly interpret the law. But sometimes they don't. When that happens at the trial court stage, your recourse will be to file an appeal.

But what happens if you believe the law itself is wrong when arguing your case before the trial judge? For typical legal issues (anything other than a human rights violation, an issue likely beyond this book's scope), you won't get far arguing "the law is wrong." Don't expect a trial judge to deviate from the law. The argument will fall flat because the judge will expect you to prove the elements of the law with evidence, not ask the judge to disregard the law itself.

Judges respect a legal principle called *stare decisis*—Latin for "let the decision stand." Unless there is an excellent reason to depart from current law (and you shouldn't assume your issue is "the one" without consulting a lawyer), judges don't. Most lawyers will tell you they've never had a trial judge disregard current law. Instead, trial judges expect litigants seeking legal change to appeal the case to a higher court with the authority to do so.

Also, judges don't want a higher court to find that the judge misapplied the law and be "overturned" on appeal. To prevent this, judges will straightforwardly decide cases within the law. Rarely will a judge's ruling require the judge to justify a significant departure from precedent (a previous decision).

The takeaway is that you shouldn't expect a judge to diverge from the law. Instead, use evidence to prove you're legally entitled to your desired result. If the judge misapplies the law, you can use the appellate process to overturn the result.

However, if Congress disagrees with a court's decision, it can usually pass a new law that contradicts it. (This isn't true if the case interprets the Constitution because Congress's power to legislate can't conflict with the Constitution.) For example, Lily Ledbetter sued her employer, claiming that it had discriminated against her by paying her less than her male peers. But the Supreme Court held that she had filed her suit too late and upheld the trial court, which had thrown the case out. (*Ledbetter v. Goodyear Tire & Rubber*, 510 U.S. 618 (2007).) The Court decided Ledbetter hadn't met the legal requirement to bring her claim within 180 days because the decision to pay Ledbetter less had happened many years before. Ledbetter argued that each time she received a paycheck for less than her peers, it was a "continuing violation" of the law, so the 180 days started to run from when she received her last paycheck. Even though the Supreme Court disagreed with Ledbetter, Congress passed the Lily Ledbetter Fair Pay Act shortly thereafter, taking Ledbetter's side. Now, employees in Ledbetter's shoes have the benefit of the act. Without it, courts would be required to treat those employees the same way the Supreme Court treated Ledbetter.

Administrative Regulations

The federal government and many state governments have administrative agencies in specific law areas. Congress and state lawmakers create these agencies and give them the authority to adopt regulations to carry out certain laws with an enabling statute. For example, the U.S. Department of Labor oversees the wages and working conditions of the nation's workers.

The regulations written by an agency typically provide the process required for oversight. For example, every state's transportation or criminal code prohibits people from driving cars with a suspended license. However, the state Department of Public Safety or the Department of Motor Vehicles oversees the process for reinstating suspended privileges and drafts regulations explaining the process, as needed.

Local Ordinances

Some areas of the law aren't covered by state or federal law, or at least aren't covered completely. In that case, local bodies like city councils or county boards have the authority to regulate. You might have encountered local ordinances if you have needed a building permit or questioned zoning laws. Often, these ordinances are enforced and regulated by the bodies that create them. Also, there are options to resolve disputes that don't involve the court system. For example, appealing a decision by the local planning commission might require a hearing before the commission rather than going to court.

State vs. Federal Law

As discussed at the beginning of the chapter, the law comes from multiple sources, with state and federal law, local law, and administrative agencies creating and enforcing law in different legal areas. Because the primary sources of law you'll likely be working with are state and federal laws, understanding the differences is essential. We'll keep the explanation simple for this book's purposes.

The U.S. Constitution is the starting point of all law in the United States. It carves out areas the federal government controls exclusively without state intervention—for example, maritime law—and what the federal government can control if it decides. Finally, the Constitution gives states the power to legislate laws in any area not explicitly retained by the federal government.

The general principle is that certain areas—federal taxes, immigration, and bankruptcy, for example—are governed solely by federal law. The states can legislate statutes and create case law in areas the federal government doesn't regulate. Over the years, what falls within the federal government's control has resulted in much judicial interpretation, and currently, federal and state law touch most other legal areas to some extent. When a conflict exists, the Constitution's "Supremacy Clause" tells us that federal law governs state law.

Issues Covered by State Law

Each state has its own set of statutes, as well as common law or case law. For instance, most states' laws cover the following areas: child custody, conservatorships, contracts, corporations, crimes (in most cases), divorce, durable powers of attorney for health care and financial management, guardianships, landlord-tenant relationships, licensing (businesses and professions), living wills, motor vehicles, partnerships, paternity, personal injuries, probate, property taxation, real estate, trusts, wills, workers' compensation, and zoning. Except in rare cases (for example, the federal government regulates the disclosure of lead-based paint hazards in residential rentals), federal law won't address these issues.

Issues Covered by Federal Law

For most of our country's history, federal law was limited to court interpretations of the U.S. Constitution, the Bill of Rights, and topics Congress is authorized to address, such as commerce and immigration. But as courts have interpreted the Constitution to allow the federal government to regulate more areas, federal law might control a broad range of social welfare, health, and environmental issues.

Federal law generally controls areas like agriculture, bankruptcy, copyright, customs, food and drug regulation, immigration, interstate commerce, maritime activity, patent, Social Security, and trademark.

Issues Covered by Both State and Federal Law

A large number of legal areas now involve both state and federal law. Federal and state governments are concerned about environmental law, consumer protection, and the enforcement of child support statutes, and the Constitution doesn't limit who can do what.

This legislative power broadened because the Constitution authorized Congress to spend money for the general welfare. Programs offering federal funds to state governments usually require the state to meet conditions and contribute financially according to the applicable federal law.

When states participate in one of these programs, federal law typically gives some latitude in how the state implements the program, allowing states to put laws and regulations in place. With time, courts interpret these statutes and regulations, creating common or case law.

Areas covered by both state and federal law include consumer protection, criminal law, employment, environmental protection, health law, labor law, occupational safety, subsidized housing, taxes, transportation, unemployment insurance, veterans' benefits, and welfare law. If you have a problem affected by federal and state law, you might have to look to state and federal law resources to get a firm handle on the issue. We'll explain more about how to do that in Chapter 4.

The Court System

As explained above, when drafting opinions that interpret the law, judges are bound by other judges' opinions. However, judges don't have to follow every prior opinion when interpreting a statute. Courts are arranged by hierarchy, and judges are only required to follow the decisions of higher-ranking courts.

How Courts Are Structured

Both state and federal courts are structured similarly. If you wish to bring a lawsuit, you will usually file a suit in the trial court. However, the names of trial courts vary significantly between states. For instance, a state might call the trial court the "superior court," "municipal court," or, in New York, the "supreme court." The function of the lowest level trial court is to conduct everything up to and including a trial. Trial courts rarely issue opinions other courts must follow.

Above the trial court is the "appellate court." If you believe the decision obtained at the trial court level is wrong, you can appeal the decision (assuming you have proper grounds). In most instances, the appellate court's role isn't to start your trial over, hearing the evidence again. Instead, it will look at what the trial court did and decide whether it made any mistakes. If an appellate court issues an opinion that sheds new light on the law, it will be published and determined to be binding on the state's trial courts below.

The highest court is usually called the "Supreme Court." In states without an intermediate appellate court, appeals go straight to the Supreme Court of that state.

The Supreme Court is another appellate court that typically decides whether the court below it correctly interpreted the law and applied it to the facts—it doesn't rehear the entire case. If you disagree with the appellate court's decision, the Supreme Court is the court you appeal to. Also, most supreme courts decide which cases they will hear, with a few exceptions, like death penalty cases. If it refuses your case, the appellate court's ruling stands.

Most Cases Don't Go to Trial

Even though our court system is designed for a judge or jury to decide a case's outcome at trial, this isn't what happens in most disputes. Here are some common reasons why most cases are resolved before trial:

- **Charges are dropped.** In criminal cases, prosecutors might decide not to pursue the case for several reasons—the evidence is inadequate to support a conviction, new evidence changes the potential outcome, or the office has insufficient resources to deal with the case.
- **The parties reach an agreement.** In criminal cases, this is called a "plea bargain." The prosecutor and defendant might agree that the defendant will voluntarily plead guilty to a lesser crime with lesser penalties—for example, a misdemeanor theft charge instead of a felony. In civil suits, the parties might settle the case, perhaps with the defendant agreeing to pay something to the plaintiff, but less than was asked for.
- **The court might rule on a "dispositive motion."** To avoid wasting court time and resources, parties can ask the judge to issue a ruling or an order before the case goes to trial. Some of these rulings have the effect of ending the case, and those decisions can be appealed. We'll explain more about dispositive motions in Chapter 9.

Federal Courts

If you have a lawsuit that involves a federal issue or is otherwise within the court's jurisdiction—meaning it covers an area that federal courts are allowed to hear—you can file it in the federal trial court, called the U.S. District Court. You can't file your lawsuit in any district court, however. As we'll explain in Chapter 9, there are rules to prevent you from showing up at a Nebraska courthouse if you and the defendant both live in Oregon, and the incident that resulted in a lawsuit took place in Oregon. Every state has at least one district court, but often more, breaking the state into regions. District courts don't usually issue "published" opinions (opinions considered binding on other courts). However, other courts might take these decisions into account.

Above the district court is the appellate court, called the "circuit court" in the federal system. There are 13 circuits, divided by area of the country. Most circuits are numbered, except for the D.C. Circuit and the Federal Circuit. The First through Eleventh Circuits all cover specific parts of the United States, while the D.C. and Federal Circuits are based in Washington, D.C. The D.C. Circuit hears appeals from cases in the District of Columbia, while the Federal Circuit deals with nationwide claims based on particular areas of law, including international trade, government contracts, patents, trademarks, specific money claims against the U.S. government, federal personnel, and veterans' benefits.

The circuit courts' decisions are binding on all the district courts that are part of that circuit but not on other circuit courts or the district courts in those other circuits. For example, the Fifth Circuit includes Texas, Louisiana, and Mississippi. If the Fifth Circuit issues a ruling, it will bind all district courts in those three states; however, it won't be binding on the Eleventh Circuit. The Eleventh Circuit might consider it "persuasive," meaning it might find the logic compelling and consider it when drafting its own decisions. But it isn't bound to do so.

RESOURCE

Want to find the federal court where you live? Visit www.uscourts. gov/federal-court-finder/search to locate both the district and circuit courts.

At the very top of the hierarchy in the federal court system is the U.S. Supreme Court. Most of us have heard of the Supreme Court, and maybe even some of the significant cases that have come out of it, like *Roe v. Wade, Brown v. Board of Education*, and *Bush v. Gore*. The Supreme Court has nine members appointed for an unlimited term by the U.S. president. As appointees who don't have to worry about reelection, the Supreme Court is supposed to be less politically biased than the legislature or president.

Except for "appeals of right"—those situations in which parties have an automatic right to Supreme Court review—the Court chooses which cases it will hear. The Court will frequently select cases involving conflicting opinions in the circuit courts. So if the Ninth Circuit says it's okay to do something and the First Circuit says it isn't, the Supreme Court might issue a rule that will bind both. All federal courts must follow the Supreme Court's decision.

State Courts

Most state court systems follow a similar structure to the federal system. Usually, the only state court opinions published are those issued by appellate courts, including the state's supreme court.

It's important to recognize that state court opinions don't generally bind federal courts, and vice versa. This makes sense. For the most part, federal courts handle federal law issues, and state courts deal with state law issues. Neither judicial system tells the other how to interpret its laws.

But this gets tricky when state or federal court systems must interpret each other's laws. For example, when both state and federal issues are part of a single lawsuit. Let's say you believe your employer discrimi-nated against you based on race. You might file a lawsuit alleging that the employer violated federal and state antidiscrimination laws. But having two cases in two different courts with two judges wouldn't make sense. So you are permitted to bring both claims in one place.

If you choose state court, the state court will have to apply federal law to decide whether your rights under federal law have been violated. If there's an issue of federal law that the judge must interpret, the judge will turn to federal law to find the answer, not state law. In that case, the judge is bound by federal law.

Exceptions to the Overall Court Structure

Not every federal and state court system functions as described above. One state exception to this structure is the state small claims court (federal courts don't offer a small claims court system). In almost all states, litigants can file claims under a certain amount in small claims court. The small claims court process is more informal than a traditional trial court, which allows people to litigate lower-stakes matters without a lawyer. If you appeal a small claims court case, you'll likely present the appeal in the state trial court, and, acting as the appellate court, the trial court will hear the entire case like new. (This is called "*de novo* review.")

Federal courts also have exceptions to the basic structure. For instance, bankruptcy falls under federal law and is filed in federal court. A basic bankruptcy case is more of an application process unless a problem arises, with bankruptcy filers receiving a debt discharge after meeting qualification requirements. However, the federal bankruptcy court judge will decide various disputes through motion and trial proceedings, when necessary. We can't point out every exception to you, so you might have to research the procedure in the applicable court system. We'll explain how to do that in Chapter 2.

Finding Legal Resources

Understanding what the law is, how it's structured, and where to find it is just the beginning of learning how to conduct legal research. In this chapter, we discuss the many types of resources available to you. In future chapters, you'll learn how you'll use these resources to find answers to your specific legal questions.

Locating Legal Information

Traditionally, legal research has occurred in one place—a law library. However, the legal community has welcomed advances in research and technology for the most part, so that's no longer the case. Most lawyers research online using sophisticated databases that can quickly find cases and statutes. Although these programs vastly reduce the time needed for research, these options are costly and require a certain degree of skill, which can be a roadblock for self-represented litigants.

To help, courts often provide onsite self-help centers to assist family law litigants and provide information about filing a small claims court action without a lawyer's help. They recognize that many people have no choice but to represent themselves and need access to user-friendly resources. Undoubtedly, these valuable resources benefit self-represented litigants greatly.

Fortunately, other advances have also made it easier to represent oneself. Over the years, more publishers have provided legal information online at no cost. For instance, researchers can easily find instructions for forming a corporation or read the Supreme Court's latest opinion on a particular topic if they know where to look. Also, with the advancement of artificial intelligence (AI) and other technology, cheaper alternatives that are easier to use could be available soon. However, we aren't quite there. AI isn't sufficiently reliable yet, so learning and utilizing traditional legal research skills is still necessary.

Despite the convenience of general online research, its usefulness is still somewhat limited. For instance, while it's great for familiarizing yourself with new legal areas, it isn't the best approach when you need accurate legal results you can rely on in court. Because of this, we explain the pros and cons of the different research options available, and how to best utilize each of them.

Law Libraries

Law libraries remain an excellent resource for legal researchers. For one thing, they usually have a lot of legal books and resources that aren't available online without paying a high fee.

In a law library, you'll gain access to all the legal resources you could need, including the expensive online databases used by lawyers. Additionally, libraries come with another helpful resource you'll have trouble replicating online—librarians. When you're having difficulty finding a source or are confused about where to begin, a librarian can help.

Law School Libraries Have Useful Websites, Too

Many law school libraries have helpful websites. Here are a few examples:

Emory University School of Law (https://law.emory.edu). Under "Law Library," you'll find links to legal materials (select "Databases : Free" under the "Electronic Resources" heading).

Berkeley Law Library (www.law.berkeley.edu/law-library). Berkeley's law school website includes several databases and research guides by subject and directions for accessing them. Select "Law Library" from the top navbar, and then "Research."

D'Angelo Law Library (www.lib.uchicago.edu/law). The University of Chicago's law library website includes research guides on various legal topics. Visit the "U.S. Legal Research for Non-Lawyers" page at https://guides.lib.uchicago.edu/c.php?g=297959.

Texas State Law Library (www.sll.texas.gov). Although not a law school library, we include the Texas State Law Library because it has an extensive digital collection of legal reference materials, including many Nolo titles. However, you must reside in Texas to use the online library. Check your state for similar resources.

When you're ready to explore a law library, you can find one online or check your local phone book if one is available. A local law school will likely have a law library and possibly states, counties, and other government agencies. Call or look online to ensure the facility is open to the public, and plan to spend most of your time researching in the library. Most won't let you check out the resources.

Court Offices and Self-Help Centers

Another good resource for a lot of legal material is your local court. Many courts recognize that litigants representing themselves need help understanding the legal process. Some courts have self-help offices or offices staffed by attorneys or clerks who help litigants with forms, deadlines, and other procedural matters. These offices also often have pamphlets explaining how to resolve a legal issue in the court system. However, these attorneys or clerks don't represent you. They can't give you legal advice—only help you understand the court process.

Many courts also have extensive resources online. It should be relatively easy to find your court's website using a search engine like Google by typing [name of county] county courthouse. You might be able to find necessary forms, court rules (discussed further below), and information about how to file a lawsuit.

Online Research

Most legal researchers will spend a lot of time researching online, and it's a perfect launching point when getting started. For instance, if you're unfamiliar with a particular area, reading articles on attorneys' websites or Nolo.com will teach you enough to zero in on specific legal principles.

Also, as discussed above, many courts include thorough information on the court's website.

Of course, the more detailed information you need, the more costly it will be to obtain online. That's when using the free online resources available in law libraries is advantageous. Many offer the same pricey services used by lawyers at no cost. You'll find more about online research in "Looking for Legal Resources Online," below.

Primary Sources and Secondary Sources

Most people—lawyers included—don't jump right into reading the actual law. There's too much of it, it's hard to find, and it isn't always easy to understand. Instead, they start by reading an article, summary, or book that explains how a particular area of law works, like family law or personal injury. These resources are known as "secondary sources." The actual statute or case law you must follow is the "primary source."

Secondary sources explain common issues and tell the reader which laws apply. Once the reader understands how the overall area of law works, the researcher reads the actual law.

So, you can expect to use primary and secondary sources when researching. Again, primary sources are the law itself—for example, the statutes, cases, or regulations that list the elements for criminal battery or tell the federal government who is entitled to Social Security benefits. A secondary source is any resource that explains how a particular area of law works but isn't the law itself. For example, a secondary source would be an article, a treatise, or a summary about preparing a contract or choosing the best structure for your business.

Primary Sources

The law found in primary sources can take many different forms. They include cases, statutes, administrative regulations, local ordinances, state and federal constitutions, and more.

Why Use Primary Sources

Using primary sources is critical because courts must follow the law itself, not a secondary source. That's why even though primary sources are often more challenging to find and read than secondary sources, it isn't wise to rely solely on secondary sources. Laws can quickly change, and you won't always see these changes reflected in secondary sources. Looking at primary sources will give you the most up-to-date information.

Another reason to rely on primary sources is that you can find cases closer to your situation. When you read a factual pattern in a case that is similar to your facts, you'll gain more insight into the possible outcome of your lawsuit.

For example, assume your dog escaped from its dog run and bit a neighbor who was stealing sports equipment from your backyard. You'll want to know whether you are liable for the trespassing neighbor's injuries. You might find secondary sources explaining your liability when your dog bites someone and your responsibility to a trespasser injured on your property. But you might need to go to primary sources to find a case involving a dog biting a trespasser. Once found, you'll have a better idea about how a court might apply the law to the facts of your case.

Where to Find Primary Sources

The most popular way to access relevant primary material is through the law library or online. But be aware that the law changes. Legislatures pass new laws, courts overrule previous decisions by lower courts, and administrative regulations are amended or repealed. So once you find a primary source, you must ensure it is still "good law." We'll explain how to check a legal source's validity in Chapter 8.

When to Use Primary Sources

As we've explained, courts only consider and follow primary sources, not secondary sources (unless there isn't any law on the issue, which is rare). So, while using a secondary source to understand general concepts is a great strategy, reading the law it refers to is essential when putting together a document or argument with legal weight. You'll often find the legal citations you need in more authoritative secondary sources. In Chapters 5 through 7, we'll explain more about reading legal documents.

Secondary Sources

By now, you get the idea that primary sources are the laws themselves, and secondary sources include anything that interprets, explains, or discusses the law. Legal journals, online articles, and law blogs—even this book—would all be considered secondary sources.

The depth of treatment you get from any given secondary source can vary greatly. Some secondary sources are very detailed, law intensive, and helpful. Others might provide only a broad, general overview of a topic. Finding the appropriate secondary source will depend, in large part, on where you are in your research.

Initially, you might need only enough information to understand the particular area of law. However, as your research progresses, you might want to find secondary sources that explain your legal issue more precisely. You'll need the specifics to know what evidence you'll need to prove or defend your case.

When to Use Secondary Sources

Secondary sources are a logical place to start when you know nothing about your research topic. A secondary source can often explain the basic concepts you'll encounter in primary sources, making it easier to read them. It will also frequently cite primary sources, which can deepen, expand, and, most importantly, speed up the research process.

Secondary sources are also helpful when learning about divergent legal approaches. Many national secondary sources comprehensively review the law, including jurisdictional differences. Keep in mind, however, that if your legal issue involves the law of one particular state, you'll be better off using a state-specific secondary source.

Where to Find Secondary Sources

Secondary sources can be found in many locations, from websites to newspapers to books to legal texts available only in law libraries. For the most part, you should be able to find more general secondary sources online. However, when you want more legally accurate information (because, let's face it, anyone can publish anything online), you'll want to head to the library or use a fee-based online research service like those described later in this chapter.

Popular Secondary Sources

The usability and helpfulness of secondary sources can vary widely. The books and online articles published on Nolo.com span many legal topics, each explaining complicated legal issues using everyday language. We recommend visiting the website early in the legal research process.

Nolo's home pages are easy to navigate using keywords or topic categories. For example, suppose you want to find out about an immigration-related issue. You can type "immigration" in the search box or click "Immigration" under "Legal Articles." Often, these resources will be a good jumping-off point, giving you a foundation to help you understand more in-depth secondary sources and, eventually, the statutes or case law that apply to your specific legal problem.

Two highly regarded secondary sources found in the law library are legal encyclopedias *American Jurisprudence* ("*Am. Jur.*") and *American Law Reports* ("*A.L.R.*"). Regularly used by attorneys and laypeople, these encyclopedias provide readers with a broad understanding of particular legal areas, and because they're more legally technical than online articles, they're natural next steps. (More about *Am. Jur.* and *A.L.R.* in Chapter 4.)

Other popular secondary sources cover state law topics in detail. For example, in California, the well-known publisher B.E.Witkin has a series of state-specific volumes used by practicing lawyers regularly, such as *Summary of California Law* and *California Procedure.* These books provide greater detail than sources like *Am. Jur.* or *A.L.R.* Lawyers frequently use them because they include pertinent statutory and case law citations and detailed topic coverage.

Finally, the websites of local, state, and federal government agencies are great secondary resources. For instance, IRS.gov has many summary documents explaining the otherwise complicated federal tax code.

Looking for Legal Resources Online

Online research can be much more efficient than doing the same research in a legal library, but not always. Narrow, focused online searches can quickly get you reliable, comprehensive results if you can access a high-quality legal database. However, if you aren't familiar with the area of law and are relying on your ingenuity and Google, you can waste a lot of valuable time.

Giving yourself a set amount of time for online research is a good idea. If you don't find what you're looking for within a reasonable period, consider taking a trip to the law library and asking the librarian to show you where to find resources about your issue. (Chapters 4, 5, and 6 discuss online research techniques in detail.)

CAUTION

Use generative AI tools with caution. If you're considering using an AI-powered search tool for legal research, you should know that the technology is in development and legal results are unreliable. We aren't including tools such as ChatGPT and other AI offerings in our current recommendations because, while the answers can appear impressive, they're sometimes misleading or wrong. Unlike traditional legal resources, the answers aren't reviewed for accuracy or attributed to a credible legal authority.

Court Websites

As explained, court websites are great resources for finding information on various legal topics, and sometimes, they provide access to primary sources like court opinions and rules. For example, visit the U.S. Supreme Court site (www.supremecourt.gov). You can look up opinions written by the Court, briefs submitted by parties, and transcripts of oral arguments made by lawyers on each side of a case. (Briefs are the legal documents explaining a position each side submits to the judge before a hearing to persuade the judge to decide a particular way.) Many other courts have similar accessibility. At www.uscourts.gov, you can find links to all the courts in the federal system using the "Court Finder" box (or go to www. uscourts.gov/federal-court-finder/search).

CAUTION

Not every opinion you find is good law. Remember, lower courts' decisions can be overruled by higher ones, and the decisions of any court can be undone by a new law created by the legislature (as long as it doesn't conflict with the state or federal constitution). In Chapter 8, we'll explain how you determine whether a source is still "good law." Remember that just because you find something online doesn't mean it holds legal weight.

The Public Access to Court Electronic Records system (PACER, www.pacer.uscourts.gov) is another excellent resource for court documents. It allows users to obtain information from various filed (not published) federal cases. PACER compiles the legal documents filed in federal lawsuits in multiple courts nationwide. For a small fee, users can download and read these documents. If you are curious about a particular case or want to know if someone has been sued in federal court before, PACER is a helpful resource.

Local state court websites also provide helpful information. Many have online filing services that allow members of the public to access legal documents like briefs and judicial opinions. Some states even compile resources in one location on the website for the entire state court system. For example, visit the New York State Unified Court System's website (www.nycourts.gov). Under the "e-Courts" heading, click "Decisions" to access rulings and opinions from the state's trial and appellate courts (you'll select the court from the menu on the left).

Legislative Websites

Many state legislatures have online information about bills under consideration or that have recently passed. You can also use these websites to find an entire set of your state's statutes. Google the state name and "state legislature" to find your site.

At the federal level, many legal researchers find GovInfo (www. govinfo.gov) particularly helpful. It's the U.S. Government Publishing Office's website, and you'll find information from all three branches of government, including Congressional legislation, the *U.S. Code*, and the *Code of Federal Regulations (C.F.R.)*.

Administrative Websites

Many state and federal administrative agencies also have websites that allow you to access legal information. For example, you can access Connecticut labor laws, regulations, and more at the Connecticut Department of Labor's website. Go to www.ctdol.state.ct.us and search for "Laws and Regulations." Similarly, on the Colorado Department of Labor and Employment website (https://cdle.colorado.gov), you can access Colorado labor laws and regulations, as well as explanatory information (click "Labor Law & Stats" from the top navbar).

Alternatively, you can go directly to the relevant administrative agency's website if you know the legal area you want to learn more about. All federal regulations are on the GovInfo website (www.govinfo.gov). Under "A to Z," click "C," and scroll down to find "Code of Federal Regulations."

Legal Research Websites

In addition to using search engines and general government sites to get legal information, you can find a lot of this information on websites specifically designed for legal research. We'll cover some of the most common ones here. Note that the skills you learn using search engines will help you here—many sites have search functions that use the same or similar logic.

LexisNexis and Westlaw

In online legal research, two players dominate—LexisNexis (www. lexisnexis.com) and Westlaw (https://legal.thomsonreuters.com/en/ westlaw)—with both sites providing access to almost any legal resource imaginable. Each site features a user-friendly platform with natural-language search capabilities that retrieve results across all databases.

While LexisNexis and Westlaw are cost-effective for large law firms with many lawyers, they're rarely realistic for the average researcher. Luckily, you'll most likely be able to gain access to Westlaw or LexisNexis in a law library. We suggest you check with nearby law libraries to determine whether they offer free public access. If not, consider some of the alternatives mentioned below.

 TIP

Have access to LexisNexis or Westlaw, and need help figuring out how to use the system? Both websites have online tutorials available—we suggest you take advantage of them before getting started, particularly if you're being charged for use. (Clicking around at random can quickly get very expensive.) Understanding what you're doing will make your research process much more efficient. Most researchers use the natural language feature, but becoming proficient at Boolean searching can also help—both databases use similar and even more complex search tools.

Nolo

As we've already mentioned, Nolo's website (www.nolo.com) has many articles and books on various legal subjects. Additionally, it provides state-by-state information on various legal topics, such as the employment discrimination laws of each state, making a will, getting a divorce, or filing a small claims court action. Nolo has other resources, such as a directory of lawyers and various legal forms.

 TIP
Try the promising legal research approach of Bloomberg Law. Bloomberg's new approach streamlines the research process by providing practical, updated guidance in certain legal areas. Bloomberg also provides traditional case law and statutory search options. Although a subscription will be too expensive for most individuals, your local law library might offer free access. A subscription isn't required for select legal news articles and podcasts (https://news.bloomberglaw.com) or legal webinars (https://learning.bloomberglaw.com), some of which offer continuing education credits.

The Law Library of Congress

The Law Library of Congress (www.loc.gov/law) is responsible for housing the Library of Congress's legal materials. In addition to its massive physical collections (more than 2.9 million items, covering domestic, foreign, and international law), the library provides free online access to many state and federal primary and secondary sources. For example, you can find links to the official versions of each state's statutes and regulations on the library's website. Librarians have also compiled research guides on many legal topics—animal law and environmental law are just two examples—to help you get started. Select "Researcher Resources" from the home page to begin exploring these materials.

The Caselaw Access Project (CAP)

An initiative of Harvard Law School, the Caselaw Access Project (https://case.law) provides free access to official book-published federal and state cases from 1658 on. You can browse cases by jurisdiction; perform full-text searches; or search by citation, date, author, or court. CAP adds new decisions to the database at the beginning of each year.

CourtListener

CourtListener (www.courtlistener.com) offers helpful resources, such as decisions from more than 2,000 state and federal courts. Also, each case in CourtListener includes "Authorities" and "Cited By" sections with links to related cases. The site allows you to schedule email alerts for developments involving a specific case or legal issue and supports Boolean operators.

Justia

Justia's BlawgSearch page (https://blawgsearch.justia.com) allows you to look for legal blogs across many legal categories. It's an excellent resource for lawyers, professors, and other legal professionals who use blogs to keep updated about legal developments.

Cheat Sheet of Legal Websites (Primary Sources)

- **The Federal Judiciary** (www.uscourts.gov) has searchable cases and other legal information from federal courts nationwide.
- **Public Access to Court Electronic Records (PACER)** (https://pacer.uscourts.gov) allows access to documents filed in federal cases nationwide for a reasonable fee.
- **GovInfo** (www.govinfo.gov) lists federal statutes and the Code of Federal Regulations (C.F.R.).
- **The Law Library of Congress** (www.loc.gov/law) includes links to the official versions of state and federal statutes, regulations, and more.
- **The Caselaw Access Project** (https://case.law) provides free access to official book-published state and federal cases.
- **CourtListener** (www.courtlistener.com) has free decisions from more than 2,000 U.S. courts.
- **Justia** (https://blawgsearch.justia.com) allows users to find blogs on various legal topics.
- **Fastcase** (www.fastcase.com) offers a lower-cost system for accessing federal and state case law and statutes, including subsequent history, and a library of secondary sources.

Fastcase

A lower-cost online option for primary and secondary law materials is Fastcase (www.fastcase.com), which includes federal and state cases, statutes, court rules, regulations, legal treatises, and more. Fastcase offers a variety of methods for sorting search results, and a feature that indicates the most-cited case among your search results. Free trial and subscription options are available, and some law libraries have subscriptions that allow researchers to access Fastcase from anywhere at no cost.

Using Search Engines

Today, many researchers turn to search engines to find relevant information on almost any topic, including legal issues. However, sometimes search engines produce more results than you need, and the results aren't always relevant or reliable. But as discussed previously, they're an excellent place to start when first becoming familiar with a topic or when you want to find out if a resource is available online to avoid a trip to the law library.

Though many search engines are available, the most popular is Google. Even though you're likely very familiar with Google, here are some basics to remember.

- **News searches.** You can search for news by going to http://news.google.com and entering your query into the search box. You'll find options to refine your search on the left of the screen.
- **News alerts.** If you want to stay abreast of a specific news subject, try "Google Alerts." You will receive daily (or "as it happens") emails based on your choice of query or topic. Go to www.google.com/alerts and type in the search terms.
- **Google Scholar.** If you'd like to limit your Google search to scholarly papers, try Google Scholar. Go to http://scholar.google.com and enter your search term. You'll get results limited to materials such as peer-reviewed journal articles, theses, books, abstracts, and technical reports from the broad research areas available online. If you're doing legal research online, you can limit your search to decisions issued by appellate courts at the state and federal levels.

Select the "Case law" radio button from the Google Scholar start page, located just below the main search query field. You can limit your search to particular jurisdictions and courts using the "Select courts" feature.

- **Advanced searches.** When performing searches with Google Scholar, you'll get better results using the advanced search feature. Select the three parallel horizontal lines on the top left of the screen (the "hamburger menu" icon). Choose "advanced search." You'll be given the option of searching for particular words and phrases. You can also search by author, publishing date, or a range of dates.

- **Quick definitions.** Type "define: (keyword)" to get the definition of a word or phrase fast. For instance, if you type "define: liability" in the search box, you'll learn that it's the "state of being responsible for something, especially by the law." Nolo's online dictionary (www.nolo.com/dictionary) will also have plain-English definitions of legal terms.

- **Searching books.** If you want to search through the complete text of millions of books to research your legal topic, you can use Google Books (http://books.google.com). Enter your search term into the query field, and you'll see a list of books containing that term or phrase. You can access a free preview of many of the books in Google's database. For some titles, the entire text is available for free online.

- **More tips.** If you'd like additional search tips, try www.tricksntech. com/best-google-search-secrets.

Boolean Searching

You want to maximize relevant results when using online research. Often, typing a few keywords, a phrase or two, or even an entire question into the search box will quickly pull up useful resources. Natural language searching has significantly improved with time, and most people have developed sophisticated search skills.

Boolean Searching Cheat Sheet

Function	Google/Bing Yahoo! Operator	Google/Bing Yahoo! Example	Westlaw Operator	Westlaw Example	Results include documents or websites which contain:
And	[space]	slip fall	&	slip & fall	both these words (slip and fall)
Or	OR	slip OR fall	[space]	slip fall	either of the words (slip or fall)
Phrase	" "	"slip and fall"	" "	"slip and fall"	the exact phrase (slip and fall)
But not	-	slip -fall	%	slip %fall	excludes the word that appears after the operator % (slip but not fall)
Near			/n	slip /4 fall	both words within a specified proximity to one another (slip within four words of fall)
Word extender			!	slip!	words that begin with the letters before the ! (including slips, slippery, slipped, and so forth)
Same sentence			/s	slip /s fall	words appear in the same sentence (slip and fall accidents happen)
Same paragraph			/p	Slip /p fall	words appear in the same paragraph (slip and fall accidents happen)

Other Common Boolean Operators

Function	Operator	Example	Results include documents or websites which contain:
Wildcard	*	F*ll or slip*	words in which one letter can differ (fall, fell, full, and fill; slips, slippery, and slipped)
Sets of conditions	( )	(slip /2 fall) and (wet or rain)	meet all the parenthetical conditions (slip within two words of fall, but must also contain either the word wet or the word rain)

However, if you're inundated with more results than you can handle, consider using a technique professional legal researchers employ to narrow results. The best way to do this is in a search engine that uses Boolean logic, as many do. Boolean logic can "read" specific words and symbols (called "operators") to help narrow our searches.

Before we explain the various Boolean search terms, we want to mention that with some search engines, you can benefit from Boolean logic without having to master the use of the various terms. On Google, for example, you'll find advanced search options.

See "Boolean Searching Cheat Sheet," below, for common Google operators. This list is incomplete and more sophisticated operators exist (search for "Boolean operators"). If you use a professional legal research site such as Westlaw, more choices will likely be available.

Here are the common Boolean operators and their functions:

- **Adj.** This operator means the words must be adjacent to each other and in the order entered. For instance, the search query *dangerous adj beauty* means that the documents must have the phrase "dangerous beauty" to end up on the search results list. Alternatively, some engines allow you to use adj/[number] in connection with a specification of how close the keywords should be. For instance, *adj/3* means the keywords must appear in the order they are entered in the search engine query box and not be separated by more than three words. Note that not all search engines recognize the *adj* operator. For example, it won't work if you try using it in a Google search, but it's useful in Bing.

- **And.** If you use the word *and* in your search, it will not be indexed like other words. That is, the search engine will not look for documents that use the word *and*. (Several other common terms, like *the* and *or*, also don't get indexed.) Instead, *and* acts as an operator. The search engine will only look for documents containing the words that appear on either side of the *and*. For example, the query *box and container* produces every document with both the word box and the word container. That is, it doesn't produce any document that doesn't have both words. Some search engines use the *+* symbol instead of the word *and* for the same purpose. As shown on the "Boolean Searching Cheat Sheet," below, Google simply gives you a text box in which to type all of your "and" words; in Westlaw, you must enter an ampersand (&) or the word *and*—if you simply list the two words, separated by a space, Westlaw will look for documents containing one term *or* the other.

- **But not.** To exclude words you don't want, you can use the operator *but not*. For example, if you are searching a legal issue in criminal law and want to exclude results that deal with civil law, you can use the *but not* operator to eliminate the word "plaintiff," which describes a party to a civil lawsuit, but not a criminal case. Just keep in mind that when using this operator, you might also exclude some relevant results, so use it carefully.

- **Or.** Using *or* instead of *and* means the engine will search for documents containing either word. You might use *or* when you're unsure which word will likely be used to describe something relevant to your search. For example, *box or container* will produce documents with either or both words. Remember, if you use Westlaw, simply separating the terms by a space will result in an "or" search.

- **Parentheses.** You can use parentheses to do a search with multiple operators. As you might recall from algebra, when you use parentheses, you tell the search engine to start the search with what's inside, then complete it with everything else. For example (*break or enter*) and (*house or car*) will look for these four combinations: break and house, break and car, enter and house, and enter and car. (Of course, it might also include results with all of those words or phrases.)

- **Quotes.** Putting quotation marks around a set of words tells the engine to search only for the exact phrase. These searches are sometimes referred to as "string searches," because they involve a specific string of alphanumeric characters (letters and numbers).

- **/[number].** This indicates words should appear in spatial proximity to each other, such as in the same sentence or paragraph. For example, using /3 means the keywords (the words on each side of /3) must not be separated by more than three words. Some search engines instead use the operator *w* (standing for within—w/3, for example. And if you're using Westlaw, /s indicates that two words must appear in the same sentence, and /p indicates that the words must appear within the same paragraph.

- *. For most search engines, the asterisk serves as a wildcard and word (or part of a word) extender. By placing an asterisk in a word in a query or at the end of a string of letters (known as the root), you are asking the search engine to search for any word that includes the letters preceding or surrounding the asterisk. For instance, if we used the word *driver* in a search request dealing with a driver's license suspension, the search engine would only look for that exact word. It would skip over documents that use closely related words such as drivers, driver's, drivers', or driving. But suppose the document with one of these variations on driver is the one you want. Typing in *drive** instead of *driver* will catch them. You can also place the asterisk within a word in a query to capture all search term variations. For example, you could type *wom*n*, and the engine will search for and return results that include the words woman and women. (Note that Westlaw, for example, uses a variation of the wildcard/word extender operator. In Westlaw, the asterisk serves as a wild-card, while the exclamation point is the word extender.)

As we've noted, not every search engine will use the same set of Boolean operators. However, the more operators available to you, the more you can narrow your search because you can combine them into one query. For example, assume you are looking for information about the circumstances that might trigger driver's license suspensions. You would want documents that contain both "license" and "suspend." But each of these documents should also have either the word "driver" or the word "operator" (since you don't know which of these two words will be used in the materials you are searching for). A query that could accomplish this search would look like this: *license and suspend and (driver or operator).*

Boolean searching takes some practice. And even once you're good at it, you might find that as you do your research, new phrases come up that you'll need to include or exclude from your query. We encourage you to remain flexible and to keep modifying your queries as you go.

Identifying Your Legal Issue

Now that you understand the basics of law and have a sense of where to find legal resources, you're ready to go, right? Well, almost. To maximize the effectiveness of your research, we suggest you first spend some time preparing. In this chapter, we'll help you do that by covering how to approach your research, frame your legal research question, and locate the resources you need.

How to Approach Your Research

Before beginning your legal research, you'll find it helpful to break the project down into small, manageable steps. You'll stay organized and focused by thinking about your legal research this way:

Step 1: What is my legal research question?

Step 2: Is this a civil issue, a criminal issue, or both?

Step 3: What area of the law should I focus on?

Step 4: What resources will help me solve my problem?

The first step asks you to identify the question you intend to research. For example, let's say you're a landlord and want to determine whether you can evict a tenant who hasn't paid rent in more than three months. You'd write that down as your legal research question.

In the second step, you'll determine whether it's a civil or criminal case. For instance, the landlord example involves a civil issue. You're not trying to throw the tenant in jail. You're just trying to get him out of the apartment.

Next, you'll determine the area of law you're researching. It's probably a matter of state law because, as explained in Chapter 1, state law deals with landlord-tenant issues almost exclusively.

The final step involves finding resources that will help you solve your landlord-tenant problem. You'll likely start with secondary sources, like online articles and court-provided resources, before moving on to statutes and other types of primary law.

Once you complete the steps, the information you find should help you plan the best course of action. For instance, in our landlord example, you might write a letter to the tenant, file an eviction suit, or pursue another measure. The rest of this chapter further explains how to approach each of the four steps effectively.

Step 1: Determine Your Legal Research Question

Before you research your question, you'll want a clear idea of the problem you must solve. Lawyers call this "framing your issue." Understanding why you are researching the problem and what you hope to accomplish is crucial. If you begin without taking this step, you'll soon see it's easy to become overwhelmed, and you'll likely find too much information to know where to start. Framing your legal research question helps avoid this problem.

Why Are You Conducting Legal Research?

You can start framing your legal research question by considering why you are conducting the research. Are you going to be filing a lawsuit? Before meeting with a lawyer, do you want to educate yourself on the law?

Another way to approach this step is by writing down your goal. For example, you might write, "My goal is to file a lawsuit against the furniture store that refused to repair the hardwood floor they damaged when delivering my dresser." Or, you might write, "My goal is to learn about estate planning strategies to avoid probate and minimize expenses."

Ultimately, your goal will be the primary issue you want to solve. However, you won't want to stop there. You'll want to identify the questions you'll need answered to achieve the goal.

What Questions Do You Need Answered?

With your goal clearly in place, you'll be ready to create a list of questions you need answered to help you reach it. For instance, you'll need to know the law that governs your problem and the procedures you must follow to resolve it. So, you'll likely have legal and procedural questions. Here are examples of questions that would probably be raised by the goals identified in the previous section.

"My goal is to file a lawsuit against the furniture store that refused to repair the hardwood floor they damaged when delivering my dresser."

- What law did the furniture store break by damaging the floor?
- Where do I file a lawsuit against the furniture store?
- When do I have to file my lawsuit?
- What kind of paperwork do I need to submit to file my lawsuit?

As you can see, these are fundamental questions. Once you begin researching, they might lead to new questions, too. For example, once you figure out what law the furniture store broke in damaging the floor (most likely, they acted negligently), you might need to research how to calculate or prove the amount the store must pay to compensate you for the damage caused by the mishap. Or, once you determine which court you must file your lawsuit in, you might explore whether the court has standard forms you can use.

"My goal is to learn about estate planning strategies to avoid probate and minimize expenses."

- What is a living trust?
- Do I need a living trust if I have a will?
- What other options avoid probate and help minimize hassle and expense?

In this instance, you might ask your attorney these questions when you meet instead of researching the answers personally.

Ultimately, your list of questions is an important starting point for conducting legal research, keeping you focused on your task.

Step 2: Is the Issue Civil or Criminal?

Understanding whether your issue is a matter of civil or criminal law is the first broad step in narrowing your research. You might know the answer to this question very clearly. For example, if you or someone you know has been arrested, you know that your issue involves criminal law. Or if you want to sue a creditor, that is a civil matter. Below, we'll explain how you can tell the difference between civil and criminal cases when you aren't exactly sure.

The issue of whether a matter is civil or criminal also has two subparts. You need to figure out whether the matter is substantive, procedural, or both. Remember, it's a substantive question if you're asking about the law. Procedural questions involve the court process. You'll also need to determine whether it is an issue of state law, federal law, or both. We'll discuss those issues in further detail, too.

Criminal Law

Generally, criminal law is involved if a specific behavior is punishable by imprisonment in a jail or prison. Because crimes are considered "offenses against the people," charges are usually initiated in court by a government prosecutor.

If you are involved in a legal dispute with a nongovernmental individual or corporation, then the matter isn't criminal. If the government is involved, it's likely criminal, but the government is involved in civil matters, too.

Substantive Criminal Law

When researching criminal law, you'll want to understand the differences between substantive criminal law and criminal procedure. Substantive law tells us what constitutes a crime and its punishment. You'd research substantive criminal law if the district attorney accused you or someone else of a crime and you wanted to know what must be proven to find you guilty and the possible punishment.

For example, suppose you want to learn the differences between burglary and larceny. You'd research the law and find that burglary is the act of breaking and entering into the premises of another with the intent to commit a theft or felony. In contrast, larceny occurs when someone takes personal property rightfully in the possession of another, intending to steal it. You'd also find out how each crime is punished. Below is a list of common criminal substantive law categories.

Criminal Law Substantive Categories

Assault and battery	Juvenile offenses	Rape
Breaking and entering	Kidnapping	Robbery
Burglary	Larceny	Shoplifting
Conspiracy	Lewd and lascivious behavior	Smuggling
Disorderly conduct	Malicious mischief	Tax evasion
Drug and narcotics offenses	Marijuana cultivation	Trespass
Drunk driving	Murder	Weapons offenses

Criminal Procedure

Criminal procedure is the process the government must follow when bringing charges against someone. For example, criminal procedure involves the types of evidence that can be used in a criminal trial, when an accused must be brought to trial, when a person can be released on bail, and so on. You might research criminal procedure when you think the criminal justice system isn't treating you or someone else fairly. For example, if you were entitled to a hearing in a criminal case and didn't receive it, that would be an issue of criminal procedure. Below is a list of common criminal procedure categories.

Criminal Procedure Topics

Arraignments	Jury verdicts	Right to counsel
Arrests	*Miranda* warnings	Search and seizure
Confessions	Plea bargaining	Sentencing
Cross-examination	Pleas	Speedy trial
Extradition	Preliminary hearings	Suppression of evidence
Grand jury	Probation	Trials
Indictments	Probation reports	Witnesses
Jury selection		

When researching criminal law, it's common to have questions of both substance and procedure. For example, let's say the police searched your house without a warrant and found an illegal drug inside. You might want to research whether police had the right to search your home—an issue of procedure. If you wanted to know whether the law requires the government to prove that the drug belonged to you, not your roommate, it would be a matter of substantive law.

Civil Law

In most cases, when you sue or someone other than the district attorney sues you, it's a matter of civil law. In a civil action, the punishment doesn't involve imprisonment except in rare circumstances—for example, when a court orders a parent to pay child support and the parent willfully refuses. The person bringing the lawsuit, "the plaintiff," wants money "damages" or an order to change behavior.

Requesting money to compensate for an injury or property damage is easy to understand. But the plaintiff can also ask the court to order the defendant to do or not do something, which can involve, for example, prohibiting an ex-employee from using a company's trade secrets, or requiring a person to honor a previous agreement.

Like criminal law, research questions about civil law can be either substantive or procedural. Substantive law is the law that establishes our rights and duties, and it is either written down in statutes or case law. For example, when someone is involved in a car accident that damages property and injures people, a set of principles called "tort law" determines who is liable and for what. It might not appear in a statute anywhere because tort law has developed in case law over many years. The case law establishes the principles that hold a negligent driver liable for damages.

Most legal research involves substantive civil law. It's a broad category encompassing many legal areas, so you'll want to know the specific area you're working in before beginning your research. To help, we've provided an extensive list of civil law categories and definitions in "Determine the Area of Law You're Researching," below.

Pro Tip: Use Jury Instructions

Using jury instructions as a basis for legal research is an excellent shortcut for lawyers and nonlawyers. It is often the quickest way to do legal research. Jury instructions explain the law simply so people without legal training understand it. Judges read jury instructions to jurors at the end of a trial.

You'll find your state's civil and criminal jury instructions published in books and online. As a researcher, you'd start by skimming the table of contents to find the cause of action you intend to pursue. The jury instruction for the cause of action will list the "elements" you must prove and the statute and case citations that apply—essentially doing the bulk of your research.

Criminal and civil jury instructions exist, and many states post jury instructions online. We discuss how the court uses jury instructions at trial in further detail and how to find them online in Chapter 9.

Civil Procedure

Civil procedure is the set of rules that govern how our civil justice system works. It controls such matters as which courts have the authority to decide different kinds of lawsuits, what types of documents must be filed, when they need to be filed, who can be sued, what kinds of proof can be offered in court, and how to appeal to a higher court.

For example, suppose you want to sue the local grocery store because you slipped and fell in the store. In that case, civil procedure will tell you where you can file your lawsuit (you won't be able to sue from Arkansas if you and the grocery store are in Michigan, for example), the documents you must file to start the lawsuit (perhaps a simple "complaint" that explains why you're suing and what you're asking for), when you must file these documents (such as within two years after the incident occurred), and how you must notify the grocer that you've filed the lawsuit (usually, by having an unrelated third party personally hand over the paperwork).

Each state has its own set of procedural rules. However, many states have procedures similar to the Federal Rules of Civil Procedure used in all federal courts. We will explain more about how to find and use the rules that apply to you in Chapter 5.

Step 3: Determine the Area of Law You're Researching

Once you know whether the area of law you're researching is criminal or civil, you'll want to determine the particular area of law and whether state or federal law applies. Many of the secondary sources discussed in Chapter 2 are organized by subject area or might be limited to a particular legal area. For example, suppose you want to determine the legal requirements for incorporating in your state. In that case, you will look at sources under "corporations" or "incorporating," but also search indexes for "business entity" law or formation.

Common Civil Law Categories

Narrowing the area of law will be slightly more manageable if you are dealing with a relatively common criminal or civil issue and know whether state or federal law applies. However, less common civil matters, especially those heard in specialized courts, can be more challenging to identify. The list below contains some common substantive civil law categories used in many research indexes, and knowing where your subject falls will narrow your search.

- **Administrative law** refers to the law regulating government agencies.
- **Bankruptcy law** covers the process that allows a debtor to liquidate assets and be relieved of further liability. It is governed primarily by federal law but also involves state property law.
- **Business and professions law** deals with restrictions and license requirements placed on professionals (for example, doctors and lawyers) and other occupational groups.

- **Business entity law** relates to creating business entities such as corporations, limited liability companies, and partnerships. It can involve both state and federal laws on how these entities can operate and be taxed, the rights of shareholders, the rights and duties of the entity's officers and directors, and more.
- **Civil rights law** means provisions that protect individuals from discrimination based on legally recognized characteristics such as race, sex, ethnic or national background, or color.
- **Commercial law** involves federal and state regulations governing commercial relations between borrowers and lenders, banks and customers, wholesalers and retailers, and mortgagors and mortgagees. Generally, this area involves disputes between businesspeople rather than between businesspeople and consumers.
- **Constitutional law** covers issues applying to federal or state constitutions.
- **Consumer law** deals with the requirements governing transactions between a seller and a buyer of personal property in a commercial setting (for example, when individuals buy products like cars or furniture from a retailer).
- **Contract law** covers written and oral agreements and what to do if they are broken or canceled.
- **Corporation law** deals with forming corporations and operational requirements.
- **Creditor/debtor law** covers how debts are collected and handled (for example, whether they can be canceled or reorganized in bankruptcy).
- **Cyberlaw** refers to how the internet affects copyright, trademark, libel, pornography, contracts, privacy, and court jurisdiction.
- **Education law** covers the rights of students and the restrictions placed on them by schools.
- **Elder law** encompasses issues relevant to seniors, such as Social Security, Medicare, Medicaid, nursing homes, and special needs trusts.
- **Employment law** means the rights of employees and the restrictions placed on employers by law.

- **Energy law** includes the state and federal laws governing the production, distribution, and utilization of energy sources like coal, natural gas, oil, electrical and nuclear power, and alternative energy.
- **Environmental law** deals with regulating the use of the environment by businesses, governments, and individuals. For example, this includes issues of air and water pollution, the environmental impact of new construction projects, the preservation of endangered species, and similar matters. It is an area regulated by both federal and state governments.
- **Estate planning** is the process people use to arrange for the distribution of their property after they die; it includes such subjects as living trusts, joint tenancies, wills, testamentary trusts, and gifts.
- **Evidence law** covers items and testimony litigants can introduce as proof in a trial or hearing.
- **Family law, divorce law, and domestic relations law** all refer to matters relating to families and family division, such as marriage, divorce, child support, and child custody.
- **Health law** relates to issues affecting health, like the type and quality of medical treatment received from hospitals or occupational health and safety requirements.
- **Housing law** covers programs involving government subsidies for construction and rental assistance, public housing, state and local planning requirements related to the type and amount of housing in different areas, and discriminatory housing practices.
- **Insurance law** encompasses problems arising under any kind of insurance contract, such as life insurance, car insurance, homeowners' insurance, fire insurance, and disability insurance.
- **Intellectual property law** is the laws and procedures governing copyrights, trademarks, trade secrets, and patents.
- **Juvenile law** deals with juvenile delinquency (when a child commits a criminal act) or dependency (when a child is abused or neglected and becomes a ward of the state).
- **Labor law** broadly covers issues surrounding unions.
- **Landlord/tenant law** concerns all issues arising from the landlord-tenant relationship, such as evictions, leases and rental agreements, rent control, and similar matters.

- **Military law** relates to all matters under the authority (jurisdiction) of the military, including discharges, enlistment, mandatory registration laws, court martials, and benefits.
- **Municipal law** includes zoning, ordinances, land use planning, condemnation of property, incorporation of cities, contracting for public improvements, and other matters of local concern.
- **Prison law** covers prison conditions, disciplinary procedures, parole, constitutional rights of prisoners, and adequate access to legal information and medical treatment.
- **Property law** encompasses the purchase, maintenance, use, regulation, and sale of real estate.
- **Public benefits law** means the administration and distribution of federal and state benefits such as TANF (Temporary Assistance for Needy Families), Social Security (SSA), Social Security Disability (SSDI), Supplemental Security Income (SSI), food stamps, school lunches, foster homes, Medicaid, Medicare, and state disability.
- **Public utilities law** covers the duties, responsibilities, and rights of public utilities that provide water, telephone service, sewage and garbage disposal, and gas and electricity.
- **Tax law** includes all issues related to federal and state taxation of such items as income, personal property, business profits, real estate, and sales transactions.
- **Tort law (personal injury law)** deals with any injury to a person or business caused by someone else's intentional or negligent actions. Many lawsuits involve torts; the most common is "negligence." This involves behavior considered unreasonably careless under the circumstances and directly results in injury to another. Medical malpractice, legal malpractice, and most automobile accidents are examples of negligence.
- **Unemployment insurance** covers all matters relating to unemployment insurance benefits.
- **Workers' compensation** concerns the rights of workers who are injured or killed in work-related accidents.

State Law or Federal Law?

When considering the area of law you must research, you'll determine whether the issue you're researching is a matter of state law, federal law, or both. It will help you narrow your research. For instance, it might help you identify whether you should look at a secondary source that deals explicitly with federal tax issues or online for your state court's small claims procedure.

It won't be immediately apparent in every case. For help, you can review a state versus federal law comparison chart on the U.S. Courts website (www.uscourts.gov/about-federal-courts/court-role-and-structure/comparing-federal-state-courts) or refer to Chapter 1 for more help. If you can't figure it out, don't worry—this will probably become clear as you start your research.

Step 4: What Resources Will Help You Find What You Need?

Once you have a sense of what you're looking for, you can start identifying the possible resources to help you find it. In the following chapters, we'll discuss locating the right resource. For now, answer these questions:

- **Do you want a general legal overview on a specific subject?** You'll probably want to start with a secondary source, like legal books, court websites, and online articles. Anything that isn't primary law counts. We'll explain how to do background research using secondary sources in Chapter 4.
- **Do you need a specific statute on a subject?** If you want a specific statute, administrative regulation, or local ordinance—for example, the definition of a crime or violation—go directly to the source. Most state statutes are on the state's legislative website. You can find federal codes at https://uscode.house.gov. As we explain in Chapter 5, a single statute can help you find other resources.

- **Are you looking for a legal case on a situation similar to yours?**
  Case law uses factual scenarios to help explain how the law works
  in different situations. Reading relevant case law is a good way to
  learn how courts interpret laws. Case law is often needed when
  writing a legal document or research paper. Read Chapter 6 to
  learn how to find cases.

We recognize that this approach won't cover every situation. For
example, international legal research is beyond the scope of this book.
But for most cases, answering these questions will help you get started
finding resources. As you explore, you'll find other sources. Just use
these questions to decide where to begin.

Using Keywords to Search Legal Resources

At some point in your research journey, you will need to rely on keywords to narrow your search results. Why? Because the secret to
successful online and library searches is understanding the terminology
used in a particular legal area.

You won't need much other than basic terms early on when using
a general search engine like Google to find topic overview articles.
However, you'll use more sophisticated legal terms when researching
in the law library or using a legal search engine to learn specific legal
requirements. So, even though you won't need extensive legal knowledge
to get started, the earlier you identify high-quality keywords, the more
successful your research will be.

You'll want to brainstorm key legal terms used in the area to get
started. If you're unfamiliar with the topic, consider reading a plain-
English online article written for laypeople, such as those on Nolo.com.
Write down any plain-English terms related to the topic and legal terms
defined in the article. They'll likely be the same terms used in legal
search engines and the law library's book indexes, and you'll naturally
add more terms to your list as your research progresses.

If you need more help developing keywords, we include the Statsky "Cartwheel" approach at the end of the chapter. It's a more detailed process that can help when you're having difficulty formulating keywords.

Online Legal Searches

Researching online is often more straightforward and quicker than using print indexes in the law library, which is why this is where most people begin. You might spend hours finding relevant words in a print index as you try phrase after phrase. In contrast, with the help of a search engine, you can type a phrase and see what it brings from various sources instead of just one. If it doesn't work, finding another phrase doesn't take long.

Once you find an online resource, your search options will likely include the following:

- **Menus.** The typical menu approach works like a nested table of contents. Click the top-level category for a list of subcategories.
- **Keywords.** Enter your search terms in the site's search or "query" box to find materials on the site that include those keywords.
- **Keyword menus.** This method presents you with a drop-down menu of keywords. Once you select a keyword, the publisher will take you to materials associated with the keyword.

If you don't find what you are looking for, keep trying. If your initial keywords don't produce anything helpful, change them. If your choice of terms in a drop-down menu doesn't work, select new ones.

Library Indexes and Topical Searches

When researching in the law library, you'll use skills similar to those you employ online. However, instead of putting queries into the search engine, you'll search for keywords in a legal index. Here's how it works.

Like the indexes in the back of ordinary books, indexes to legal texts are usually alphabetical lists of subjects, with volume and page numbers directing you to where you can find particular information. This system applies when researching secondary sources, statutes, and cases (we describe this further in Chapter 6). When using your terms to search a legal index in the law library, this five-step approach should help:

Step 1: Use your keywords to select one or more probable legal categories in the index.

Step 2: Find the main entry relevant to your problem and be prepared to follow up cross-references.

Step 3: Search for relevant subentries under the main entry.

Step 4: Return to another main entry if your first choice fails.

Step 5: Once you find a relevant main and subentry, think even smaller and more detailed.

For instance, suppose your research question is whether a drunk driving conviction results in losing a driver's license. You list "drunk driving" and such variations as "operating a motor vehicle under the influence of intoxicating beverages" or "driving while intoxicated" as likely search terms. You also include "driver's license," with possible alternatives being "operator's permit" or "operator's license."

The first step is to decide which legal category your search terms would most likely fall under. You decide that starting with the vehicle index would be logical because driver's licenses and drunk driving fall within the larger "vehicle" category.

The second step is to search the index for your terms and follow up cross-references. For instance, if you started with "vehicles," you would probably be referred to "motor vehicles."

The third step is to search for subentries under the main entry. For instance, if you looked for "drunk driving" under "motor vehicles," you might find an alternative term, such as "operating under the influence" listed below it as a more specific and relevant topic.

The fourth step is returning to another main entry if your first choice doesn't pan out. For example, if you found no reference to "drunk driving" or its equivalent under "motor vehicles," consider looking under "alcohol," "traffic offenses," "alcoholic beverages," or "automobiles." You also might come up with some more variations of your specific terms.

The fifth step is to conceptualize even more detailed entries that will likely refer you to material on your specific question. For instance, once you find an entry that covers drunk driving under the main entry "motor vehicles," you might consider looking for such specific terms as "license," "suspension," "revocation," "restriction," and "forfeiture."

If you run into a brick wall, take a deep breath and start over. Restructure your question, develop new terms, and find a different substantive category. We can't emphasize strongly enough that most research fails because the researcher runs out of patience at the index-searching stage.

We'll show you how to find particular indexes later in the book.

Understanding Index Jargon

Indexes themselves use jargon that can be confusing. Here are definitions of some of the more commonly used indexing terms:

- *Generally, this index.* When a term is followed by a "Generally, this index," it means that the term can be found as a main entry in its alphabetical place in the index. For instance, if you find "child support" under the larger heading of "Minors," and it is followed by "Generally, this index," look for it as a main entry.
- *See also.* The terms following the "see also" may produce related subject matter.
- *See.* The material you seek will be found directly under the term following the "see" rather than under the original term.
- *See ____ infra.* The entry is found under the same main entry but further down alphabetically. It's Latin for "below."
- *See ____ supra.* The entry is found under the same main entry, but further up alphabetically. It's Latin for "above."

MOTOR VEHICLES—Continued
Horns and warning devices—Continued
    Necessity of flags where explosives transported, 75 § 409.
    Penalty for violation of regulations concerning, 75 §§ 401, 405.
    Repair or emergency vehicles, warning devices, 75 § 352.
    Requirement of, 75 § 401.
    Siren, bell, compression or sparkplug whistle, attachment to, purpose, 75
       § 401.
    Use of flag in connection with towing other vehicles, 75 § 452.
Hunting from,
    Permit, 34 § 1311.401.
       Disabled veteran, 34 § 1311.418a.
    Prohibited, 34 § 1311.704.
       Penalty for, 34 § 1311.731.
Hydrants, parking near prohibited, 75 § 612.
Incorporated towns, enforcement of Vehicle Code by officials, 75 § 731.
Infants, see Minors, post this head.
Information,
    Supplied by secretary of revenue, 75 § 787.
    To be shown in record, etc., 69 § 612.
    Violation of,
       Speed laws, 75 § 501.
       Vehicle Code, time of filing, 75 § 731.
Inspection of equipment,
    Exemption from fee for inspection certificate, 75 § 331.
    Fee for certificate, 75 § 306.1.
    Official, 75 § 431.
    Penalty for violation of regulations as to, 75 § 431.
Insurance, see Insurance and Insurance Companies.
Intersections,
    Acquisition of land by township of first class to afford unobstructed view, 53
       § 57040.
    Center, 75 § 546.
    Definition, Vehicle Code, 75 § 2.
    Duty to keep to right in crossing, 75 § 522.
    Grade crossings, generally, see Grade Crossings.
    Interpretation of traffic signals at intersections, 75 § 635.
    Keeping to right in crossing, 75 § 522.
    Parking near intersection prohibited, 75 § 612.
    Parking prohibited within, 75 § 612.
    Pocono Mountain Memorial Parkway, restrictions. 36 § 655.2.
    Right of way, 75 § 573.
       Pedestrians, 75 § 572.
    Rim Parkway, restrictions, 36 § 655.2.
    Rules at intersections,
       Center of intersection, 75 § 546.
       Right of way, 75 § 572.
       Right to turn and manner of making turn, 75 § 546.
    Speed on approaching or traversing, 75 § 501.
    State highways, see State Highways.
    Stopping before entering or crossing, 75 §§ 591, 712.
    Through highways, establishment, 75 § 712.
    Traffic signals, duty to obey and interpretation thereof, 75 § 635.
    Turn by vehicles and manner of making turn, 75 § 546.
Interstate bridges, driving on with excessive weight, 75 §§ 1231, 1232.
Interstate commerce,
    Size, weight or construction of vehicles, violation of federal statute or regula-
       tion, 75 § 457.
    Violation of federal statute or regulation, 75 § 435.
Intoxicating liquor,
    Operating while under the influence of as unlawful, 75 § 231.
    Revocation of license of vehicles used in violating law, 47 § 6—604.
    Revocation of operator's privilege for driving while under influence, 75 § 191.
Jobber defined, 75 § 2.
Judgments for damages,
    Certified copies forwarded to secretary of revenue, 75 § 1265.
    Failure to forward certified copy to secretary of revenue, penalties, 75
       § 1265.

MOTOR VEHICLES

MOTOR VEHICLES (cont.)

Interstate Compact for Motor Vehicle Safety Equipment, this index

Jitneys and Taxis, this index

Joyriding, penalty, 23 § 1094

Junior operator,
    Defined, 23 § 4
    Drivers' licenses, ante

Junk motor vehicles. Junkyards, this index

Leased vehicles,
    Trucking units, registration, 23 § 301a

Lienholder. Uniform Motor Vehicle Certificate of Title and Anti-Theft Act, this index

Lights. Equipment, ante

Log-haulers, registration, fees, 23 § 366

Manufacturers. Motor Vehicle Manufacturers, Distributors and Dealers, this index

Minors,
    Driver's license certificate, color, 23 § 610a
    Junior operator's license, 23 § 607
    Learners' permits, 23 § 617
    Parental consent,
        Junior operator, 23 § 607
        Learners' permits, 23 § 617
    Provisional licenses, 23 § 607a
    Re-examination, provisional licenses, 23 § 607a

Misrepresentation, license and registration applications, 23 § 202

Mo-peds, this index

Motor Buses, this index

Motorcycles, this index

Motor Trucks, this index

Motor vehicle, defined. Defined, ante

Motor vehicle law book, 23 § 112

Moving violations, point system, 23 § 2501 et seq.
    Legislative review, 23 § 2507
    Notice of points assessed, 23 § 2504
    Procedures, 23 § 2506
    Records, period for maintaining, 23 § 2503
    Schedule, 23 § 2502
    Suspension or revocation of license, 23 § 2505

MOTOR VEHICLES (cont.)

Municipal regulation, 24 § 2291

Negligent and careless operation, 23 § 1091

Non-gasoline driven motor vehicle,
    Defined, 23 § 4
    Registration, fee, 23 § 362

Odometers, alteration, penalties, 23 § 1704a

Offenses,
    Generally, 23 § 1701 et seq.
    Nolo contendere pleas, effect, 23 § 1710
    Police Courts, generally, this index
    Reporting convictions to commissioner, 23 § 1709
    Traffic Rules and Regulations, this index

Operating vehicle under influence of intoxicating liquor, drugs, 23 § 1201 et seq.

Operation, emergency vehicles, 23 § 1015

Operation of. Traffic Rules and Regulations, generally, this index

Operator, defined, 23 § 4
    Licenses. Drivers' licenses, ante

Overweight vehicles, fines for operating, 23 § 1391a

Ownership and possession, odometers, alteration, 23 § 1704a
    Serial numbers, obliterated or defaced, 23 § 1701
    Assignment, new numbers, 23 § 1702
    Evidence of violation, 23 § 1704
    Penalty, 23 § 1703
    Title to, post

Parking. Police Courts. Traffic Rules and Regulations, this index
    Credit card or check, payment for towing by, 23 § 1754

Pleasure car,
    Defined, 23 § 4
    Registration,
        Fees, 23 § 361
        Period of, 23 § 302

Point system,
    Assessment of points, 23 § 2502
        Recording, 23 § 2503
    Established, 23 § 2501
    Legislative review, 23 § 2507

Vermont Index

TRAFFIC

330

The Statsky "Cartwheel" Approach

The Statsky approach uses a diagram—called the "Cartwheel"—which prompts the reader for different word categories. Below, we illustrate how you'd use the Cartwheel structure when researching who is authorized to perform a wedding and particular ceremony type.

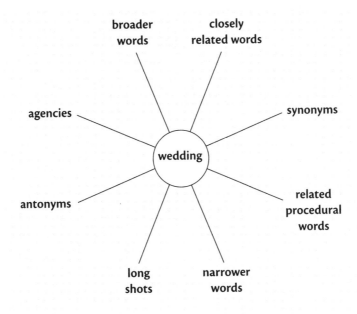

Reproduced by permission from *Domestic Relations*, by William P. Statsky, copyright © 1978 by West Publishing Company (out of print). All Rights Reserved.

The first step would be to look up the keyword—in this example, "wedding"—in the legal resources's index and table. If that's unsuccessful, the second step would be to think of as many different phrasings and contexts of the word "wedding" as possible.

The Cartwheel method has 18 steps to help you come up with terms to look up in an index or table of contents, as follows:

1. Identify all significant words using the facts of the research problem. Place each word or small set of words in the center of the Cartwheel.
2. Look up the words in the index and table of contents.
3. Identify the broader categories of significant words.
4. Look up all broader categories in the index and table of contents.
5. Identify the narrower categories of these words.
6. In the index and table of contents, look up the narrower categories.
7. Identify all synonyms of the words.
8. Look up all synonyms in the index and table of contents.
9. Identify all the antonyms of these words.
10. In the index and table of contents, look up all antonyms.
11. Identify all closely related words.
12. Look up all these closely related words in the index and table of contents.
13. Identify all procedural terms related to these words.
14. Look up these procedural terms in the index and table of contents.
15. Identify all agencies, if any, which might have some connection to these words.
16. Look up all agencies in the index and table of contents.
17. Identify all long shots.
18. Look up these long shots in the index and table of contents.

If we were to apply these 18 steps of the Cartwheel to the word "wedding," here are some of the words and phrases that you would check in the index and table of contents of every law book that deals with family law:

- **Broader Words:** celebration, ceremony, rite, ritual, formality, festivity
- **Narrower Words:** civil wedding, church wedding, proxy wedding, sham wedding, shotgun marriage
- **Synonyms:** marriage, nuptial
- **Antonyms:** alienation, annulment, dissolution, divorce, separation

- **Loosely Related Words:** matrimony, marital, domestic, husband, wife, bride, anniversary, custom, children, blood test, premarital, spouse, relationship, family, home, consummation, cohabitation, sexual relations, betrothal, minister, wedlock, oath, contract, name change, domicile, residence
- **Procedural Terms:** application, petition, authorization
- **Agencies:** Bureau of Vital Statistics, County Clerk, License Bureau, Secretary of State, Justice of the Peace, and
- **Long Shots:** dowry, common law, single, blood relationship, fraud, religion, license, illegitimate, remarriage, prenuptial, antenuptial, alimony, bigamy, pregnancy, gifts, chastity, community property, impotence, incest, virginity, support, custody, consent, paternity.

Perhaps you might think that some of the word selections in the above categories are a bit far-fetched. But you simply won't know for sure whether a word will be fruitful until you try it. To be successful, you must be imaginative.

Finding and Using Secondary Sources

Once you've classified your problem and settled on the terms and keywords defining your issue, you're ready to begin your research. But where do you start?

As we've explained, the number of available resources can seem overwhelming. And if you go straight to the text of the law itself, you might find it difficult to understand or too "lawyerly" to make much sense of it.

That's why we recommend that you start by using secondary sources. In Chapter 2, we discussed how secondary sources explain and interpret primary sources like statutes, cases, and regulations. Using them helps you familiarize yourself with the overall legal area, ultimately making understanding the law easier. Once you have a grasp of the basic concepts in the applicable legal area, you'll likely find that primary sources aren't as challenging as they might first seem.

However, not all secondary sources are created equal. This chapter discusses where to find secondary sources and how to use them.

Online Resources

As you likely know, going online and using a search engine to find information on almost any topic is simple. Type "driving under the influence" into Google, for example, and you'll get more than 1.2 billion results from government websites, individual lawyers' websites, and more.

RELATED TOPIC

Need to figure out how to narrow your online search? Go back to Chapter 2, where we explained how to brainstorm topical keywords and use Boolean searching if you're not finding the information you need. Also, recognize that search engines have formulas called "algorithms" to make sure you get the most relevant results first. These algorithms are proprietary, so you won't know how they work. But it explains why one search engine might give you different results than another. Because of these limitations, you should verify online research results with treatises in the law library.

However, this approach doesn't guarantee you'll find the information you need—and what you find might not be accurate. Because it's crucial to understand how to refine your results from the most credible sources, below we explain some ways to determine the reliability of an online source and how to eliminate results you don't want.

Deciding Whether Information Is Reliable

When you pull up a legal article, you won't know if a lawyer who posts information on a website is a legal expert in the field or right out of law school. It's even possible that the writer doesn't have any legal training at all. Here are some indicators to help you decide when to trust online information:

- **Does it cite primary sources?** You'll need to know where to find the law to verify it. A source that provides legal citations to the actual law will be more reliable than one lacking citations or with inaccurate citations. Question the source if the citations don't check out or aren't present. (We discuss using primary source materials in Chapters 5 to 7.)

- **What is the website's motive?** A website trying to entice you to buy legal services will likely provide less helpful information than a website that a state bar organization suggests that self-represented litigants use. For instance, a government website (usually ending in ".gov") is rarely interested in selling you something and is considered the most reliable. Also, a nonprofit's website (typically ending in ".org") often strives to educate the public and provide information. However, websites ending in ".org" aren't always as reliable as those ending in ".gov."

- **What can you tell about the author?** The first consideration should be whether the author is an area expert. You'll want to verify that the writer is a lawyer, preferably with experience in the area. Second, consider the author's purpose. An academic paper written for a scholarly publication might include many primary source citations but be difficult to understand and provide little practical information.

- **When was the resource written?** Don't waste time learning about unusable, outdated laws. The older the information, the more likely it is to have changed. A copyright date can be a good clue, but it won't ensure content accuracy.
- **Do other reputable websites cite it?** If the website you're using is accurate and reliable, the websites it refers you to will likely also be high quality. After all, the website you trust probably became trustworthy by carefully vetting the sites it uses.
- **Can users change the information?** While users' input might not necessarily be inaccurate, there's no promise of accuracy. You'll want to be sure primary law citations verify what you're reading.

RESOURCE

Nolo has easy-to-understand materials online. Nolo is dedicated to making legal concepts understandable for nonlawyers. Nolo's commitment extends to providing accurate, up-to-date, free legal information in articles across various legal areas. Visit Nolo.com for articles on small business; wills and estate planning; employment; patent and copyright; debt and credit; and more.

Where to Look Online

A reliable place to look for secondary sources online is the Cornell University Law site's Wex, a free legal dictionary and encyclopedia. It provides comprehensive, easy-to-read summaries in many areas of law. To access this information:

- Go to www.law.cornell.edu/wex.
- Click the "Browse" button in the middle of the page. This will produce an alphabetical list of all legal terms and topics.
- Find the area of your research on the alphabetical list.

You will find definitions of legal terms and brief overviews of legal topics with links to resources such as relevant laws and cases, other websites on the subject, and pages for related Wex keywords and topics.

If you are looking for additional background materials in a specific area of law, we suggest using the list in the appendix at the back of this book. For general online searches, which will often lead you to helpful background resources, refer back to Chapter 2.

CAUTION
Use generative AI tools with caution. If you're considering using an AI-powered search tool for legal research, you should know that the technology is in development and legal results are unreliable. We aren't including tools such as ChatGPT and other AI offerings in our current recommendations because while the answers can appear impressive, they're sometimes misleading or wrong. Unlike traditional legal resources, the answers aren't reviewed for accuracy or attributed to a credible legal authority.

Self-Help Legal Books

Today, many publishers provide guides to help nonlawyers understand complicated legal concepts. The publisher of this book, Nolo, has the longest list, with titles ranging from *How to File for Chapter 7 Bankruptcy* and *How to Form a Nonprofit Corporation* (both nationwide) to *Patent, Copyright & Trademark*. Most of Nolo's books are written or edited by attorneys and are updated frequently to stay current with the law. A complete list of Nolo publications is available on its website at Nolo.com.

The reliability of other self-help books varies greatly. Online booksellers like Amazon (www.amazon.com) have systems allowing you to see how others have reviewed a book, which can be helpful if you have numerous choices. Consider using the article evaluation system described above when evaluating how valuable any source will likely be, including books.

To find these materials, look first in a law library or public library. Many carry complete sets of Nolo books and other publishers' self-help books. You can find self-help books in a bookstore or go online to buy one. Some publishers sell their books directly on their websites or through a bookseller like Amazon.

Some publishers (including West and Foundation Press) also publish books specifically for law students called "hornbooks." While more "legal" than self-help books, these resources help readers grasp the general principles and concepts in a particular area of law. You can find most of these books in any law bookstore (usually near law schools) or law library.

Other good background resources are the concise law summaries intended as study guides for law students. Titles such as *Gilbert Law Summaries*, *Black Letter Outlines*, *Emanuel Law Outlines*, *Legalines*, and *Law in a Nutshell* can be found in legal bookstores and law libraries. All provide an up-to-date framework or overview of a legal subject area, making it easier to understand the law you are researching.

Legal Encyclopedias

While some books and resources are developed specifically for self-help researchers and law students, many legal books are published primarily for attorneys. Most books provide a broad overview of a legal topic, often with citations to primary sources. As a result, they're not only an excellent resource for learning information about your legal topic, but they can serve as a bridge to the next phase of your research—reading the law itself. The most common of these sources are legal encyclopedias.

Legal encyclopedias contain detailed discussions of virtually every area of the law. The most helpful are those created for your specific state because that will be the law that will apply in most cases. More general encyclopedias usually focus on broad overviews of the law that explain universal practices and notable differences between states.

These encyclopedias are usually multivolume sets, organized alphabetically by subject matter like regular encyclopedias, but with broader main entries and many more subentries. Also, they contain thorough indexes, so you can find relevant sections using the keywords you identified in the previous chapter.

Legal encyclopedias are often an excellent place to start your research. Because they cover the entire range of law and their entries are broken into small segments, you will likely find material relevant to your research problem. Each entry provides treatment of the particular topic. You'll get a good overview of your issue and the specific statutes and cases (the actual law) you'll need to advance your research.

The main drawback to comprehensive legal encyclopedias is that they're more challenging to access. You won't find them in a bookstore or on a free website. Instead, they're primarily located in law libraries or as part of large legal databases like Westlaw or LexisNexis. As we explained in Chapter 2, using Westlaw or LexisNexis is prohibitively expensive for most people, so if you want to access these sources, consider going to the local law library.

National Legal Encyclopedias

Two encyclopedias, *American Jurisprudence* (commonly called "*Am. Jur.*") and *Corpus Juris Secundum* (abbreviated "*C.J.S.*"), provide a national overview of American law. The entries are generalized and don't necessarily provide state-specific information. However, they contain footnoted references to court decisions from many different states and federal courts, where relevant.

The table of contents and a firearm discussion by *Am. Jur.* are shown below to give you an idea of how these books are set up.

Which legal encyclopedia should you use if your law library has both? Many researchers favor *Am. Jur. 2d* over *C.J.S.* because they feel that *C.J.S.* tends to have too much unnecessary information. Although these two encyclopedias used to compete with each other, they're now both published by the same parent company, Thomson Reuters (which also owns Westlaw). These encyclopedias use the "Key Number" system to organize or tag the legal issues they discuss. To learn about the Key Number system, see Chapter 6.

Am. Jur. 2d, Part of Table of Contents for Topic "Weapons and Firearms"

§ 3. —Unloaded firearm.

Generally, it is held that an unloaded gun, used as a firearm and not as bludgeon, is not a dangerous weapon within the contemplation of statutes punishing assaults made with dangerous or deadly weapons, although there is substantial authority to the contrary.[36] It is generally, but not universally, considered to be a matter of defense to show that the weapon was unloaded, rather than a substantive part of the state's case to aver and prove that it was loaded.[37] There also is authority that an unloaded revolver or gun merely pointed at the person is not a dangerous weapon within the meaning of statutes defining assault and robbery while armed with a dangerous weapon, although many courts hold that an unloaded gun or pistol is a dangerous weapon within the meaning of such statutes;[38] and generally, an unloaded pistol or revolver is regarded as within the meaning of statutes against carrying concealed "dangerous or deadly weapons"[39] or denouncing the carrying "of any concealed and dangerous weapon."[40] It has been held that a statute prohibiting the carrying of a weapon capable of inflicting bodily harm, concealed on or about the person, did not apply to an unloaded pistol found in the glove compartment of the defendant's automobile, no ammunition having been found on or about the defendant's person or in the vehicle.[41] In a few cases the courts have recognized that if the gun was unloaded, that fact would have a bearing on the determination as to whether it was carried as a weapon.[42]

Generally an unloaded gun or pistol used to strike with is not necessarily a dangerous weapon, but is such, or not, according to its size, weight, and the manner of using it.[43] Accordingly, to resolve the factual question whether a

---

36. See 6 Am Jur 2d, ASSAULT AND BATTERY § 54.

As to whether a simple criminal assault may be committed with an unloaded firearm, see 6 Am Jur 2d, ASSAULT AND BATTERY § 34.

As to civil action for damages for an assault by pointing unloaded firearm, see 6 Am Jur 2d, ASSAULT AND BATTERY §§ 109, 123.

37. See 6 Am Jur 2d, ASSAULT AND BATTERY § 93.

As to presumption as to whether gun was loaded, see 6 Am Jur 2d, ASSAULT AND BATTERY § 94.

38. See 67 Am Jur 2d, ROBBERY § 5.

39. Asocar v State, 252 Ind 326, 247 NE2d 679; Mularkey v State, 201 Wis 429, 230 NW 76.

Annotation: 79 ALR2d 1430, § 8.

40. Mularkey v State, 201 Wis 429, 230 NW 76.

A pistol mechanically capable of being fired is a deadly weapon within the meaning of the statute prohibiting the carrying of a concealed

"deadly weapon," even though it was unloaded and no ammunition was on the carrier's person or was readily available. Commonwealth v Harris (Ky) 344 SW2d 820.

41. State v Haugabrook, 31 Ohio Misc 157, 57 Ohio Ops 2d 322, 272 NE2d 213.

42. State v Larkin, 24 Mo App 410.

Annotation: 79 ALR2d 1432, § 8.

In Carr v State, 34 Ark 448, in reversing a conviction under a statute making it a misdemeanor to wear any pistol concealed as a weapon unless upon a journey, the evidence being that defendant was carrying two unloaded pistols, the court said that it must be shown that the pistols were carried as weapons, for the purpose of convenience in a fight, and that in the instant case the pistols were useless for that purpose.

43. State v Mays, 7 Ariz App 90, 436 P2d 482; State v Jaramillo (App) 82 NM 548, 484 P2d 768; Hilliard v State, 87 Tex Crim 15, 218 SW 1052, 8 ALR 1316.

Annotation: 79 ALR2d 1423, § 6[a]; 8 ALR 1319.

Am. Jur. 2d, "Weapons and Firearms"

State Encyclopedias

In addition to national encyclopedias, there are several state-specific encyclopedias. State-specific and national encyclopedias are organized the same way. When researching a question of state law, it is almost always best to start with a state-specific encyclopedia, if one exists. A more direct approach will help you avoid sifting through legal discussions that don't apply to your state's law.

RESOURCE

Some state-specific legal encyclopedias (alphabetized by state):

- *California Jurisprudence 3d* (Thomson Reuters)
- *Florida Jurisprudence 2d* (Lawyers Cooperative Publishing)
- *Illinois Jurisprudence* (LexisNexis Publishing)
- *Indiana Law Encyclopedia* (Thomson West)
- *Michigan Law and Practice Encyclopedia* (Michie)
- Strong's *North Carolina Index 4th* (Lawyers Cooperative Publishing)
- *New York Jurisprudence 2d* (Lawyers Cooperative Publishing)
- *Ohio Jurisprudence 3d* (Lawyers Cooperative Publishing)
- *Pennsylvania Law Encyclopedia* (Michie)
- *Tennessee Jurisprudence* (LexisNexis Publishing), and
- Michie's *Jurisprudence of Virginia and West Virginia* (Michie).

American Law Reports

This series of books has two titles: *American Law Reports* (*A.L.R.*) and *American Law Reports, Federal* (*A.L.R. Fed.*). *A.L.R.* covers issues primarily arising under state statutes and in state cases, as well as federally oriented issues that arose before 1969, the year *A.L.R. Fed.* was first published. *A.L.R. Fed.* covers issues that arise primarily under federal statutes or in federal cases. Both publications are multivolume sets that contain discussions of narrow issues addressed in newly decided court cases. Each discussion comments on the case itself and other cases that have considered the same or similar issues.

A.L.R. and *A.L.R. Fed.* are different from the legal encyclopedias described earlier in that they don't attempt to cover every subject. So, although you might not find what you're looking for, you'll be well rewarded if you do. Fortunately, *A.L.R.* has an excellent index that lets you quickly determine whether you're on the right track.

A.L.R. comes in seven series (*A.L.R.–A.L.R. 7th*). Unlike the legal encyclopedias, the newest series doesn't replace previous ones. *A.L.R. 7th* might contain an almost entirely new set of topics not covered in *A.L.R. 4th.* The older series are updated with "pocket parts" (inserts in the back of each hardcover volume) and hardbound volumes called "the Later Case Service." *A.L.R. Federal* is still in its third series.

Form Books

Form books are pretty much what their name suggests: collections of legal forms, usually in a fill-in-the-blanks format. They're handy if you're looking for a form. They're also helpful because they typically discuss the procedural rules relevant to each form's use. In other words, when you find the form you need, chances are you'll also find an overview of the procedure and instructions on making the most common modifications. A typical form book entry from *American Jurisprudence Legal Forms, Second Series* is shown below. We show the form as well as the accompanying material about the law governing the procedure.

RESOURCE

Most states and individual courts have websites that contain or link to all the forms required to file claims. You can also obtain many federal court forms at www.uscourts.gov/services-forms.

NAME   § 182:52

---

of __18____, State of __19____, and since such time has resided with her husband at the above address.

4. Applicant desires to change her name to __20____, her maiden surname, for the following reasons: __21____ *[specify reasons, such as* to continue her professional or business use of her maiden name *or* to avoid confusion between her professional or business relations with those of her husband *or* to assert her equal partnership with her husband in the marital relation *or* to assert her ethnic heritage, of which she is proud, *or other legally permissible reason]*.

5. __22____ *[State information as to publication of notice of intent to change name, if required by statute.]*

Dated: __23____, 19__24__.

                                                              [Signature]

[Jurat]

☑ **Notes on Use:**

See also Notes on Use following § 182:43.

Annotations: Right of married woman to use maiden surname. 67 ALR3d 1266.

*Circumstance justifying grant or denial of petition to change adult's name. 79 ALR3d 562.

Cross references: For other change of name forms, see § 182:54 et seq.

V. CHANGE OF NAME

§ 182:51 Scope of division

Material in this division consists of forms related to change of name. Included are such matters as application to a court of record for change of name and relevant affidavits arid notices.

§ 182:52 Introductory comments

Unless applicable statutes provide otherwise, a person may change such person's name at will, without any legal proceedings, merely by adopting another name. In most states, however, statutes set forth specific procedures and requirements for change of name; such procedure usually includes filing a petition or application with a court of record. The court hearing a petition or application for change of name has discretion to either grant or deny it, the general rule being that there must exist some substantial reason for the change.[8]

8. *Text references:* Change of name, generally. 57 Am Jur 2d, Name §§ 10–16.

Annotations: Circumstances justifying grant or denial of petition to change adult's name. 79 ALR3d 562.

(For Tax Notes and Notes on use, see end of form)

Form and Explanation From *Am. Jur. Legal Forms, 2d Series*

§ 182:53   NAME

§ 182:53 Annotation references

ALR annotations treating the subject of change of name by an individual are set forth below.

ALR annotations:

Circumstance justifying grant or denial of petition to change adult's name. 79 ALR3d
562.
Change of child's name in adoption proceeding. 53 ALR2d 927.

§ 182:54 Application for change of name

To: __1_____ *[court of record]*

APPLICATION FOR CHANGE OF NAME

Applicant states:

1. Applicant resides at __2_____ *[address]*, City of __3_____, County of
__4____, State of __5_____, __6____ *[ZIP]*, and has resided there for
more than __7__ *[number of months or years]* prior to filing this application.

2. Applicant was born __8_____ *[in the City of __9_____, County of
__10____, State of __11_____ or set forth foreign address]* on __12____,
19_13_. Applicant was named __14_____ and has always been known by that
name.

3. The name of applicant's father is __15_____, and the name of applicant's mother is __16_____. They reside at __17_____ [__18_____ *(address)*,
City of __19____, County of __20____, State of __21_____, __22____ *(ZIP)*
or set forth foreign address].*

4. Applicant __23_____ *[is or is not]* married. __24_____ *[If married, give
information as to date and place of marriage, spouse's name, and date and
place of spouse's birth.]*

5. Applicant desires to change applicant's name to __25_____ for the
following reasons: __26_____.

6. __27_____ *[State information as to publication of notice of intent to
change name, if required by statute.]*

7. __28_____ *[State information required by statute as to financial matters,
any criminal records, and pending actions or other proceedings in which the
applicant may be a party.]*

Dated: __29_____, 19_30_.

[Jurat]   *[Signature]*

☑ **Notes on Use:**

Text references: Statutory regulation of change of name, generally. 57 Am Jur
2d, Name §§ 11–16.

(For Tax Notes and Notes on use, see end of form)

324   **13A Am Jur Legal Forms 2d (Rev)**

Form and Explanation From *Am. Jur. Legal Forms, 2d Series*

TIP
Are you actually looking for forms? If you are, form books are a great resource, but so are:
- **Court websites.** We suggest you start with the court's website if you need to file a document with a specific court. Many courts have standard forms for this purpose.
- **Reliable publishers.** We recommend browsing www.nolo.com for helpful forms. If you find forms elsewhere, make sure you know how they were developed, who created them, whether they are state specific, and so forth.

The forms in *Am. Jur. Legal Forms* are national in scope and often lack the specificity found in a form book prepared for a particular state. When looking for an appropriate form or the procedure that goes with it, it is best to start with a publication specific to your state or topic, if there is one. As in the case of state encyclopedias, state form books are generally published only in the more populous states.

Practice Manuals

There are practice manuals for torts, contracts, family law, real estate transactions, search and seizure, and many other issues. Some are state specific, while others are national in scope. For example, a publication called *Defense of Drunk Driving Cases*, by Richard Erwin; Harvey M. Cohen, Ph.D.; David Slavin; and Richard J. Essen tells you everything you need to know when handling a drunk driving offense ($6,891 as of February 2024).

Many of these books are well written and organized. They can give you a good understanding of the procedural and substantive law and the hands-on instructions necessary to prosecute or defend your case. These resources are generally available in law libraries.

Continuing Legal Education Publications

Some publishers are dedicated to providing practicing lawyers with continuing education. Two of these—Continuing Education of the Bar (CEB) and the Rutter Group—direct their materials toward California lawyers. The Practising Law Institute (PLI) focuses on New York lawyers. Publishers in some other states produce similar resources, often called "CLE" ("continuing legal education") books.

Continuing legal education publishers produce detailed practice guidelines, instructions, and forms for many different areas of law and practice, both state and federal. They also publish written materials for continuing legal education seminars they sponsor. Continuing education materials are usually available in the law libraries in the states for which they are published.

To find these publications, ask the law librarian or go to the publisher's website to see what's available (the books will probably be too expensive to buy, but then you'll at least know what you're looking for in the law library). A list of popular publishers appears below.

RESOURCE

Popular CLE publishers:

- CEB, www.ceb.com
- Rutter Group, www.theruttergroup.com
- PLI, www.pli.edu, and
- West LegalEdcenter, https://westlegaledcenter.com.

Law Reviews and Other Legal Periodicals

Legal professionals constantly analyze the law's evolution because it is continually developing and changing. You can find articles about new legislation, current legal theories and viewpoints, and important cases in law journals published by law schools, commercial publishers, and professional legal societies, such as bar associations.

The articles in journals produced by law schools are written by law students, professors, and even practicing attorneys, and sometimes present a whole new view of an area of the law. They tend to focus on where the law is going instead of where it is or where it's been, although they might provide some history to set the stage for the discussion. Even if articles are more academic than practical, they still might contain valuable descriptions of the state of the law in the specific area being discussed and can provide you with research leads.

On the other hand, journals produced by bar associations and other professional groups tend to be much more practical, emphasizing recent developments. Many law reviews and journals are general, covering subjects across the legal spectrum. But increasingly, legal periodicals specialize in such fields as taxation, environmental law, labor, entertainment and communications, and women's studies.

Because these publications are so often academic or esoteric, in most cases, we'd recommend you first try to find a basic summary or another practical publication. Even if you don't find the answer you're looking for, you'll at least understand the subject, which will make it easier to digest the more challenging law review articles.

Finding Law Review Articles in the Library

Most law libraries contain the more influential journals and law reviews, and some libraries (especially in large law schools) have complete sets. You can find articles using an electronic index called LegalTrac or either of two printed indexes, the *Index to Legal Periodicals & Books* or the *Current Index to Legal Periodicals*.

All indexes are organized by subject, author, and title, and contain an abbreviated reference to the review or journal in which the article is located. The printed indexes contain numerous volumes organized according to the publishing year.

The LegalTrac computerized index to legal periodicals is part of a more extensive database called Infotrac, which contains information on many additional resources, including business and general periodicals. Instructions for using LegalTrac are shown on the screen and are easy to follow. If you get confused, ask a law librarian for help.

18   INDEX TO LEGAL PERIODICALS

Constitutional theory—United States—cont.
Twentieth century Jeffersonian: Brandeis, freedom of speech, and the republican revival. H. Garfield. 69 *Or. L. Rev.* 527-88 '90
Construction industry
See also
Architects and engineers
The Kentucky no action statute: down for the count?. 79 *Ky. L.J.* 159-75 '90/'91
The qualification of arbitrators for construction disputes. M. F. Hoellering. 45 *Arb. J.* 34-41+ D '90
Construction of statutes *See* Statutory interpretation
Constructive trusts *See* Implied trusts
Consumer credit *See* Credit
Consumer protection
See also
Advertising
Credit
Health
Loans
Prices
Products liability
Unfair insurance settlement practices
Advanced Hair Studio Pty Ltd. & Anor v. TVW Enterprises Limited [[1987] 77 A.L.R. 615]. 17 *Melb. U.L. Rev.* 527-32 Je '90
Consumer problems and ADR: an analysis of the Federal Trade Commission-ordered General Motors mediation and arbitration program. A. Best. 1990 *J. Dis. Res.* 267-92 '90
Leases of personal property: a project for consumer protection. J. J. A. Burke, J. M. Cannel. 28 *Harv. J. on Legis.* 115-66 Wint '91
Shysters, sharks, and ambulance chasers beware: attorney liability under CUTPA. 11 *U. Bridgeport L. Rev.* 97-125 '90
Contempt
Current problems in the law of contempt. J. Laws. 43 *Current Legal Probs.* 99-114 '90
A new perspective on the judicial contempt power: recommendations for reform. L. Raveson. 18 *Hastings Const. L.Q.* 1-65 Fall '90
Continental shelf
See also
Exclusive economic zone
Territorial waters
The EEC's continental shelf: a "terra incognita". J. E. Harders. 8 *J. Energy & Nat. Resources L.* 263-79 '90
Secured transactions affecting the federal outer continental shelf. M. C. Maloney. 34 *Inst. on Min. L.* 47-78 '87
Contracts
See also
Conflict of laws—Contracts
Government contracts
Sales
Contract versus contractarianism: the regulatory role of contract law. J. Braucher. 47 *Wash. & Lee L. Rev.* 697-739 Fall '90
Contractual concerns for hospitals and other health care organizations. M. L. Malone, R. C. Beasley. 32 *S. Tex. L. Rev.* 77-104 D '90
The myth that promisees prefer supracompensatory remedies: an analysis of contracting for damage measures. A. Schwartz. 100 *Yale L.J.* 369-407 N '90
Reconsidering the reliance rules: the Restatement of Contracts and promissory estoppel in North Dakota. T. C. Folsom. 66 *N.D.L. Rev.* 317-447 '90
Strategic bargaining and the economic theory of contract default rules. J. S. Johnston. 100 *Yale L.J.* 615-64 D '90
Unconscionable conduct and small business: possible extension of section 52A of the Trade Practices Act 1974. G. Q. Taperell. 18 *Austl. Bus. L. Rev.* 370-88 D '90
Acceptance
See Contracts—Offer and acceptance
Consideration
La opcion de compra en Puerto Rico. M. J. Godreau. 53 *Rev. Jur. U.P.R.* 563-608 '84
Covenants
Flats: mutual enforceability of covenants. Two views. J. E. Adams, S. Baughen. 134 *Solic. J.* 1504-5 D 14 '90
Offer and acceptance
See also
Options
Liability for mistake in contract formation. M. P. Gergen. 64 *S. Cal. L. Rev.* 1-49 N '90

The strategic structure of offer and acceptance: game theory and the law of contract formation. A. Katz. 89 *Mich. L. Rev.* 215-95 N '90
Performance
La clausula penal. P. F. Silva-Ruiz. 54 *Rev. Jur. U.P.R.* 89-112 '85
Expectations, loss distribution and commercial impracticability. S. Walt. 24 *Ind. L. Rev.* 65-109 '91
Punitive damages for breach of contract—a principled approach. F. J. Cavico, Jr. 22 *St. Mary's L.J.* 357-453 '90
Contributory negligence
See also
Comparative negligence
Controlled substances *See* Narcotics
Conversion
Commercialization of human tissues: has biotechnology created the need for an expanded scope of informed consent?. 27 *Cal. W.L. Rev.* 209-30 '90/'91
Moore v. The Regents of the University of California: balancing the need for biotechnology innovation against the right of informed consent. M. S. Dorney. 5 *High Tech. L.J.* 333-69 Fall '90
Tort law—informed consent—California Supreme Court recognizes patient's cause of action for physician's nondisclosure of excised tissue's commercial value.—Moore v. Regents of the University of California, 793 P.2d 479 (Cal.). 104 *Harv. L. Rev.* 808-15 Ja '91
Conveyancing *See* Title to land
Convicts *See* Prisons and prisoners
Cook, Rebecca J.
International human rights law concerning women: case notes and comments. 23 *Vand. J. Transnat'l L.* 779-818 '90
Cooperative federalism
See also
Federalism
States' rights
Cooperatives
See also
Condominium and cooperative buildings
IRS expands availability of patronage dividend deductions and tax-exempt status for cooperatives but restricts benefit of package design expenditures. D. W. Butwill. 12 *J. Agric. Tax'n & L.* 342-51 Wint '91
Copyright
See also
Authors and publishers
The 101st Congress: a review of amendments to the Copyright Act. 37 *J. Copyright Soc'y U.S.A.* 462-98 '90
Accounting for profits gained by infringement of copyright: when does it end?. L. Bently. 13 *Eur. Intell. Prop. Rev.* 5-15 Ja '91
Applying the merger doctrine to the copyright of computer software. 37 *Copyright L. Symp. (ASCAP)* 173-214 '90
Computer protection against foreign competition in the United States. 10 *Computer L.J.* 393-412 O '90
The continuing battle over music performance rights in television programming. 36 *Copyright L. Symp. (ASCAP)* 167-91 '89
Contribution of the Bar to the development of copyright law. S. Rothenberg. 37 *J. Copyright Soc'y U.S.A.* 453-61 '90
Copyright and computer databases: is traditional compilation law adequate?. 37 *Copyright L. Symp. (ASCAP)* 85-125 '90
Copyright law—Fifth Circuit interprets Copyright Act to allow copying of software for any legitimate reason—Vault Corp. v. Quaid Software Ltd., 847 F.2d 255. 23 *Suffolk U.L. Rev.* 905-12 Fall '89
Copyright ownership of commissioned computer software in light of current developments in the work made for hire doctrine. 24 *Ind. L. Rev.* 135-59 '91
Copyright protection of computer "interfaces" in Japan. O. Hirakawa, K. Nakano. 7 *Computer Law.* 1-16 D '90
Copyright wrong: the United States' failure to provide copyright protection for works of architecture. 47 *Wash. & Lee L. Rev.* 1103-27 Fall '90
Copyrighted software and tying arrangements: a fresh appreciation for per se illegality. 10 *Computer L.J.* 413-52 O '90
Copyrighting "look and feel": Manufacturers Technologies v. CAMS [706 F. Supp. 984]. 3 *Harv. J.L. & Tech.* 195-208 Spr '90
Copyrights and copyremedies: unfair use and injunctions. J. L. Oakes. 18 *Hofstra L. Rev.* 983-1003 Summ '90

Listings in the *Index to Legal Periodicals & Books*

Finding Law Review Articles Online

If you're researching from your home or office, you'll likely want to find law review and journal articles online. The Law Review Commons provides access to more than 220,000 articles from roughly 300 law reviews and journals at no cost. Journals indexed in the Commons include *Cornell Law Review, Duke Law Journal, Emory Law Journal, Notre Dame Law Review,* and the *University of Pennsylvania Journal of Constitutional Law.* You can browse journals by subject or title and search by keyword or publication date. To get started, go to https://lawreviewcommons.com.

Specialized Loose-Leaf Materials

Most attorneys specialize in a particular field because there's too much law to learn every area well. Before the advent of comprehensive legal databases like Westlaw and LexisNexis, many legal publishers catered to the need for specialized and up-to-date information by offering loose-leaf compilations of recent developments in particular fields and weekly or monthly loose-leaf supplements.

While most of these publications are now available electronically (either as part of a more extensive legal database or through an individual subscription), some still exist in print. These materials provide information about new legislation, regulations, and judicial and administrative decisions that might affect the field of law covered by a publication.

Unless your research topic falls squarely within one of these special categories, you will probably find these resources too specialized for your purposes. If it does, locate the appropriate service, read the instructions on using it at the front of the first volume, and check the index.

A benefit of these resources is that using one might solve your problem almost immediately. All the loose-leaf services listed here can be found in a good law library.

Selected Loose-Leaf Services

Wolters Kluwer

Bankruptcy Law Reporter

Consumer Credit Guide

Employment Safety and Health Guide

LLCs and Partnerships: Law, Finance, and Tax Planning

Medicare and Medicaid Guide

Standard Federal Tax Reporter

Unemployment Insurance Reporter

Wage-Hour Compliance Handbook

West Group

Bankruptcy Practice Handbook

Employment Coordinator

Estate, Tax and Personal Financial Planning

Family Estate Planning Guide

Labor and Employment Law: Compliance and Litigation

Social Security Law and Practice

Treatises and Monographs

Like experts in every field, legal experts publish books. When a book attempts to cover an entire area of the law, it is called a "treatise." Typically, law treatises have titles like *Prosser on Torts, Powell on Real Property,* and *Corbin on Contracts.* When a book covers just a small portion of a general legal field or introduces a new concept into the legal realm, it is called a "monograph." Hundreds—or even thousands—of these books can be found in the stacks of a typical law library and can provide an overview of a subject.

There is a big difference between these resources and the textbooks discussed earlier in this chapter. While textbooks cover entire legal topics with the intent to teach, treatises and monographs exist to provide in-depth reference materials. Generally, they delve much deeper into an area than you would care to go. They also become dated more quickly despite periodic supplementation.

Restatements of the Law

Legal scholars always try to pinpoint what the law "is" on a particular subject. In some cases, groups of scholars have convened under the auspices of an organization called the American Law Institute (ALI) to put into writing definitive statements of the law in various areas. These statements are termed "Restatements" and cover topics like contracts, torts, and property.

While these tomes cover their subjects exhaustively, they are usually of little help to the beginning researcher looking for a good background resource. First, they are not in a narrative form but rather consist of very terse summations of legal principles and longer comments explaining them. Second, the language in these comments is generally arcane, and third, the various restatements aren't well indexed or organized for efficient information retrieval. Because these publications often try to reconcile unreconcilable contradictions in the law, they tend to produce more confusion than enlightenment. They're not a good place to start your research, and you'll probably find you don't need them once you get going.

Finding and Using Constitutions, Statutes, Regulations, and Ordinances

At some point during your legal research, you will probably find yourself reviewing legislatively or administratively created materials, such as statutes, regulations, and ordinances. These sources are at the heart of what most of us think of when we think of "the law." In this chapter, we'll explain how to find and use them.

Finding and Using Constitutions

As a legal researcher, we doubt you'll spend much time examining constitutional issues. As the supreme law of the land, the U.S. and state constitutions are very broad documents that lay out the basic framework of how our law operates. In fact, the U.S. Constitution is a relatively short document you can skim through in minutes. To see for yourself, take a look at a copy at www.archives.gov/founding-docs/constitution-transcript.

You'll notice that the Constitution describes the responsibilities of various branches of government using broad, flexible language that allows the law to change along with societal values. The Constitution doesn't address the detailed issues most of us need answered, like how to calculate child support or whether you're entitled to accrued vacation time when you quit your job. Instead, you'll often find the answers to these questions in statutes and regulations.

Fortunately, most of us can trust that the laws we rely on for answers are constitutionally valid. While proving that the federal or state legislature passed an unconstitutional statute or that a court created unconstitutional case law is possible, it would be time-consuming and beyond the ability of most individuals. Courts have interpreted constitutions over many years, and the research required would extend far beyond the literal words on the Constitution's page.

That's not to say you can't do it, because all research is possible with enough effort. If you plan to challenge a law that conflicts with the U.S. Constitution or a state's constitution, consider starting with one of the secondary sources described in the last chapter. Reading about constitutional history will help you understand the area and provide context.

More information about the federal constitution is on the National Archives webpage (www.archives.gov/founding-docs/constitution). This site organizes the Constitution by article and amendment, discussing each separately, and provides multiple links to additional resources. You can also find information on the Library of Congress's website.

To find state constitutions, start at the NBER/Maryland State Constitutions Project (www.stateconstitutions.umd.edu/Search/Search.aspx). Federal and state constitutions will also be available in a law library.

The Bill of Rights

First Amendment: freedom of speech, freedom of religion, freedom of association, separation of church and state

Second Amendment: right to bear arms

Third Amendment: right not to have soldiers quartered in homes

Fourth Amendment: right of privacy, right against unreasonable searches and seizures, right to confront adverse witnesses

Fifth Amendment: right to trial by jury, right to due process of law (life, liberty, property), right against self-incrimination, freedom from double jeopardy

Sixth Amendment: speedy and public trial, right to representation by counsel, right to confront witnesses (cross-examination), right to subpoena witnesses

Seventh Amendment: right to trial in civil cases

Eighth Amendment: right to reasonable bail, ban on cruel and unusual punishment

Ninth Amendment: people retain rights in addition to those granted in the Constitution

Tenth Amendment: everything not prohibited is allowed

Finding Federal Statutes

If you are researching an area of federal law, you will most certainly have to look at a federal statute or two. These laws are enacted by Congress and signed by the president (or passed over a veto). But before you figure out how to interpret and use federal statutes, you should know where to find them.

Where to Find Federal Statutes

Federal statutes are located in law libraries. You can also find them online on the Office of the Law Revision Counsel of the U.S. House of Representatives website (https://uscode.house.gov). You'll have several search options, including searching by section or keywords. You can also browse the popular name list. Helpful search tips are available online at https://uscode.house.gov/static/help.html.

Federal statutes are also published in several books in the law library, the most popular being the *United States Code (U.S.C.)*, or the *United States Code Annotated (U.S.C.A.)*. The second set is "annotated."

If you need only the statute, going to the *U.S.C.* will meet your needs. But if you need more, use the *U.S.C.A.* It has the statute itself and other related resources, such as relevant cases that explain how the courts have interpreted the statute in specific factual scenarios. Statutes available for free online are typically not annotated.

How Federal Statutes Are Organized

Federal statutes are organized by subject in 54 separate numbered titles, and each title covers a specific subject. For instance, Title 35 contains the statutes governing patent law. Title 11 includes the bankruptcy statutes. In the library, these titles can span multiple volumes or only take up part of one volume, depending on how much law falls under that title. There's no other rule or set structure.

Ways to Find a Federal Statute

There are several approaches to finding statutes in the *U.S. Code*, depending on how much information you have:

- **Do you know the citation?** If so, you can look it up directly by typing it into a search box or finding the appropriate volume. You'll search for the title number and section.
- **Do you know the "popular name"?** Sometimes, you might only have the act or statute's name but not the specific citation. You can look it up in the Popular Names Index in print or by using the Popular Name Tool in the online version of the *U.S. Code*.
- **Do you know the subject area?** If you can pinpoint the title you need, use the subject index for the specific title.
- **Do you have keywords?** If you followed our advice in Chapter 3, you should have them. At the end of the entire print series is a general subject index that allows you to search by keyword. Typing the right combination of words using natural language or a Boolean search should also yield relevant results if you're searching online.

Using Citations

The reference to any primary law source—including a federal statute—is called a "citation." Once you understand how to read a citation, you'll recognize them in the future because they're written in a standard form to tell you precisely where the law is located. Citations to federal statutes contain the title of the *U.S. Code* where the statute is found and the section number.

EXAMPLE: The citation for the Civil Rights Act of 1964 is:

42	U.S.C.A.	§ 2000	a-h
title number	United States Code Annotated	section number	subsection letters

Sample Federal Statute Citation

If you are looking for this statute online, you can simply type it into the search box (you probably won't need the "§" sign, which means "section"). Finding this statute in the law library is also easy. Locate the set of books labeled *U.S.C.A.* (maroon) or *U.S.C.* (black and blue). Look at the spine of the volumes marked 42 to find the one that includes § 2000a-h. Within the title, you'll find sections arranged numerically.

Using the Popular Name

You might hear a federal statute referred to by its popular name—for example, the "Civil Rights Act," the "Taft-Hartley Act," or the "Marine Mammal Protection Act." You can find such a statute by using the *Popular Names Index* that accompanies the *United States Code Annotated* (*U.S.C.A.*), the "popular names table" volume that accompanies the *United States Code Service, Lawyers' Edition* (*U.S.C.S.*); or *Shepard's Acts and Cases by Popular Names: Federal and State.* This last publication is particularly useful for finding state and federal statutes and cases through their popular names. If you're searching online, you can use the Popular Name Tool at https://uscode.house.gov/popularnames/popularnames.htm.

Finding Statutes by Chapter, Section, or Title Number

Sometimes statutes are commonly known by a title, chapter, or section number that refers to how they are organized, not to the book they are in. For instance, many people might have heard of Title VII, the statutes that address discrimination in the workplace. But it's not part of Title VII of the U.S. Code—it's actually in Title 42.

Where did the "Title VII" come from? When written, bills are assigned internal organizing labels for legislative purposes. A bill isn't assigned to a title of the federal code until it passes and becomes a law.

When researching a statute that you know only by one of its internal organizing designations—such as Title VII, Chapter 7 (Bankruptcy Code), or Section 8 (Low-Income Housing Assistance)—first see whether it is listed that way in a popular names index. If not, focus on the subject of the statute—for instance, "civil rights" or "job discrimination"—and use one of the code indexes discussed below.

POPULAR NAME TABLE 832

Civil Rights Act of 1957
Pub. L. 85–315, Sept. 9, 1957, 71 Stat. 634 (See Title 5, § 5315(19); Title 28, §§ 1343, 1861;
Title 42, §§ 1971, 1975, 1975a, 1975b, 1975c, 1975d, 1975e, 1995)
Pub. L. 86–383, title IV, § 401, Sept. 28, 1959, 73 Stat. 724 (Title 42, § 1975c)
Pub. L. 86–449, May 6, 1960, title IV, title VI, 74 Stat. 89 (Title 42, §§ 1971, 1975d)
Pub. L. 87–264, title IV, Sept. 21, 1961, 75 Stat. 559 (Title 42, § 1975c)
Pub. L. 88–152, § 2, Oct. 17, 1963, 77 Stat. 271 (Title 42, § 1975c)
Pub. L. 88–352, title V, July 2, 1964, 78 Stat. 249 (Title 42, §§ 1975a–1975d)
Pub. L. 90–198, § 1, Dec. 14, 1967, 81 Stat. 582 (Title 42, §§ 1975c, 1975e)
Pub. L. 91–521, §§ 1–4, Nov. 25, 1970, 84 Stat. 1356, 1357 (Title 42, §§ 1975a, 1975b, 1975d, 1975e)
Pub. L. 92–64, Aug. 4, 1971, 85 Stat. 166 (Title 42, § 1975e)
Pub. L. 92–496, Oct. 14, 1972, 86 Stat. 913 (Title 42, §§ 1975a–1975e)
Pub. L. 94–292, § 2, May 27, 1976, 90 Stat. 524 (Title 42, § 1975e)
Pub. L. 95–132, § 2, Oct. 13, 1977, 91 Stat. 1157 (Title 42, § 1975e)
Pub. L. 95–444, §§ 2–7, Oct. 10, 1978, 92 Stat. 1067, 1068 (Title 42, §§ 1975b, 1975c, 1975d, 1975e)
Pub. L. 96–81, §§ 2, 3, Oct. 6, 1979, 93 Stat. 642 (Title 42, §§ 1975c, 1975e)
Pub. L. 96–447, § 2, Oct. 13, 1980, 94 Stat. 1894 (Title 42, § 1975e)

Civil Rights Act of 1960
Pub. L. 86–449, May 6, 1960, 74 Stat. 86 (Title 18, §§ 837, 1074, 1509; Title 20, §§ 241, 640;
Title 42, §§ 1971, 1974–1974e, 1975d)

Civil Rights Act of 1964
Pub. L. 88–352, July 2, 1964, 78 Stat. 241 (Title 28, § 1447; Title 42, §§ 1971, 1975a–1975d, 2000a–2000h–6)
Pub. L. 92–261, §§ 2–8, 10, 11, 13, Mar. 24, 1972, 86 Stat. 103–113 (Title 42, §§ 2000e, 2000e–1 to 2000e–6, 2000e–8, 2000e–9, 2000e–13 to 2000e–17)

● ●

Manpower Development and Training Amendments of 1966
Pub. L. 89–792, Nov. 7, 1966, 80 Stat. 1434 (Title 42, §§ 2572b, 2572c, 2582, 2583, 2601, 2603, 2610b, 2611, 2614)

Marihuana and Health Reporting Act
Pub. L. 91–296 title V, June 30, 1970, 84 Stat. 352 (Title 42, § 242 note)
Pub. L. 95–461, § 3(a), Oct. 14, 1978, 92 Stat. 1268 (Title 42, § 242 note)

Marihuana Tax Act of 1937
Aug. 2, 1937, ch. 553, 50 Stat. 551

Marine Corps Personnel Act
May 29, 1934, ch. 367, 48 Stat. 809

Marine Insurance Act (District of Columbia)
Mar. 4, 1922, ch. 93, 42 Stat. 401

Marine Mammal Protection Act of 1972
Pub. L. 92–522, Oct. 21, 1972, 86 Stat. 1027 (Title 16, §§ 1361, 1362, 1371–1384, 1401–1407)
Pub. L. 93–205, § 13(e), Dec. 28, 1973, 87 Stat. 902 (Title 16, §§ 1362, 1371, 1372, 1402)
Pub. L. 94–265, title IV, § 404(a), Apr. 13, 1976, 90 Stat. 360 (Title 16, § 1362)
Pub. L. 95–136, §§ 1–4, Oct. 18, 1977, 91 Stat. 1167 (Title 16, §§ 1372, 1380, 1384, 1407)
Pub. L. 95–316, §§ 1–4, July 10, 1978, 92 Stat. 380, 381 (Title 16, §§ 1379, 1380, 1384, 1407)

The *U.S.C.A. Popular Names Index* is included with the *U.S.C.A.* set of books, directly following it on the shelves. This index gives a citation that refers to the correct title and section of the named statute (for example, Title 20, § 607). Above are the popular names index entries for two of the three acts mentioned above. As you can see, the Civil Rights Act of 1964 is in Titles 28 and 42, and the Marine Mammal Protection Act is in Title 16 of the federal code.

Using Indexes

If you don't have the name or citation of the statute, start with the index. Each title of the code has a separate index located at the back of the last book of the title. There is also a general index for all the titles as a whole. If you know what title your statute is in—or likely to be in—start with the index for that title. Use the general index if you aren't sure which title your statute is in. Work from the keywords list you created in Chapter 2.

Some titles contain a variety of subject matter. For instance, Title 42 contains statutes relating to water resources, water planning, voting rights, civil rights, and the National Science Foundation, in addition to its general topic of public health and welfare. If you looked up any of these subjects individually in the general index, they'd all refer you to Title 42.

Making Sure Federal Statutes Are Current

Once you've found the statute or statutes you need, you will want to ensure they are still current. After all, the series of books that publish statutes are only published occasionally, and Congress can change or update those statutes at any time. Indeed, many laws are completely changed by amendment and deletion in just a few years.

Fortunately, there's a simple way to stay up to date using the "pocket part system." Pocket parts are paper supplements that fit inside each hardcover volume, usually at the back. They are published once a year and contain any statutory changes occurring in the interim. Sometimes, the pocket parts get too bulky because of legislative changes. In that case, either a new hardcover volume incorporating all of the changes gets published, or you'll find a separate paperback volume on the shelf next to the hardcover book.

Always check the pocket part to see if a statute you're reading has been amended or repealed. Usually, the pocket parts will reprint the sections of any statutes that have been amended in the hardcover version. Sections of the statute that haven't been amended aren't reproduced in the pocket part. Instead, you'll use the hardcover volume for the text. If you don't check the pocket part, you might find that the statute you discovered in the hardcover volume has long since been amended or even repealed. If a book older than a year doesn't have a pocket part, ask the librarian if there is one.

 TIP

If you're working online, find out how up to date the statutes are. Even on the most advanced systems, statutes aren't updated as soon as they're passed. You might have to check the congress.gov website for any recent changes (more on that below).

After you do this, there will be another step in the process, commonly called "Shepardizing." Using a volume called *Shepard's Citations for Statutes*, you'll look up each time a case has mentioned a particular statute and provides a reference (citation) to the case. In addition, *Shepard's* provides references to amendments that have been made to the statute and instances when attorney general opinions and some secondary sources have mentioned the statute. We'll explain how to use this resource in Chapter 8.

Finding Recently Passed Federal Law

Sometimes, the statute you seek won't be in the code because it has passed only recently. Federal statutes start as "bills" introduced in a session of Congress. They are assigned labels and numbers depending on which house of Congress they originate in. For example, a bill introduced in the U.S. Senate might be called Senate Bill 2 (S.2).

You can search bills using the congress.gov website (www.congress. gov). On the home page, top and center, you see a box with the heading "Current Congress" on its left side. If you then click "More Options," you can search for a pending bill by sponsor (the Congress member responsible for introducing the bill) or when it was introduced. Use the search bar at the top of the page to search using a word or phrase in the bill or the bill number. The list your search produces will have entries that briefly describe bills and their current status—for example, "in committee," "passed from the Senate to the House," "engrossed" (in its final form), "enrolled" (sent to the president), and so on.

To search for a previous bill that recently became law, use the advanced search feature and select "Laws" in the "Quick List" menu.

Few of the many bills introduced in Congress become law. To do so, they must be passed by both houses and signed by the president or passed over the president's veto. Once a bill becomes law, it is assigned a new label. The basic label is Public Law (Pub. L.). Following the "Pub. L.," the statute will have one number that corresponds with the number of the Congress (for example, 94th) that passed it, followed by another number that is simply the number assigned to that specific bill by the Congress. So Pub. L. No. 94-586, for example, refers to Public Law 586 passed by the 94th Congress.

Bill drafters are aware that their handiwork will end up in codes. Much of the new law organized in Public Laws is published in various parts of the *U.S. Code*, because each law might amend different statutes or add new sections to other titles. For example, a new tax provision might also affect the education system; in that case, both might be part of one bill (and one Public Law), but once "codified," will go into two different titles (the tax title, Title 26, and the education title, Title 20).

Finding Out-of-Date Federal Statutes in the Law Library

If you are looking for a specific statute that has been amended or deleted and no longer appears in the *United States Code*, you can find it in two publications: the *Statutes at Large* (www.loc.gov/collections/united-states-statutes-at-large/about-this-collection) and the *U.S. Code Congressional and Administrative News*.

The *Statutes at Large* series contains statutes organized by their public law numbers instead of their federal code citations. The *U.S. Code Congressional and Administrative News* publication also carries statutes by their public law number but is annotated and generally an easier resource to use.

Finding State Statutes

You can use many principles that apply to researching federal statutes when dealing with state statutes. However, there are some differences in federal and state legislative processes and the resources you use to find and interpret state statutes.

Ways to Find a State Statute

As with federal statutes, you can find state statutes in different ways. If you are starting from square one, you can use an index (or online keyword search) to find relevant statutes. If you have the citation for the statute, you can look it up that way.

Every state maintains its statutes online in some form. The websites vary in format, but almost all allow you to search for statutes by topic, keyword searches, and specific code numbers. You can start your research by visiting your state's legislative website. Another approach is to search the Law Library of Congress's "Guide to Law Online" section (www.loc.gov/research-centers/law-library-of-congress/researcher-resources/guide-to-law-online/states-and-territories). Click your state and select "Legislative Branch" to be taken to a page with links to your state's statutes and other legislative materials.

CAUTION
Sometimes it's necessary to expand your search. Often statutes within a particular category are found in different parts of a code and even in different codes entirely. A single search might get you to some of the statutes you seek, while missing other relevant ones. Make sure you browse the statutes surrounding the particular statute you find in a topical search. Also, when possible, do a keyword search of the entire code to pull up any additional statutes that might appear in other parts.

Of course, you can still use the law library to look up state statutes if that's your preferred choice. Just recognize that not every law library will have every state's statutes. For example, if you're located in California and you want to look up a statute in Arizona, your law library might not have Arizona's state statutes.

Using State Statute Indexes

Many print collections of state statutes have indexes for each subject (that is, for each title, code, or chapter) and for the collection of laws as a whole. As with indexes to the federal code, you will probably find a general index at the end of the series, with indexes to each title distributed throughout the volumes at the beginning or end of each title.

If your state's statutes are found in two or more publications, use either index. For example, the California statutes are published both in *West's Annotated Codes* and in *Deering's Annotated Codes* (LexisNexis Publishing). Because both publications index the same statutes and citations, you can look up any citation you find in the *Deering* index in the *West* code, and vice versa.

If you are working online, you might not have access to this type of index. However, you should be able to search by keyword. For more on keyword searching, go back to Chapter 2.

Using State Statutory Citations

You can also use a citation to find a state statute. Citations to state statutes typically refer to the title (or volume) and section numbers. The three examples shown below are typical.

23   Vt. Stat. Ann.   § 1185

title (volume   Vermont Statutes   section
number)   Annotated   number

N.J. Stat. Ann.   2A: 170-90.1

New Jersey Statutes   volume   section
Annotated   number   number

Mich. Comp. Laws Ann.   421.27   (c)(2)(ii)

Michigan Compiled Laws   section   subsection
Annotated   number   letter

Sample State Statute Citations

In states with separate codes, like New York and California, citations look like those shown below.

P.C.   § 518
Penal   section
Code   number

Penal Law   § 14025
Collection of   section
Penal Statutes number

Sample California and New York Citations

If you are looking for a statute online and have located the state's statutes, you can usually type the citation into the search box. Sometimes, you might have to select the correct title or section from a list and select the code from within the title. This works much like it does if you're looking in the law library. First, locate the correct title (by looking at the first number of the citation); second, turn to the section number.

Making Sure State Statutes Are Current

As with federal statutes, you will want to use the pocket part system to ensure state statutes are current. Functionally, this will happen the same way when dealing with federal statutes—you'll check the back of the volume for a pocket part, then ask the librarian if there isn't one.

Pocket parts show updates in one of two ways. In most states, the part of the statute that has been amended is shown in the pocket part, with additions underlined and deletions marked by asterisks. For example, a California statute from the hardcover volume in its original form and the amended version from the pocket part are shown below. As you can see, words that have been added to the statute are underlined. Removed words are represented by asterisks.

---

§ 1942.   **Repairs by lessee; rent deduction; limit**

If within a reasonable time after notice to the lessor, of dilapidations which he ought to repair, he neglects to do so, the lessee may repair the same himself, where the cost of such repairs do not require an expenditure greater than one month's rent of the premises, and deduct the expenses of such repairs from the rent, or the lessee may vacate the premises, in which case he shall be discharged from further payment of rent, or performance of other conditions. (Enacted 1872. As amended Code Am.1873–74, c. 612, p. 246, § 206.)

Main Volume Statute

§ 1942. Repairs by tenant; rent deduction or vacation of premises; presumption; limit; nonavailability of remedy; additional remedy

(a) If within a reasonable time after <u>written or oral</u> notice to the * * * <u>landlord or his agent, as defined in subdivision (a) of Section 1962,</u> of dilapidations <u>rendering the premises untenantable</u> which * * * <u>the landlord</u> ought to repair, * * * <u>the landlord</u> neglects to do so, the * * * <u>tenant</u> may repair the same himself where the cost of such repairs does not require an expenditure * * * <u>more</u> than one month's rent of the premises and deduct the expenses of such repairs from the rent <u>when due,</u> or the * * * <u>tenant</u> may vacate the premises, in which case * * * <u>the tenant</u> shall be discharged from further payment of rent, or performance of other conditions <u>as of the date of vacating the premises.</u>

Pocket Part Statute

In some states, the pocket parts reprint the sections of any statutes that have been amended. Statute sections not yet amended aren't reproduced in the pocket part. Instead, you'll go to the hardcover volume for the text.

Finding Recently Enacted State Legislation

As we've already discussed, if your research involves a newly passed, repealed, or amended statute, it might not be reflected in the version of the statute you are looking at. If you're online, you can usually find the updated version by going to the state legislature's website and looking up the bill number, if you have it. If not, you can search recently enacted bills by keyword in a section of the legislature's website called "session laws."

Of course, if you use the hard-copy volumes, the changes might not yet be reflected in the pocket parts, which come out only once a year. Fortunately, most states publish newly passed statutes in legislative update publications, which appear more frequently than the pocket parts. These updated publications are under different names, such as *McKinney's New York Session Law Service* and *Vernon's Texas Session Law Services*. Advance legislative update services are usually shelved next to the annotated state statutes. If you can't find them, ask a law librarian.

All update publications are organized pretty much the same way, and there are several ways to get to the statutes you seek. First, the statutes appear in numerical order according to the number given them by the state legislature. Second, in many states, statutes appear according to their "chapter" number; in others, they are listed by "session law" number. You can get to it directly if you already know which number statute you're looking for.

Using the annotated code or collection citation is another way to use the advance legislative service. If you know, for example, that Labor Code § 560.5 has been amended, a table at the front or back of each legislative service volume will convert your "code" citation to the appropriate chapter number.

Finally, all advance legislative services have a detailed alphabetical table of contents at the front and a cumulative subject index in the back.

Finding Pending State Legislation

As with newly enacted legislation, in most states, the easiest way to find pending state legislation is to go online and look at the state legislature's website. If you know what bill you're looking for, you can look it up by bill number. If you don't, you could try looking up the citation for a statute you know has changed, or you can do a keyword search to find the bill.

 TIP

If you don't use online resources, the alternatives are time-consuming and will probably require you to have a bill number or know the subject being considered. Rather than spending your time figuring this out in a law library, we suggest you call your local elected representative's office and ask for a copy of the bill.

Understanding and Using Federal and State Statutes

Most legal research projects involve determining how the law works in a particular circumstance. This situation usually arises when you aren't sure how a court would apply a statute to the facts in your situation. If a statute is unclear, the court will try to figure out what the legislature intended and explain it in its decision, which has the effect of assisting other courts. Only if the legislature exceeded its powers or intended something unconstitutional will courts disregard a statute, which doesn't happen often.

However, determining what the legislature intended is often challenging, sometimes because of poorly drafted legislation. Occasionally, it's because legislators compromise, delete words, and add more words to get enough votes to pass the bill. What might have begun as straightforward and clear language often becomes so riddled with exceptions and conditions that the result presents serious difficulties to anyone who wants to understand what the legislature intended. In the words of one frustrated judge:

I concur in the opinion of the majority because its construction of Code of Civil Procedure Section 660 seems plausible and hence probably correct, although—given the cosmic incomprehensibility of the section—one can never be absolutely sure.

It occurs to me that Section 660 illustrates poignantly the maxim so useful in statutory construction—that if the Legislature had known what it meant, it would have said so.

It seems to me shameful, however, that large sums of money should change hands depending upon one's view of what this dismal, opaque statute means.

(Bunton v. Arizona Pacific Tanklines, 141 Cal.App.3d 210, 190 Cal. Rptr. 295 (1983).)

Interpreting Statutes

Understanding what a statute says and what it means is your first goal. To get a grasp on understanding statutes, we suggest you follow these eight rules.

Rule 1: Read the Statute at Least Three Times, Then Read It Again

Often, a different and hopefully more accurate meaning will emerge from each reading. Never feel that somehow you are inadequate because, after reading it several times, you aren't sure what a particular statute means. Many lawsuits result from the fact that lawyers disagree about confusing statutory language.

Rule 2: Pay Close Attention to "Ands" and "Ors"

Many statutes have lots of "ands" and "ors" tucked into different clauses, and the thrust of the statute often depends on which clauses are joined by an "and" and which by an "or." When clauses are joined by an "or," it means that the conditions in at least one of the clauses must be present, but not all. When clauses are joined by an "and," the conditions in all the clauses must be met.

Rule 3: Assume All Words and Punctuation in the Statute Have Meaning

Often, statutes seem to be internally inconsistent or redundant. Sometimes they are. However, courts presume that every word and comma in a statute means something, and you should do the same. If you're unsure what a word or phrase means, look it up in a law dictionary or a multi-volume publication titled *Words and Phrases*, discussed further below.

Rule 4: Interpret a Statute So That It Is Consistent With All Other Related Statutes, If Possible

Although one statute might conflict with others on the same subject, a judge who examines the statutes will attempt to reconcile the meanings so that no conflict exists. Ask yourself whether any interpretation of the statute will make it consistent rather than inconsistent with other statutes.

Interpreting "Ands" and "Ors"

Consider the following provision taken from 42 U.S.C.A. § 416:

An applicant who is the son or daughter of a fully or currently insured individual, but who is not (and is not deemed to be) the child of such insured individual under paragraph (2) of this subsection, shall nevertheless be deemed to be the child of such insured individual if:

(A)   *in the case of an insured individual entitled to old-age insurance benefits (who was not, in the month preceding such entitlement, entitled to disability insurance benefits)—*

   (i)   *such insured individual—*

   (I)   *has acknowledged in writing that the applicant is his or her son or daughter*

   (II)   *has been decreed by a court to be the mother or father of the applicant, or*

   (III) *has been ordered by a court to contribute to the support of the applicant because the applicant is his or her son or daughter, and such acknowledgment, court decree, or court order was made not less than one year before such insured individual became entitled to old-age insurance benefits or attained retirement age (as defined in subsection (l)), whichever is earlier ...*

Interpretation: To be considered a child of an insured individual, a person must satisfy at least one of the three conditions under Section (A)(i)—because of the use of the word "or"—and the condition must be met within one year of when the insured individual became entitled to old-age insurance benefits or attained retirement age, because of the "and."

Rule 5: Interpret Criminal Statutes Strictly

Courts apply a doctrine called "strict interpretation" to criminal law, to further the policy that no person should be held accountable for a crime without adequate notice that their behavior would be considered criminal. The only way to provide this type of notice is to insist that criminal laws be interpreted literally, interpreting any ambiguities in favor of the defendant. For example, to convict somebody of "breaking and entering a building belonging to another with the intent to commit theft or a felony therein" (a common definition of burglary), a prosecutor has to prove each element of the crime—that the person broke into and entered a building and intended to commit a felony inside.

> EXAMPLE: A young man in Vermont was charged with the felony of breaking and entering into the county courthouse. He was found in the morning passed out under the judge's desk with some rare coins that he had taken from the desk.
>
> At his trial, the young man testified that he thought the courthouse was a church and that he simply broke in to get some sleep. However, once inside, he decided to look around and ended up stealing the coins. He didn't remember passing out. The trial judge (not the coin collector, but a more disinterested jurist) instructed the jury that unless they found beyond a reasonable doubt that the young man actually intended to commit the theft or another felony at the time he entered the courthouse, they couldn't convict him of breaking and entering. He was acquitted.

Rule 6: Interpret Ambiguities in Statutes in Ways That Seem to Best Further the Purpose of the Legislation

Much legislation is designed either to protect the public from ills or to provide various benefits. When ambiguities exist in these types of statutes—commonly called "social welfare legislation"—the courts tend to interpret them so that the protection or benefit will be provided, rather than the other way around.

EXAMPLE: A statute allows public assistance recipients to "earn" up to $500 a month without losing any benefits. The purpose of the statute is to provide an incentive for those receiving public assistance to find work. Tom's father gives him $500 a month to stop drinking. Tom reports this to the state's social services department, which promptly reduces Tom's monthly grant by $500. Tom goes to court, arguing that he is "earning" the money by not drinking and is entitled to the $500 exemption. The social services department contends that since the statute was intended to stimulate employment, the term "earns" means income from employment. The social services department's argument will probably win since its interpretation is more consistent with the statute's underlying objective.

Rule 7: Interpret the Statute So That It Makes Sense and Doesn't Lead to Absurd or Improbable Results

Courts are sometimes called on to interpret statutes that, if taken literally, would lead to a result that the legislature couldn't have intended. In such an instance, a court will try to interpret the statute so that it makes sense or leads to a logical result.

EXAMPLE: A California statute imposed a $100 daily penalty on landlords who interfered with a tenant's utilities with the intent to evict the tenant. The California Supreme Court ruled that the legislature couldn't have intended this harsh result and instead interpreted the statute as allowing a penalty of *up to* $100 per day.

Few things are more challenging for a layperson than when the judge rejects a literal interpretation of a statute because "the legislature couldn't have intended it." When reading a statute, ask whether your interpretation is grounded in common sense and how the legislature likely intended the law to work. But remember that many laws aren't applied how we assume they should be or how we would like them to be. It's one of the primary reasons we must research the law.

Rule 8: Track Down All Cross-References to Other Statutes and Sections

People who draft statutes regularly reference other statutes and subsections of the same statute. When faced with such a statute, the human tendency is to ignore the cross-references and hope that they don't pertain to your situation. Our advice, quite simply, is to track down each cross-reference and make sure you understand how it relates to the main body of the statute you are analyzing. If you don't, you could overlook something crucial.

Tools for Interpreting Statutes

Although we recommend you start by reading a statute multiple times so you understand it as best you can, other resources are available to help you interpret statutes.

Reading Cases That Interpret Statutes

It would be nice if research into the meaning of statutes began and ended with reading the statutes themselves. But as we've explained, the judiciary is charged with interpreting statutes when a dispute over their meaning arises in a lawsuit. Court interpretations of statutes are as much a part of the law as the words of the statutes themselves.

For example, the California statute mentioned earlier provided that landlords were liable to tenants for $100 every day the landlord shut off utilities to force the tenants out. When a landlord appealed a judgment against him under this statute, the California Supreme Court decided that it would be unconstitutional to penalize a landlord $100 per day regardless of circumstances (*Hale v. Morgan*, 22 Cal.3d 388, 149 Cal. Rptr. 375, 584 P.2d 512 (1978)). The Court interpreted the statute to allow a penalty of up to $100 per day, depending on circumstances. Immediately after this court decision, California utility shut-off law could be determined only by reading the statute and the court case together. (The California legislature later amended the statute to comply with the Court's ruling.)

It can be challenging to read and understand case law. We'll discuss how to do so in the next chapter.

Using Attorney General Opinions to Interpret Statutes

Government agencies often ask attorneys general, the highest legal officers in government, to interpret the meaning of statutes. When they do, they frequently issue written opinions. These attorney general opinions aren't binding on the courts. Still, they have influence, especially when there is no precedent (relevant case law) to the contrary. And they can help decipher an otherwise hopelessly complicated statute.

You can find these opinions online by visiting the National Association of Attorneys General (NAAG) website (www.naag.org), which links to each state attorney general's website and provides information such as bios and phone numbers. You can also try using a search engine to search for your state attorney general's website.

You can also find these opinions in the library, collected in publications usually called something like *Opinions of the Attorney-General of the State of [State]*. Both federal and state sets exist. If a statute is the subject of an attorney general's opinion, the citation to the opinion citing the statute will appear after the case citations in *Shepard's Citations for Statutes*. (See Chapter 8 for more on how to use this valuable tool.)

Using *Words and Phrases* to Interpret Statutes

To interpret a statute correctly, you might need to know how courts have interpreted one or more of its specialized words and phrases. One tool to help you do this is a multivolume set called *Words and Phrases* (Thomson West). It contains one-sentence interpretations of common words and phrases pulled from cases and organized alphabetically. This publication allows you to determine whether courts have interpreted or used any particular word or phrase you are interested in and, if so, how.

In a real sense, *Words and Phrases* offers contextual definitions instead of the abstract and disconnected entries found in most law dictionaries. Below is part of the *Words and Phrases* entry for "Landlord and Tenant."

As with other hardbound legal resources, don't forget to check the pocket part in the back of each book for the newest entries.

LANDLORD AND TENANT

In general

The relation of "landlord and tenant" depends upon agreement. Estes v. Gatliff, 163 S.W.2d 273, 275, 291 Ky. 93.

A "landlord and tenant relationship" will be implied from occupancy of premises with owner's consent. Crawford v. Jerry, 11 A.2d 210, 211, 111 Vt. 120.

The relation of "landlord and tenant" arises only where one in possession of land recognizes another as his landlord. Hoffmann v. Chapman, Tex.Civ.App., 170 S.W.2d 496, 498.

A contract establishing "landlord and tenant relationship" does not include principal and agent or master and servant relationships. Butler v. Maney, 200 So. 226, 228, 146 Fla. 33.

The relation of "landlord and tenant" may arise by express or implied contract and on slight evidence. Delay v. Douglas, Mo. App., 164 S.W.2d 154, 156.

Words and Phrases

Using Legislative History to Interpret Statutes

You might be uncertain about the meaning of a statute no matter how much you study it. For instance, many statutes provide that certain government employees are entitled to an administrative hearing if they lose their jobs. Such statutes often don't say whether the agency must provide the hearing before or after the discharge.

In all likelihood, if it's confusing to you, it was previously confusing to someone else, too, and that means you'll be able to find a case discussing it. But if not, how should you proceed? In those rare cases, one common way (and in many cases, the only way) is to find out what the legislators intended at the time they passed the statute. Their intent can be inferred from legislative committee reports, hearings, and floor debates that comprise the statute's "legislative history."

When you investigate legislative history, keep a couple of points in mind. First, as mentioned earlier, what the legislature intended in a statute is supposed to be gleaned from the "plain words" of the statute itself. So, if a judge believes the words of a statute are reasonably clear, there will be no inquiry into the legislative intent.

The second point is that you often won't find clear legislative intent despite your best efforts to unearth it. Typically, a few legislators know what's intended by the words of any particular statute, while the great majority who haven't even read it vote for or against the bill for reasons unrelated to how it's worded. For that reason, some judges stick to the words of the statute, no matter how difficult it is to understand.

Finding Federal Legislative History

Most legislative history for federal statutes is reported in committee reports. You can use Congress's website (www.congress.gov) to find legislative history for the last several sessions of Congress. You'll get the history session by session—that is, each history will discuss only the change or changes made in that session.

To find federal legislative history in the library, look at the annotated federal code for the statute. Most include a reference to the *U.S. Code Congressional and Administrative News*, which contains federal legislative history. If the federal statute doesn't have a citation to its legislative history, you can check the subject index, popular names table, and statutory reference table in each volume of the *U.S. Code Congressional and Administrative News*. However, there is one major limitation to the value of these indexes and tables. They are not cumulative. In other words, they index only materials from the legislative session covered by that volume.

If you have the public law number of a statute, find the volume containing the public laws for the Congress indicated in the public law number. For instance, if the number is 94-584, find the volume containing material for the 94th Congress. Then, use the statutory reference table to locate the committee reports. If you don't know the public law number, the *U.S. Code* citation, or the approximate year the statute was passed, you will have difficulty finding the appropriate committee reports. Your best bet is to search for the *U.S. Code* citation.

It is important to remember that the typical statute is amended many times over its lifespan, and each amendment has its own committee reports. Therefore, the legislative history of a statute generally refers to a collection of legislative histories. You must search each of these legislative histories, because any given *U.S. Code Congressional and Administrative News* volume contains only the committee reports for the session covered by that volume.

Finding State Legislative History

State legislative history is usually more difficult to uncover than federal legislative history. The chances of finding state legislative history online vary widely, depending on your state and the dates you're interested in. Your best bet is to use a commercial legal database, such as Westlaw or LexisNexis, if you can access one. If not, you can try searching your state legislature's website. The California Legislative Information website (https://leginfo.legislature.ca.gov), for example, includes bill analyses dating back to 1999. And the Maine Legislature has compiled and posted legislative histories for all bills since 1983 (www.maine.gov/legis/lawlib/lldl/legishistory.htm). Note, though, that not all states will make all of the legislative history materials you'll likely be searching for freely available online.

Fortunately, your local law library will have print materials to help you access this information. Many states have legislative analysts (lawyers who work for the legislature), whose comments on legislation are considered by the state legislators in the same way as Congress considers committee reports. These comments are sometimes published in the advance legislative update services as an introduction to the new statute.

Statutes and accompanying comments printed in these advance legislative services are later bound and retained in volumes called *Session Laws*, according to the year passed. It is some-times possible to discover the legislative history of an older state statute by finding these legislative analysts' comments with the statute in the bound *Session Laws*. To find a statute in the *Session Laws*, you need the chapter number assigned by the legislature. That number appears directly after the statute's text as printed in a code.

It is also common for legislative committees to have their staff lawyers draft memoranda to guide them in their deliberations. These memoranda are usually unavailable in law libraries but might be kept on file with the legislature. The best course for a researcher is probably to ask a law librarian about the available legislative history for laws in that state.

Using Uniform Law Histories to Interpret Statutes

Since 1892, there has been an effort to make several substantive areas of the law uniform among the states. A group of lawyers, judges, and law professors called the Uniform Law Commission (U.L.C.) drafts legislation covering certain areas of law, and then tries to get as many states as possible to adopt the "uniform" legislation. The packages drafted by the U.L.C. aren't law and don't affect our legal system until one or more state legislatures adopt them. Also, the fact that the package is adopted in one or more states doesn't make it law in any state that hasn't adopted it.

If the statute you are researching was a uniform law adopted by your state (you'll find this information in the annotations to the statutes, explained below), you can get some help interpreting its meaning by looking at a series of books called the *Uniform Laws Annotated (U.L.A.)*, published by Thomson West (also available on Westlaw). It contains all of the uniform laws, the original comments accompanying them, a listing of the states that have adopted them, notations of how states have altered each provision in the course of adopting it, summaries of case opinions that have interpreted each statute, and references to pertinent law review discussions. If your annotated state statutes are published by Thomson West (almost all are), the annotation following the statute will tell you. In addition, the annotation will reproduce the Uniform Law Commission's comment that accompanied the statute as initially proposed. It will also contain comments about how the state version of the statute differs from the original.

States seldom adopt uniform law packages without change. Usually, they add to or delete some of the statutes in the package. By the time the various states have adopted uniform laws, they are no longer, strictly speaking, "uniform." Still, for the most part, if you have an overall understanding of the package as the U.L.C. produced it, you will have a good grasp of the final result in any given adopting state.

To read a uniform law's text or find out which states have adopted it, go to the U.L.C.'s website (www.uniformlaws.org). Selecting "Acts" from the top navbar allows you to browse or search for an act.

Uniform Laws Adopted by Many States

- Uniform Commercial Code
- Uniform Controlled Substances Act
- Uniform Gifts to Minors Act
- Uniform Transfers to Minors Act
- Uniform Partnership Act
- Uniform Child Custody Jurisdiction Act

Using Statutes to Conduct Additional Research

Up to this point, we've referred you to other resources to help you understand the statute or statutes you're reading. But statutes serve another important function: They help you conduct additional research.

Reading the Statutory Scheme

Statutes aren't arranged haphazardly. Usually, legislatures arrange them into clumps called "statutory schemes." If you are interested in a particular area of law (small claims court, for example), you will usually find that the statutory scheme appears in one central location, and you can read that entire scheme at once. You might find that you can sue for up to $10,000 in one statute before finding a lower limit set for cases involving evictions, for example.

Reading the statutory scheme will help you answer the direct question in front of you and understand the legal principles in the field more generally. And it might also lead you to additional information you need. We suggest you browse or read the scheme anytime you review a statute for the first time.

Using Annotations

Statutes can either be "annotated" or "unannotated." Unannotated statutes have only the statute's text. Most statutes found online are unannotated. An unannotated version will work if you only need to read the statute. However, the annotated code is beneficial if you need to conduct additional research. Annotated codes contain cases and secondary sources that interpret or explain the statute.

Two versions of the *U.S. Code* are published in annotated form: the *United States Code Annotated,* or *U.S.C.A.* (Thomson West), and the *United States Code Service*, or *U.S.C.S.* (LexisNexis Publishing). These annotated codes include:

- one-sentence summaries of court cases that have interpreted the statute
- notes about the statute's history (such as amendments)
- cross-references to other relevant statutes
- cross-references to administrative regulations that might help interpret the statute
- citations to the legislative history of the statute, and
- research guides (references to relevant materials by the same publisher).

Finding and Using Regulations

Legislatures often pass laws that need active enforcement. For example, a complex series of federal statutes govern the collection of the federal income tax. However, the federal government wouldn't be solvent very long if it relied on everyone to pay their tax bill voluntarily. Accordingly, Congress created the Internal Revenue Service (IRS) to resolve questions about how the tax laws should be interpreted, provide specific guidance to help people prepare their tax returns, and keep a close watch on us all to ensure we pay our share.

The IRS is one of many "administrative agencies" created by Congress over the years to implement its programs. State legislatures have created a similar host of agencies to carry out their programs. Legislatures give such agencies the power to make rules and guidelines to carry out the goals of the statutes that authorized the creation of the agencies and the programs over which they have authority.

These rules and guidelines are collectively termed "regulations." Some are directed at the general public, some at business entities, and some at the agency itself. As long as they are consistent with the legislation that created them, they are just as binding and enforceable as statutes. Courts are willing to overturn an agency's regulations only when they conclude that the agency misinterpreted the law or issued a regulation without authority.

Finding Federal Regulations in a Law Library

Most federal regulations are published in the *Code of Federal Regulations (C.F.R.)*, a multivolume and well-indexed paperbound set organized by subject. The *C.F.R.* is organized into 50 separate titles, each covering a general subject. For instance, Title 7 contains regulations concerning agriculture, Title 10 contains energy regulations, and so on. *C.F.R.* titles often, but not always, correspond to the *U.S.C.* titles in terms of their subject matter. For example, Title 7 of the *United States Code* covers statutes relating to agriculture, and Title 7 of the *C.F.R.* contains agriculture regulations. But Title 42 of *U.S.C.* contains statutes on the

Medicaid program, while the Medicaid regulations are found in Title 45 of the *C.F.R.*

Along with each regulation, the *C.F.R.* provides a reference to the statute that authorizes it and a reference to where (and when) the regulation was published in the *Federal Register.* (All regulations are supposed to be published first in the *Federal Register*, as discussed below.)

The best way to find a federal regulation published in the C.F.R. if you don't already have the citation is to start with the general subject index that comes with this series. If you already know which title your regulation is likely to be in, use the table of contents at the end of each individual title.

Once you've found a regulation, you must be sure it's current. A new edition of the C.F.R. is published yearly with volumes staggered quarterly. Titles 1–16 are published on January 1, Titles 17–27 are published on April 1, Titles 28–41 are published on July 1, and Titles 42–50 are published on October 1.

When a new annual edition is published, its regulations are current as of that date. But how can you make sure you're up to date if the C.F.R. volume that contains the regulation you are interested in was published January 1, 2024, and you are doing your research in July 2024? First, consult the latest monthly pamphlet called *C.F.R., L.S.A.*, which stands for "List of *C.F.R.* Sections Affected." Find the title and section number of the regulation you are interested in. Second, see if any changes have occurred between the last published *C.F.R.* volume (January 1 in our example) and the pamphlet date (July 2024). Below is a typical page from *C.F.R., L.S.A.*

Suppose now that you are doing your research on July 15, and the July version of the *C.F.R., L.S.A.* hasn't yet hit the library shelf.

You would first use the *C.F.R., L.S.A.* for June. Second, you can use the *Federal Register*, where all new federal regulations are published initially. The *Federal Register* also contains proposed regulations, schedules of government agency meetings, presidential documents, and lists of bills that have been enacted.

The *Federal Register* can be hard to use because it contains many pages of very small type on newsprint. It is published daily, and a cumulative monthly index is available to help you find the regulation you're after. However, this index is generally organized according to the agency that initiated the action, so unless you know which agency you're dealing with, it can be of little help.

If you have a *C.F.R.* citation to the new regulation, or you want to bring your *C.F.R.* search entirely up to date (see above), you can consult the *C.F.R.* sections affected list in the latest issue of the *Federal Register*. This will give you a listing of all *C.F.R.* sections affected during the current month of the *Federal Register*.

Summing Up ...
How to Find Federal Regulations in the Law Library

✓ Consult either the general subject index to the *Code of Federal Regulations (C.F.R.)*, or the *Index to the Code of Federal Regulations* (commercially published by the National Archives and Records Administration, Office of the Federal Register).

✓ After you find the regulation, read the latest monthly issue of the *List of C.F.R. Sections Affected (C.F.R., L.S.A.)* to see whether changes in the regulation have been made since the *C.F.R.* volume was published.

✓ Consult the *List of C.F.R. Sections Affected* in the latest daily issue of the *Federal Register* for the most current status of a regulation.

✓ For regulations that have been issued since the latest *C.F.R.* volume was published, consult the cumulative index to the *Federal Register* under the appropriate agency.

92   **LSA—LIST OF CFR SECTIONS AFFECTED**

CHANGES APRIL 1, 1991 THROUGH NOVEMBER 29, 1991

TITLE 19 Chapter I—Con.   Page
171.33 (b)(1) and (d) heading
   revised.. 40780
   (b)(1) and (d) corrected.............. 48823
172.22 (e) added............................40780
   (e) corrected.............................. 48823
172.33 (b)(1) revised.................... 40780
177 Interpretive rule................... 46372
177.22 (b) introductory text
   amended...................................46115
178.2 Table amended...................32087
191.10 (e)(1)(i) amended............. 46115
191.21 (c) and (d) amended......... 46115
191.27 (c) amended....................... 46115

Chapter II—United States International Trade Commission (Parts 200—299)

200 Authority citation re-
   vised..36726
200.735-102 (g) removed..............36726
200.735-103 (a) and (c) introductory text amended; (b)
   and (c)(2) revised.....................36726
200.735-114 Nomenclature
   change....................................... 36726
200.735-115 Nomenclature
   change....................................... 36726
200.735-116 (b) revised................. 36726
200.735-121 Nomenclature
   change....................................... 36726

Chapter III—International Trade Administration, Department of Commerce (Parts 300—399)

356 Revised................................... 37804

Title 19—*Proposed Rules:*

4....................................40283, 48448, 51762
10.. 48448, 51762
19.. 22833, 33733
24.. 31576
101... 21111,
   22369, 55102, 56179
102.. 48448, 51762
113.. 22833, 33733
118... 33734
134.. 48448, 51762
142... 42568
141... 56608
142... 56608
144.. 22833, 33733
162... 25363
177............................... 46134, 48448, 51762

Note: **Boldface entries indicate November changes.**

TITLE 20—EMPLOYEES' BENEFITS

Chapter I—Office of Workers' Compensation Programs, Department of Labor (Parts 1—199)

                                    Page
10.305 Revised............................. 47675
10.306 (a) revised........................47675
10.311 (c) revised.........................47675

Chapter II—Railroad Retirement Board (Parts 200—399)

200.8 (b) amended; (d)(1), (2),
   (3), (f), (g) and (h) redesignated as (d)(2), (3), (4), (g),
   (h) and (i); (d)(1), (f) and (j)
   added.................................... 50247
216 Revised................................. 28692
236 Removed................................55073
240 Removed................................55073
323 Added.....................................26328
330 Revised................................. 28702
367 Added.....................................46375

Chapter III—Social Security Administration, Department of Health and Human Services (Parts 400—499)

404.362 (b)(1) revised; (b)(2) removed; (b)(3) redesignated
   as (b)(2)................................ 24000
404.367 Introductory text and
   (b) revised.............................. 35999
404.401—404.499 (Subpart E)
   Authority citation revised...... 41789
404.401 (d) revised........................ 41789
   Technical correction.................. 50157
404.402 (d)(1) revised................... 41789
   Technical correction.................. 50157
404.469 Added................................41789
   Technical correction.................. 50157
404.501—404.515 (Subpart F)
   Authority citation revised...... 52468
404.520 Added................................52468
404.521 Added................................52468
404.522 Added................................52469
404.523 Added................................52469
404.524 Added................................52469
404.525 Added................................52469
404.526 Added................................52469
404.621 (a)(2)(i) and (ii) re-
   moved; (a)(2)(iii) and (iv)
   redesignated as (a)(2)(i) and
   (ii)... 58846

List of C.F.R. Sections Affected (C.F.R., L.S.A.)

Finding Federal Regulations Online

The entire *Code of Federal Regulations (C.F.R.)* is available online. Also, many special law collections that are put together for online research (see Chapter 4) contain federal regulations relevant to the collection's specific topics.

You can find the *C.F.R.* online in several places. The best online source for the *C.F.R.* is the National Archives' eCFR website (www.ecfr. gov). You can browse by topic, search the section headings by keyword, or search by citation (if you have one). You can also track recent regulatory amendments and even trace the changes over time. Plus, you can view historical versions of the *C.F.R.* back to January 2017 if you're interested in the text of a regulation at a specific point in the past. Go to www.ecfr. gov/reader-aids/using-ecfr/getting-started for helpful search tips.

Or, if you know which regulatory agency issued the regulation you're looking for, you can go directly to the agency's website (www.<agency acronym>.gov; for example, www.fcc.gov).

Finding State Regulations in a Law Library

State regulations can be more challenging to locate than federal regulations. While most states have an administrative code containing at least a portion of the state's regulations, each agency typically keeps regulations in loose-leaf manuals published by the individual agency. It's often necessary to know which state agency is responsible for writing a particular regulation before you can find it. However, some larger law libraries carry all or most of the state regulations.

Agencies regularly change regulations, so checking that the regulation you've found is up to date is crucial. The easiest way to do so is to contact the agency directly.

Finding State Regulations Online

There are several ways to find a state's regulations online. Many of the sites we list for finding state statutes online will also provide links to state regulations. Your state's website will provide links to state agencies and regulations. You can likely do keyword searches or browse drop-down menus for the appropriate title.

Reading and Understanding Regulations

The general rules of statutory interpretation also apply to interpreting regulations. However, there are some additional factors to consider when interpreting regulations. The most important things to remember are:

- Agency interpretations of a regulation should be followed or argued against, but not ignored. Because regulations are often written to implement a general statutory scheme, they tend to be wordy and hard to understand, even more so than statutes. However, regulations are increasingly being written so that they can be more clearly understood.
- Regulations should be interpreted in a way that best fulfills the intent of the authorizing statute.

 Summing Up …
How to Find State Regulations in the Law Library

✓ If your state's regulations have been collected and published in an "Administrative Code," use the subject index. If there is no index, find the place in the publication that covers the agency issuing the regulations and check the table of contents.

✓ If there is no administrative code or analogous publication, find out what agency issued the regulations. Then ask the law librarian whether the library carries that agency's regulations.

✓ If the regulations can't be found in the law library, check with the nearest large public library.

✓ If the regulations aren't kept there, contact the agency issuing the regulations and ask how you can get a copy of them.

A typical regulation consists of the actual rule and a paragraph or two of agency interpretation. Sometimes, it will give examples of how the regulation should apply to a specific set of facts. Only the rule part of the regulation acts like a law. The interpretation and examples are designed only to explain its application.

Finding and Using Procedural Statutes and Rules

If your research involves procedural issues—such as getting a case into court and keeping it there—you need to pay special attention to several types of laws, all of which can usually be found in a law library with the help of a law librarian. We'll discuss these materials further in Chapter 9.

Rules of Civil Procedure

Rules of Civil Procedure are usually statutes passed by a legislature or rules issued by a state's highest court. They govern such matters as:

- who can sue whom, for what kinds of wrongs, and in which courts
- which types of documents must be filed to initiate and respond to a lawsuit
- time limits for filing various court papers
- what court papers must say to be effective
- the ways each side to a lawsuit can find out necessary facts from the other side and third-party witnesses (discovery)
- how a case is brought to trial
- what kind of trial you are entitled to (that is, by judge or jury)
- what kind of judgment and relief you are entitled to if you win
- what happens to you if you lose
- how you can enforce a judgment
- how you can appeal a judgment if you lose, and
- what kind of appeal is available if the court doesn't comply with the laws in the pretrial stage of the case.

You must follow these rules exactly. While some procedural mistakes can be fixed, especially if done very promptly, many violations mean your case is lost, just as surely as if you went to trial and the court or jury found against you.

Rules of Civil Procedure for the federal courts are found in Title 28 of the *U.S.C.A.*; Rules of Civil Procedure for state courts are usually found among the other state statutes in a code, title, or chapter titled "Civil Procedure" or "Court Rules."

Rules of Court (If Any)

Your state might have another publication called *Rules of Court* or something similar. If so, it will contain rules issued by the state's highest court and specify in more detail the procedures that must be followed. For example, a statute might specify that a certain document must be filed with the court. The Rule of Court would specify the precise form the document must be in.

Local Rules (If Any)

Many courts have their own local rules that get even more detailed. A local rule might specify the paper size or where an attorney's name must be placed on the page. Although these housekeeping matters might not seem as important as the accuracy of the facts and the law in your papers, many lawyers have learned that you ignore them at your peril. Some judges and clerks love to use deviations from local rules as the basis for returning your papers or even denying your motion.

Finding Court Rules Online

Like other government entities, trial courts often provide online access to the same information provided by the clerk's office, including the daily court calendar, personnel and filing information, recent court rulings, and the local court rules.

RESOURCE

Check desk references. It is no secret that administrative assistants and paralegals are critical in getting the proper papers to the right courts on time. These details are commonly put into step-by-step form and published in handbooks and "desk references." You can find information about filing fees, service of process, statutes of limitation, time limits, common motions, and similar nitty-gritty matters in these publications, which exist in larger states. For example, in California, you can use *California Paralegal's Guide 6th*, by Zella Mack (LexisNexis Publishing). Ask a legal assistant, paralegal, or law librarian if this resource is published in your state.

A good list of court websites can be found at the National Center for State Courts (www.ncsc.org). Under "What We Do," click "Information & Resources," then "Court websites."

Finding and Using Local Laws or Ordinances

Counties, cities, and special districts, such as school districts or sanitation districts, have significant power over day-to-day life. The amount of rulemaking authority afforded these local entities is usually set out in the state constitution and statutes. Subject to these higher forms of law, cities commonly have the authority to:

- divide their domain into zones of activity (called "zoning power")
- set requirements for new buildings and the refurbishing of old buildings
- pass and enforce local parking and driving rules
- set minimum standards for health and safety in rental properties, and
- issue fire and police regulations.

Local laws are usually called "ordinances." Ordinances are like statutes and regulations in that they have the force and effect of law, assuming they are within the local government's lawful authority. Special districts are usually empowered to pass regulations that are also binding law.

Finding Ordinances and Local Laws in the Law Library

Because of the many different forms of local government, it is difficult to specify how to research these ordinances or specialized regulations. Here are some general suggestions:

- Ordinances are often divided into local codes such as the "traffic code," "planning code," "building code," and the like. These codes are usually available in your local public library or law library. You can also get them from the pertinent city office for free or at a small cost.
- City and county agencies keep collections of ordinances that pertain to their agency.
- Special districts provide regulations in paperbound pamphlets at no cost or for a low price.

Ordinances, like statutes, are occasionally interpreted by the courts. If you want to find out whether a court has considered an ordinance you're interested in, you can do an online search of case law with keyword searches. In the law library, use *Shepard's Citations for Statutes*. (For instructions on Shepardizing statutes or ordinances, see Chapter 8.)

Finding Local Laws Online

The Municipal Code Corporation maintains a helpful site for finding local laws (https://library.municode.com). If you come up empty there, you might be able to access your codes or ordinances on a city or county website, especially if you're looking for ordinances for large cities or populous counties. Just type the name of your city, county, or other municipality into Google or another search engine. Many local government websites will have drop-down menus with relevant codes or allow you to do keyword searches.

6

Finding Cases

U sing secondary sources, as described in Chapter 4, and statutes, as described in Chapter 5, is almost certainly going to lead you to citations or references to case law relevant to your topic. But you'll also want to know how to find cases intentionally. In this chapter, we explain how to locate cases. In the next chapter, we'll cover how to read and understand the cases you find.

Using Citations to Find Cases

A case citation is a shorthand way of referring the reader to a case's location. To start, it will tell you in which book or "reporter" the case can be found.

Reporters contain decisions by appellate courts, federal trial courts, and specialty courts, such as bankruptcy. Each set of reporters contains opinions from a particular court or group of courts. For example, state reporters have only one state's appellate decisions ("Cal.App." contains appellate cases from California). Subject matter reporters contain decisions affecting a particular area of law ("B.R." contains federal bankruptcy opinions). Also, federal cases are reported in their own sets, one for trial-level decisions (called "F.Supp.") and one for appellate opinions from the Circuit Courts of Appeals (abbreviated as "F."). A new series begins when they reach the maximum number of cases that can fit in a volume. It is identified as "2d" or "3d," and so on. We explain more about the different types of reporters in Chapter 7.

Every reported (published) case has a unique citation. You can find any case published in a standard case reporter if you have the citation. We'll use the example below to walk through the different elements.

Lukhard v. Reed	95	L.Ed. 2d	328	(1987)
case name	volume number	name of reporter	the page number	year of the decision

Citation Form

Citations often take slightly different forms because each state can develop a citation system, so you'll want to check your state court's website for format information. For example, it's typical for the date, volume number, and case reporter abbreviation to follow the case name. *A Uniform System of Citation*, 21st ed., known as the "Blue Book" because of its blue cover, provides a nationwide system of citations. Although developed primarily for law school use, federal courts and some state courts use it. We follow it here for consistency.

The elements are:
- **Case name.** The first element of a case citation is the case name; here, *Lukhard v. Reed*. There are usually two names, the plaintiff's and defendant's, on either side of a "v." (short for "versus"). Usually, the plaintiff's name is first, but not always. In *Lukhard v. Reed*, the original plaintiff was Reed, but Lukhard's name was put first when he appealed a lower court decision in favor of Reed. Other times, there will be only one name: for example, *In re Gault* is the name of a juvenile case; the "in re" means "in the matter of." These types of case names typically appear when the state brings the proceeding for the individual's best interest or when the proceeding isn't considered an adversary proceeding that warrants the "v." Finally, cases are sometimes referred to by the subject matter of the dispute. For instance, divorce cases commonly carry such names as *Marriage of Sullivan* (last name of the divorcing couple) or *In the Matter of Schmidt*.
- **Volume number.** A case citation provides as the second element the volume number of the reporter in which the case is located. The volumes of each separate reporter are numbered consecutively.

- **Name of reporter.** A citation wouldn't be much help without the name of the reporter. That information comes third, immediately after the volume number. In the *Lukhard* case, the full name of the reporter is *United States Supreme Court Reports, Lawyer's Edition*. Most reporters have been published in two or more series. For example, the *Lukhard* case is published in the second series of the *L.Ed.* reporter (L.Ed.2d). Cases decided in the 19th and early 20th centuries were published in the first series (L.Ed).
- **The page number.** You have undoubtedly already figured out what the fourth item of a citation is for. It provides the page number the case starts on. You'll need this number to look up the case in the law library or to cite the case in a court document, even if you are doing your research online.
- **Year of the decision.** Citations also carry the year the case was decided. This fifth element can be helpful because newer cases reflect current legal trends better than older ones. When researching, you usually want first to check the most recent cases relating to your problem or issue.

Citing Federal Cases: The Circuit, State, or District

Citations to cases decided by the federal Courts of Appeal usually include the circuit of the court deciding the case. A case decided by the Court of Appeals for the Third Circuit is cited as 654 F.2d 917 (3d Cir. 1984). A U.S. District Court citation should indicate the state and judicial district of the case; for example, in *Staffin v. Greenberg*, 509 F.Supp. 825 (E.D. Pa. 1981), the "E.D. Pa." means "Eastern Judicial District for Pennsylvania."

Parallel Citations

Cases are often found in more than one reporter. For example, U.S. Supreme Court cases can be found in three separate reporters. When you see a U.S. Supreme Court case referred to (that is, "cited"), you might see multiple citations following the case name.

> EXAMPLE: *Lukhard v. Reed*
> - 481 U.S. 368: *United States Reports*
> - 95 L.Ed.2d 328: *Lawyer's Edition, 2d Series*, and
> - 107 S.Ct. 1807 (1987): *Supreme Court Reporter.*

These three citations are known as "parallel citations" because they parallel each other (refer to the same case).

Citing to Advance Sheets

The next chapter explains that advance sheets are the newest cases that haven't yet appeared in a reporter. But functionally, they're no different. Advance sheets are numbered and paginated to fit with the reporters in which the cases will appear. In other words, a case's volume and page numbers will be the same in the advance sheets and permanent hardcover edition.

Internet Citations

As a rule, citations to very recent cases from online services such as LexisNexis or Westlaw will be accepted by a court. Also, cases published by the LexisNexis, Westlaw, and Fastcase services typically include the hard copy citation, which is always acceptable. However, you could run into trouble if you want to specifically cite or quote a particular page of the official reporter in a court document (called a "pincite" because you're pinpointing the exact page), particularly if you are using a free online site. Although LexisNexis and Westlaw have this functionality, other free websites might not. To get the pincite, you'll have to either look at the official reporter or look in an online service that provides it, often for a fee.

Finding Cases Online

Cases are now widely available online, and that's often the easiest way to access them if you know a few significant facts. For example, websites might allow you to limit your search by party name, location or court, and date. You might also be able to limit your search by using keywords. When combined with the power of Boolean searching (discussed in Chapter 2), you should be able to locate new and existing cases in narrow subject areas.

To find online cases for free, try the Caselaw Access Project (www.case.law), CourtListener (www.courtlistener.com), or Google Scholar (https://scholar.google.com).

> CAUTION
> **Use generative AI tools with caution.** If you're considering using an AI-powered search tool for legal research, you should know that the technology is in development and legal results are unreliable. We aren't including tools such as ChatGPT and other AI offerings in our current recommendations because while the answers can appear impressive, they're sometimes misleading or wrong. Unlike traditional legal resources, the answers aren't reviewed for accuracy or attributed to a credible legal authority.

Finding State Cases Online

To find state cases online, visit one of the websites identified above. If you already know the address for your state judiciary's website or another site where it maintains its cases, you can go there directly.

Not every website will have all cases for each state from the beginning of time. Still, most websites are pretty comprehensive, going back at least to the early 1900s. If you need case law older than that—which is rare—you might have to use the law library or an online service that costs money, like Westlaw or LexisNexis. A cheaper alternative, as explained in Chapter 2, is Fastcase.

Finding Federal Cases Online

As we'll cover in detail in Chapter 7, there are essentially three types of federal opinions. The type will depend on the court in which the lawsuit was litigated: U.S. Supreme Court opinions, federal Circuit Court of Appeal opinions, and U.S. District Court opinions. There are several specialty courts under the U.S. District Court category, including bankruptcy courts.

Here is a rough description of what you can find for free online at this time:

- all U.S. Supreme Court opinions
- most Federal Court of Appeals opinions, depending on the circuit
- recent District Court opinions, depending on the district, and
- most bankruptcy court opinions.

The Supreme Court has its own website (www.supremecourt.gov). The circuits, districts, and bankruptcy courts have sites as well. Generally, the circuit sites follow the form of www.ca<circuit number>.uscourts.gov, such as www.ca9.uscourts.gov for the Ninth Circuit. District court addresses are more variable. If you don't have your circuit, district, or bankruptcy court's direct address, you can find a link at the website for the federal judiciary (www.uscourts.gov/federal-court-finder/search).

Also, as we explained in Chapter 2, most primary online legal resources can be found through a basic keyword search and by using one of the dedicated legal information sites mentioned above. For instance, if you know of a federal district court case you want to read, enter the case name or keywords describing the case's subject matter into a search engine. You will likely get a direct link to the case.

Using Westlaw or LexisNexis to Find Cases

If your law library offers free access to Westlaw or LexisNexis (and many do), you're in luck. You can locate the case you're looking for (and all other cases that cite it) by entering the citation or the case name into the search box at the top of the page.

For example, if a case name is *Fisher v. Priceless*, you could enter "Priceless" in the search box and pull up all cases containing that name. You could also use "Fisher" in the search, but as a rule, using one name is more efficient as long as it is uncommon.

Finding Cases in the Law Library

There are several ways to find cases in the law library, depending on where you are coming from in your research:

- If you have found a relevant statute and want to read cases that interpret the provisions you are interested in, you can probably find an appropriate citation in the case notes in the annotations (see "Case Notes That Follow Statutes," below), or in the listings for that statute in *Shepard's Citations for Statutes* (discussed below, and further in Chapter 8).
- If your research involves primarily common law (cases), you might find a helpful case citation in a background resource (see "Background Resources," below) or in the subject index to a case digest (see "The Case Digest Subject Index," below).
- If you know the name of a case you want to find but not its citation, you can use the table of cases in a case digest (see "The Digest Table of Cases," below). If the case is very recent (within the past several months) and not yet listed in the case digest table of cases, you can find it by searching the tables of cases in the advance sheets or recently published hardcover case reporter volumes (see "The Case Reporter Table of Cases," below).
- If you have a case citation for one reporter and you need the citation for a second reporter (that is, the parallel citation), you can find it by using *Shepard's*. (See Chapter 8.)

Below, we examine these approaches to finding an appropriate citation for that one good case in more detail.

Background Resources

Many background materials discussed in Chapter 4 (known as "secondary sources") are copiously footnoted with citations to cases that discuss specific points of law covered in the main discussion. For example, consider the page from *California Jurisprudence*, a California legal encyclopedia, shown below.

Although we generally recommend that you go directly from secondary sources to pertinent statutes—and then to cases—researchers sometimes go directly to any case that appears relevant (or they at least note the citation for later reference). For example, if you want to know your constitutional rights if you are accused of a zoning violation, the case of *Los Angeles v. Gage* (cited in Footnote 42 on the page shown below) appears directly on that point. Before you search for a statute related to this issue, you might first read this case to see what light it sheds on your problem. The case itself might even discuss relevant statutes.

Finding Recent Cases That Have Interpreted a Statute

Each volume of a case reporter has a "table of statutes" that is mentioned by the cases reported in that volume. The table is usually in the front of the volume. It can be helpful if you know that a statute has been interpreted within a specific period.

For example, suppose you hear of a 2022 Illinois court decision that interprets that state's statute governing stock issuances of small corporations. You are familiar with the statute and would like to read the case but don't know its name or where to find it. What to do? If you aren't going to do an online search, you can check the particular statute in the table of statutes in each volume of the *North Eastern Reporter* that contains 2022 Illinois cases. If a case interpreted the statute you are interested in, the table of statutes will tell you precisely which one and provide its citation. Remember to check the advance sheets for the reporter if you think the case was very recent.

§ 210   ZONING AND OTHER LAND CONTROLS

additional time not exceeding a specified number of days as the
court may, within the original number of days, allow, but in no
event later than a designated number of days after entry of the
order, petition the proper reviewing court to review such order by
writ of mandate. No such order of vacation is effective, nor may it
be recorded in the office any county recorder, until the time
within which a petition for writ of mandate may thus be filed has
expired.[41]

§ 211. Defenses

Generally speaking, any matter that is germane to a cause of
action to enforce a zoning or planning enactment and that
presents a legal reason why the plaintiff should not succeed
therein may constitute a good defense. It is a good defense, for
instance, that the enactment under which complaint is made is
unconstitutional or invalid, either in toto or as applied to the
defendant's property.[42] In order to plead this defense, however, the
defendant must have exhausted the administrative remedies available to him under the enactment.[43] And the partial invalidity of

41. *Deering's Gov C § 65908 subd*
(b).

42. *Los Angeles v Gage, 127 CA2d
442, 274 P2d 34; People v Gottfurcht
(2d Dist) 62 CA3d 634, 133 Cal Rptr
270.*

Regarding validity of zoning enact-
ments generally, see §§ 43 et seq., supra.

Practice References: 8 POF2d p.
53, Unreasonableness of Zoning Restriction §§ 1 et seq.; 13 POF2d p.
373, Vested Right in Continuation of
Zoning §§ 1 et seq.; 14 POF2d p. 117,
Zoning—Nonconforming Use §§ 1 et
seq.

43. *San Mateo v Hardy, 64 CA2d
794, 149 P2d 307.*

A church and a member thereof
failed to exhaust their administrative
remedies before defending on constitu-

tional grounds against the enforcement
of an ordinance requiring a use permit
as a prerequisite to operation of
church on property in a residential
zone, where it did not appear that the
member even applied for any such
permit, and the church dismissed its
appeal from the planning commission's
decision to the city council before
decision by the council. *Chico v First
Ave. Baptist Church, 108 CA2d 297,
238 P2d 587.*

Property owners whose auto wreck-
ing yard was found to be a nonconforming use and was ordered terminated by the county board of supervisors on recommendation of the county
planning commission were not denied
procedural due process, where a public
hearing after 15 days' notice was held
by the planning commission at which
hearing the property owners were represented by counsel and witnesses were

Page From *California Jurisprudence*

Case Notes That Follow Statutes

If you are searching for a case that has interpreted a relevant statute, check the listings after the statute's text in an "annotated" version of the code. In the annotated code, one-sentence summaries of court cases that interpret the statute directly follow the notes on the statute's history. These summaries are headnotes (discussed below) that have been lifted from the case reporter. Some statutes have been interpreted by the courts so often that the publisher includes a little index to the case summaries organized by issues raised by the statute. The example below is from the *Michigan Compiled Laws Annotated.*

It is often difficult to tell from such a summary whether a case is relevant to your research problem. Fortunately, the summaries also contain a case citation that allows you to look up the case and read it yourself. It is essential that you read the case itself and not rely solely on the annotation. It's common to find an annotation that seems right on point, but after reading it, you realize it isn't helpful to your matter.

Shepard's Citations for Statutes

Several different research tools are provided by a service known as *Shepard's. Shepard's Citations for Statutes* provides a complete listing of each time a particular statute, regulation, or constitutional provision has been referred to and perhaps interpreted by a published decision of a federal or state court. We'll discuss how to use this important tool in Chapter 8.

Using Digests

Digests are collections of headnotes—one-sentence summaries of how a particular case decided specific legal issues—taken from cases as reported in case reporters and grouped by topic. These headnotes are at the beginning of cases cited in West reporters. For example, in *Nationwide Insurance Co. v. Ervin*, 231 N.E.2d 112 (1967), one of the issues is classified under "Insurance." The court's holding on that issue

Historical and Statutory Notes

Source:
P.A.1931, No. 328, § 451a, added by P.A.
1969, No. 243, § 1, Eff. March 20, 1970.

C.L.1948, § 750.451a.
C.L.1970, § 750.451a.

Statute text

750.452. House of ill-fame; keeping, maintaining or operating

Sec. 452. KEEPING, ETC., A HOUSE OF ILL-FAME—Any person who shall keep, maintain or operate, or aid and abet in keeping, maintaining or operating a house of ill-fame, bawdy house or any house or place resorted to for the purpose of prostitution or lewdness shall be guilty of a felony, punishable by imprisonment in the state prison for not more than 5 years or by a fine of not more than 2,500 dollars.

Historical and Statutory Notes

Source:
P.A.1931, No. 328, § 452, Eff. Sept. 18.
C.L.1948, § 750.452.
C.L.1970, § 750.452.

Prior Laws:
R.S.1846, c. 158, § 10.
C.L.1857, § 5865.

C.L.1871, § 7700.
How. § 9286.
P.A.1887, No. 34.
C.L.1897, § 11697.
C.L.1915, § 15471.
P.A.1927, No. 37, § 1.
P.A.1927, No. 40, § 1.
C.L.1929, §§ 16826, 16860.

Cross References

Disorderly persons, see § 750.167.
Public nuisances, abatement, see § 600.3801.

Library References

Disorderly House ⇔5.
WESTLAW Topic No. 130.
C.J.S. Disorderly Houses § 5.

Notes of Decisions

Mini-index

Conduct or use of house 3
Elements of offense 1
Evidence 6–8
  In general 6
  Reputation 7
  Weight and sufficiency of evidence 8
House, building or place 2
Indictment or information 5
Instructions 10
Jury questions 9
Keeping of house 4
Reputation, evidence 7
Review 12
Sentence and punishment 11
Weight and sufficiency of evidence 8

Case summaries

1. Elements of offense

Under this section providing that "Any person who shall keep, maintain or operate, or aid and abet in keeping, maintaining or operating a house of ill-fame, bawdy house or any house

or place resorted to for the purpose of prostitution * * * shall be guilty of a felony, * * *,", it is only where the operation or maintenance of a house of ill fame is charged that the reputation of the premises is an essential element. People v. Mayes (1973) 205 N.W.2d 212, 44 Mich.App. 482.

A person who solicited a female, who was at the time a prostitute, and inmate of a house of ill fame, to become an inmate of another such house, was not guilty of a violation of How. § 9286, which provided for the punishment of any person who solicited a female to enter such house for the purpose of "becoming" a prostitute. People v. Cook (1893) 55 N.W. 980, 96 Mich. 368.

2. House, building or place

Evidence that defendant kept a house to which men resorted for purposes of prostitution, that frequent acts of prostitution were there committed with her, and that the house

362

Michigan Statute

is summarized in Headnote 5, shown below, and has been assigned a topic key number, 435.3(1). (LexisNexis has a similar system—but it is only available online, and it isn't as extensive as the West system—called the "Key Number" system.) If you are interested in cases that deal with the same subject matter, you can use that headnote and its key number to look up similar cases.

> ## A Shortcut When Using the *General Digest*
>
> Each volume of the *General Digest* includes all West key topics and numbers. So, when you are chasing down the key topic and number of a particular headnote, a relevant case summary might appear in any or all volumes. To make your search more efficient, each 10th volume of the *General Digest* contains a Table of Key Numbers that tells you which of the preceding 10 volumes have entries under your key topic and subtopic number.

West has divided this huge digest into smaller ones:
- The *U.S. Supreme Court Digest* covers only U.S. Supreme Court cases.
- The *Federal Practice Digest* covers all federal courts (including the U.S. Supreme Court).
- State digests (for example, the *Illinois Digest* covers only the cases from that state). Thomson West publishes digests for every state, except for Delaware, Nevada, and Utah.
- Regional digests (the states have been grouped into four regions: *Atlantic, Pacific, Northwestern,* and *Southeastern*).

As you can see, some digests overlap. For instance, both the *U.S. Supreme Court Digest* and the *Federal Practice Digest* cover U.S. Supreme Court cases. And both the *Pacific Regional Digest* and the *California Digest* cover California cases. All entries in these digests are duplicated in the *Decennial* and *General Digests*.

NATIONWIDE INSURANCE COMPANY v. ERVIN
Cite as 231 N.E.2d 112

1. Insurance ⚖138(1)

Parties to insurance contract are free to incorporate such provisions into it, if not unlawful, as they see fit and it is then the duty of the court to enforce those provisions.

2. Insurance ⚖146.7(8)

Rule that all ambiguities in policy will be construed most strongly against insurance company, as the party that drafted the policy, only has application where ambiguity in fact exists and court may not distort the contract to create the ambiguity itself.

3. Insurance ⚖146.2

Insurance contract should be construed in accordance with the general contract rule of construction that the agreement should be ascertained as a whole to determine intention of parties and purpose which they sought to accomplish.

4. Insurance ⚖435.2(2)

Enumeration in automobile policy of those few situations where coverage is afforded to the insured with reference to other than named automobile serves to limit areas of risk assumed by insurer.

5. Insurance ⚖435.3(1)

Provision of automobile policy limiting coverage for additional owned automobile to 30 days after acquisition by insured permits owner adequate opportunity to acquire necessary additional insurance and is not intended to cover two automobiles for any protracted period.

6. Insurance ⚖435.2(4)

Provision in automobile policy granting coverage to insured for temporary substitute automobile, not owned by the insured, applies to those situations where the named automobile is in repair shop or withdrawn from use for short period.

7. Insurance ⚖435.3(1)

Where insured had bought second automobile in July 1964 after transmission "went

231 N.E.2d—8

out" of automobile which was named in policy and which remained inoperable in driveway of his home until repair in spring of 1966, and had accident with second automobile on September 26, 1964, the second automobile was not a "replacement" for the named automobile within policy provision extending coverage to replacement automobile.

———•———

Barrick, Jackson & Switzer, Rockford, for appellant.

Nordquist & Anderson, Rockford, for appellees.

ABRAHAMSON, Justice.

The Nationwide Insurance Company brings this appeal from a decree of the Circuit Court of the 17th Judicial Circuit, Winnebago County, entered December 29, 1966, that found that an automobile insurance policy issued by it to Douglas Ervin "covered" an accident that had occurred on September 26, 1964, and that a certain automobile operated by Ervin at the time of the accident was a "replacement" as defined in the policy.

On August 16, 1963, Nationwide issued its policy of automobile insurance number 94–441–489 to Ervin for coverage of his 1958 Chevrolet. In July of 1964 the transmission of the Chevrolet, according to Ervin, "went out" and he purchased a 1958 Cadillac. The Chevrolet was retained by Ervin, although inoperable, and left in the driveway of his home.

On September 26, 1964, Ervin was in an automobile accident with the Cadillac that involved a truck owned by the Jones Transfer Company, an Illinois Corporation, and another automobile in which Robert Holmes was a passenger. Holmes subsequently brought suit against Ervin and Jones Transfer for injuries allegedly suffered as a result of that accident. Nationwide was called upon by Ervin to defend him in that suit pursuant to the policy.

Headnotes From *Ervin*

CAUTION
Always remember to check the pocket part of any digest you use to get the most recent cases.

The Case Digest Subject Index

If you haven't found a helpful case through one of the above methods, you can proceed directly to a case digest. Even without a relevant head-note, you can use the subject index (called the "Descriptive Word Index" in the West digest system) in a digest to discover "that one good case."

For example, if you want to know whether a father who doesn't support his child after a job loss can legally be denied visitation rights, you would be dealing with the topics of "child visitation," "child support," and "child custody." You could use the subject indexes (and tables of contents) in a case digest for your state to find a relevant case that deals with your questions.

The Digest Table of Cases

It is common to hear well-known cases referred to by name only. Lawyers might talk about *Roe v. Wade*, or a criminal defendant might claim that the police violated the rules established by the *Miranda* case. If you know the name of a case but need its citation to locate and read it, it might be easy to find online. For very famous cases like those mentioned above, you can probably even type the case name into a search engine and get the result you're looking for. For all others, you can use features on websites like CourtListener (www.courtlistener.com) that allow you to look up cases by limiting by the parties' names, the court, or the case year. And, of course, a well-written keyword search might yield a relevant result.

The West digest system is also an option if you're in the law library and using print materials. Each digest is accompanied by a table of cases that lists all the cases referred to in that digest. Using the correct digest and accompanying table of cases, you can find the name of any case that was decided long enough ago—usually a year or more—to find its way into the table of cases. The table of cases is organized with the plaintiff's name first. If you don't find your case in the table of cases, consult the Defendant-Plaintiff table.

Summing Up ...
How to Find Federal Cases in a Law Library When You Don't Know the Citation

✓ Locate the table of cases for *West's Federal Practice Digest 5th* for the most recent cases (2003 to the present); *4th* for cases reported from 1989 to 2002; *3d* for cases between 1975 and 1989; *2d* for cases between 1962 and 1975; and *Modern Federal Practice Digest* for earlier cases.

✓ Find the case name in the hardcover volume or pocket part and note the citation.

✓ If there is more than one entry for the case name, determine from the information provided with each entry (its date and issues decided) which case is the correct one. If cases involve the same topic, note both citations and read both cases.

✓ If you don't find an entry for the case name, reverse the names and look again. If you still don't find it, look in the Defendant-Plaintiff Table of Cases under both names.

When a case starts in the trial court, the first name is the plaintiff's, and the name after the "v." is the defendant's. However, if the defendant appeals, the defendant's name is sometimes put first in the appeal. Because most cases are opinions issued by appellate courts, a case name might consist of the defendant's name in front of the "v." and the plaintiff's name after. If you can't find a case under one name, reverse the names and try again.

Federal cases can be found in the *West Federal Practice Digest*, which has multiple series based on date; Supreme Court cases can also be found in the *U.S. Supreme Court Digest*. If, for example, you are interested in the rights of unwed fathers with respect to decisions affecting their children and have heard that a U.S. Supreme Court case called *Caban v. Mohammed* is relevant, you can use the *West Federal Practice Digest* Table of Cases (start with the *Third Series*) and look it up. In the table of cases for the *Second Series*, you would find what is shown below.

82 F P D 2d—61

CALIFANO

References are to Digest Topics and Key Numbers

C., Inc. v. Brookside Drug Store, Inc., Bkrtcy.Conn., 3 B.R. 120. See Brookside Drug Store, Inc., Matter of.

Caban v. Mohammed, U.S.N.Y., 99 S.Ct. 1760, 441 U.S. 380, 60 L.Ed.2d 297.— Adop 2, 7.2(3), 7.4(1); Const Law 70.- 3(1), 70.3(6), 224(1), 224(2).

Caban v. Nelson, D.C.Conn., 475 F.Supp. 865. See Velez v. Nelson.

Caban, U. S. ex rel., v. Rowe, D.C.Ill., 449 F.Supp. 360. See U. S. ex rel. Caban v. Rowe.

Cabezal Supermarket, Inc., Matter of, D.C.N.D., 406 F.Supp. 345.—Bankr 303(6), 441.5, 442, 446(8.1).

Caesars Palace Securities Litigation, D.C.N.Y., 360 F.Supp. 366.—Fed Civ Proc 161, 176.

Cafeteria and Restaurant Workers Union, Local 473, AFL–CIO v. McElroy, U.S.Dist.Col., 81 S.Ct. 1743, 367 U.S. 886, 6 L.Ed.2d 1230.—Const Law 278.- 4(3), 278.6(1).

Cafferty v. Trans World Airlines, Inc., D.C.Mo., 488 F.Supp. 1076.—Fed Cts 1145; Labor 416.4, 968.

Cagle's, Inc. v. N. L. R. B., C.A.5, 588 F.2d 943.—Labor 290, 367, 379, 382.2, 388.1, 394, 574, 577, 705.

& Supply, Inc., 98 Idaho 495, 567 P.2d 1246.

Calderon v. McGee, C.A.Tex., 589 F.2d 909.—Elections 12; Fed Cts 922.

Calderon v. McGee, C.A.Tex., 584 F.2d 66, vac in part and reh 589 F.2d 909.— Schools 53(1).

Caldwell v. Board of Ed. of City of St. Louis, C.A.Mo., 620 F.2d 1277. See Adams v. U. S.

Caldwell v. Califano, D.C.Ala., 455 F.Supp. 1069.—Social S 142.30.

Caldwell v. Camp, C.A.Mo., 594 F.2d 705. —Courts 508(1), 508(2), 508(7); Fed Civ

Table of Cases in *Federal Practice Digest*

If you're looking for a citation for a state case, use the West state or regional digests. For example, suppose you want to read the landmark Oregon Supreme Court case of *Burnette v. Wahl*. To find the citation, locate the West *Regional Digest* that covers Oregon (the *Pacific Digest*) or the *Oregon Digest* and get the volume containing the table of cases.

Summing Up ...

How to Find State Cases When You Don't Know the Citation

✓ Locate the table of cases for the state or regional digest that covers your state's cases.

✓ Find the case name in the hardcover volume or pocket part and note the citation.

✓ If there is more than one entry for the case name, determine from the information provided with each entry (its date and issues decided) which case is the correct one. If two cases involve the same topic, note both citations and read both cases.

✓ If you don't find an entry for the case name, reverse the names and look again. If you still don't find it, look in the Defendant-Plaintiff Table of Cases under both names.

The Case Reporter Table of Cases

Each case reporter volume has a table of cases, usually at the front. This table lists all cases in that volume of the reporter and their page references. It's a very valuable tool if you are searching for a case you know only by name that was decided too recently to be listed in a digest table of cases (generally, within the previous six months to one year).

If the case is more recent than the dates of the cases in the latest hardcover case reporter, use the table of cases in the advance sheets. But remember that there is usually a one- to two-month lag between the decision in a case and its publication in an advance sheet. If the case is old enough to be in the hardcover volumes, start with the table of cases in the latest hardcover volume and work backward.

The Case Reporter Subject Index

Each case reporter volume has a subject index, usually at the back. If the reporter is published by West (most are), the index is organized according to the key numbers assigned to the cases in the volume. If you know that a case involving a specific topic was decided during a certain period but don't know its name, you might be able to find it by looking in the subject index for each volume containing cases for that period.

For example, suppose you want to read a 1992 Illinois court decision that interprets that state's statute governing stock issuances of small corporations. You could find it using the subject index for the volumes containing cases decided in 1992. Look under "corporations," "stock," or "business" until you find what you are looking for, and the index will refer you to the correct case. (See Chapter 3 for help in using a legal index.)

Be prepared to look under more than one topic when trying to find a case through this method. Also, be aware that the volume might contain the case you're looking for, even though it's not described in the subject index.

The Next Step

Suppose you find a good, relevant case or cases—then what? It is at this point that your research efforts become productive. Once you have located even one relevant case, you have the key to all other relevant case law using many tools discussed here.

We'll cover one additional tool, which helps you do further research while verifying that your research still accurately reflects the law, in Chapter 8. But first, we will cover how to read and understand the cases you've discovered.

Using Case Law

Finding the cases you need is your first step. Your second step is to read and understand them. In this chapter, we explain the fundamental structure of a case so you'll know what you're reading and why it's important.

What Is a Case?

In law, we use the term "case" rather liberally. For instance, we refer to any legal matter filed in court as a "case." However, when referencing legal research, a "case" refers to a unique lawsuit important enough to be published and create law. Because published case opinions are law, we must find and cite to them as legal authority when they apply.

Although all lawsuits begin when a plaintiff or prosecutor files a complaint against a defendant, very few cases become published law. Not only does it take a long time for a case to establish law, but most cases don't involve unique issues that the courts or legislature haven't yet addressed.

For instance, most participants in a lawsuit settle the dispute without going to trial. Hundreds more are decided daily at trial before a judge or jury nationwide without incident. For the most part, these unremarkable cases aren't published and don't become law (with some exceptions).

Typically, the process of becoming law begins when trial litigants believe a trial judge committed an error and misapplied the law to the litigant's detriment. Because of the large volume of litigation, such problems occasionally arise. The remedy is to appeal to a higher court—most likely the court of appeals—to decide whether an error occurred. If the appellate court also makes a mistake, a litigant can appeal to the highest court, the Supreme Court. The federal court and most state courts work this way.

So why is understanding the appeals process important? Most published opinions in the law library are appellate and Supreme Court opinions—not trial court decisions (federal trial court opinions are an exception). However, not all appellate and Supreme Court opinions are published. The court will order the case published if it creates new law, modifies existing law, or provides needed guidance.

KEYWELL CORP. v. WEINSTEIN   159
Cite as 33 F.3d 159 (2nd Cir. 1994)

Parties

KEYWELL CORPORATION,
Plaintiff-Appellant,

v.

Daniel C. WEINSTEIN and Anthony
Boscarino, Defendants-Appellees.

Docket Number

No. 1208, Docket 93-7994.

The Court

United States Court of Appeals,
Second Circuit.

The Dates

Argued March 7, 1994.

Decided Aug. 23, 1994.

Summary

Purchaser of metal recycling plant brought suit under CERCLA against two shareholders, officers, and directors of selling corporation to recover environmental cleanup costs. The United States District Court for the Western District of New York, William M. Skretny, J., granted summary judgment for defendants, and purchaser appealed. The Court of Appeals, Jacobs, Circuit Judge, held that: (1) genuine issue of material fact on reasonableness of purchaser's reliance on seller's misrepresentations precluded summary judgment on fraud claims, but (2) purchaser was not entitled to recover cleanup costs under CERCLA, since parties clearly allocated risk of CERCLA liability to purchaser under terms of purchase agreement.

Decision

Affirmed in part, and reversed and remanded in part.

1. Federal Courts ⬩766

When reviewing district court's grant of summary judgment, Court of Appeals must determine whether genuine issue of material fact exists and whether district court correctly applied law.

2. Federal Civil Procedure ⬩2470.1

Summary judgment is appropriate only if, resolving all ambiguities and drawing all factual inferences in favor of nonmoving party, there is no genuine issue of material fact to be tried. Fed.Rules Civ.Proc.Rule 56(c), 28 U.S.C.A.

3. Federal Civil Procedure ⬩2544

Party seeking summary judgment bears burden of demonstrating absence of any genuine factual dispute. Fed.Rules Civ.Proc. Rule 56(c), 28 U.S.C.A.

4. Federal Civil Procedure ⬩2504

Purchaser raised genuine questions of fact on reasonableness of its reliance on sellers' misrepresentations regarding release of hazardous substances on property, precluding summary judgment for sellers on its claim of fraudulent misrepresentation under New York law, since reasonable jury could conclude that purchaser, having conducted environmental due diligence and received report that was consistent with sellers' representations that there had been no dumping or other release of hazardous waste on property, had no obligation to investigate further, despite recommendation for additional testing in environmental audit.

5. Contracts ⬩2

New York law applied to claim questioning validity of contract, though parties chose Maryland law to govern their contract, where contract was made in New York.

6. Contracts ⬩2

Questions concerning validity of contract should be determined by law of jurisdiction in which it was made.

7. Fraud ⬩3

In New York, plaintiff claiming fraudulent misrepresentation must prove that defendant made material false representation, defendant intended to defraud plaintiff thereby, plaintiff reasonably relied on representation, and plaintiff suffered damage as result of such reliance.

8. Fraud ⬩22(1)

When party is aware of circumstances that indicate certain representations may be false, that party cannot reasonably rely on those representations, but must make additional inquiry to determine their accuracy.

9. Fraud ⬩31

Defrauded party is permitted to affirm contract and seek relief in damages, rather than choose remedy of rescission.

Opinion in *Keywell Corp. v. Weinstein*

160   **33 FEDERAL REPORTER, 3d SERIES**

10. Health and Environment ⟐25.5(5.5)

Purchaser of metal recycling plant was not entitled to recover costs of environmental cleanup from two officers, directors, and majority shareholders of selling corporation as signatories to purchase agreement, where agreement clearly allocated risk of CERCLA liability, which purchaser assumed when indemnity period expired, as shortened by the signing of release. Comprehensive Environmental Response, Compensation, and Liability Act of 1980, §§ 107(a), 113(f), 42 U.S.C.A. §§ 9607(a), 9613(f).

11. Health and Environment ⟐25.5(5.5)

Private parties may contractually allocate among themselves any loss they may suffer by imposition of CERCLA liability. Comprehensive Environmental Response, Compensation, and Liability Act of 1980, § 107(e)(1), 42 U.S.C.A. § 9607(e)(1).

Stuart A. Smith, New York City (Alfred Ferrer III, Piper & Marbury, Joseph G. Finnerty, Jr., Charles P. Scheeler, of counsel) for plaintiff-appellant.

Thomas E. Lippard, Pittsburgh, PA (Craig E. Frischman, Thorp Reed & Armstrong, of counsel) for defendant-appellee Weinstein.

Jeremiah J. McCarthy, Buffalo, NY (Phillips, Lytle, Hitchcock, Blaine & Huber, of counsel) for defendant-appellee Boscarino.

Before: WALKER, JACOBS, Circuit Judges and CARMAN,* Judge.

JACOBS, Circuit Judge:

Keywell Corporation ("Keywell") has incurred costs for environmental cleanup at an industrial facility that it purchased in 1987 from Vac Air Alloys Corporation ("Vac Air"). Defendants–Appellees Daniel C. Weinstein ("Weinstein") and Anthony Boscarino ("Boscarino") were shareholders, officers and directors of Vac Air prior to the purchase and at the time of the transaction, and were signatories to the Purchase Agreement. Keywell has brought suit against Weinstein

*Honorable Gregory W. Carman of the United States Court of International Trade, sitting by

and Boscarino, (i) alleging that they induced Keywell to buy the property by making misrepresentations bearing upon the environmental risks at the premises, and (ii) alleging that, as owners and operators of Vac Air, they are strictly liable to Keywell for their equitable share of response costs pursuant to §§ 107(a) and 113(f) of the Comprehensive Environmental Response, Compensation, and Liability Act ("CERCLA"). 42 U.S.C. §§ 9607(a) and 9613(f). Following the parties' submission of cross-motions for summary judgment, the district court dismissed Keywell's claims, finding as a matter of law that Keywell could not have reasonably relied on the allegedly fraudulent misrepresentations, and that Keywell had contractually released its right to sue defendants under CERCLA.

We affirm the dismissal of the CERCLA claims on the ground that the parties allocated the risk of CERCLA liability in their Purchase Agreement, the terms of which establish that such risk now falls on Keywell. However, we reverse the dismissal of the diversity fraud claims and remand for further proceedings.

Summary

BACKGROUND

The facts, drawing all justifiable inferences in favor of the non-movant Keywell, are as follows. Weinstein founded Vac Air in 1966 and, until the time Keywell purchased certain Vac Air assets in December 1987, was a principal shareholder, president, chief executive officer, and member of the board of directors of the company. Boscarino joined Vac Air in 1971 as an assistant to the secretary/treasurer, and by 1978 he had become a stockholder, director, and vice-president of the company. Both Weinstein and Boscarino took an active part in conducting the business of Vac Air, which included the operation of a metals recycling plant located in Frewsburg, New York (the "Frewsburg plant").

From the time Vac Air was founded in 1966 until Keywell's acquisition of assets in December 1987, the Frewsburg plant recycled scrap metal—a process that entailed the

designation.

The Nuts and Bolts of a Case

When you turn to a case in a reporter, you'll find identifying information on the first page. We explain the importance of each item using the *Keywell* case, which we have reproduced above.

The Citation. The editors of the *Federal Reporter* make it impossible for you to forget which case you're reading. The case name appears at the top of each page, along with instructions on how to cite the case—for example, here you're told to "Cite as 33 F.3d 159 (2d Cir. 1994)."

The Parties. In a civil case, the plaintiff is the person or company who filed the lawsuit and is listed above or in front of the "v.," which stands for "versus." The defendant, the party sued, is listed after the "v." In a federal criminal case, the plaintiff is the prosecutor or "the People" of the U.S. government. The state is the prosecutor or "the People" in a state case. The defendant is the person charged with a crime.

Some reported federal cases are from the trial level. For example, all of the cases in the *Federal Supplement* (F.Supp) are from U.S. District Courts, and, in those cases, the parties are identified as "plaintiff" and "defendant." When a reported case is from an appellate court, the appellant is the party who lost and is bringing the appeal. The appellee won the lower case and must defend that victory.

In the *Keywell* case, Keywell Corporation is the "Plaintiff-Appellant," which tells you Keywell initiated the lawsuit at the trial level and filed the present appeal. Weinstein and Boscarino were the defendants at the trial level and are the appellees now.

The Docket Number. The court clerk gives a case filed in the trial court a "docket number," which is used to identify the case while in the trial court. If appealed, it receives a different number from the appellate court clerk. The docket number is used when it's first issued as a "slip opinion." It gets a permanent citation when published in the reporter series.

In the *Keywell* case, the docket number is "No. 1208 Docket Number 93-7994." When this case was first listed in *Shepard's*, the listing would have looked like this: "Dk2 93-7994." The "Dk2" tells you this is a slip opinion from the Second Circuit.

The Court. This is the court that wrote the decision. In the *Keywell* case, the decision was written by the U.S. Court of Appeals for the Second Circuit, which heard the case. To learn which trial court had the case initially, read The Summary, discussed below.

The Dates. Many opinions include the date the case was argued and the opinion date. The issue date is essential if the decision announces a new rule of law or invalidates a statute. But watch out: Opinions don't become "final" until the time for granting a rehearing has passed. The local rules for each court will specify how long that period might be.

The Summary. The editors write a one-paragraph summary of the decision to help readers understand the case quickly. You can't cite this text because it isn't part of the decision itself. If the opinion is from a trial court (such as in "F.Supp.," the reporter series containing federal district court cases), it will list the issue and the decision. If the opinion is from an appellate-level court, the summary will describe the trial court's decision and explain the holding of the appellate court.

The Decision. Many summaries end with a one-line phrase describing the holding of the court. In *Keywell*, the lower court's decision was "Affirmed in part, and reversed and remanded in part." The trial court's decision was upheld as to one or more issues but reversed on others, and the case was sent back to the trial court for further proceedings.

How the Opinion Itself Is Organized

As we've explained, a party who disagrees with the trial outcome can file an appeal. In most appeals, the appealing party is limited to disputing mistakes the lower court made when applying the law. Except in rare circumstances, there's no fresh look at the facts presented at trial. Instead, the appellate court reviews the trial court's rulings to decide whether the court followed the law when applying it to the facts. Then, the appellate court issues an opinion.

Typically, every intermediate appellate or supreme court opinion contains four basic elements:

1. **A statement of facts.** The higher court accepts facts taken from the lower court's factual determination as accurate unless the lower court's determinations were clearly in error.

2. **A statement of the legal issue or issues.** Put another way, this is the legal question at issue—in what way do the parties disagree about how the lower court handled the case?

3. **A ruling or holding.** The ruling is the court's answer to or decision on the issues presented for resolution. If the court agrees with the lower court's conclusions and the relief it ordered for one or both parties, the lower court decision is "affirmed." If the court disagrees with either or both of these aspects of the lower court's decision, the decision is "reversed."

   Sometimes, lower court decisions are affirmed in part and reversed in part. If the intermediate appellate or supreme court agrees substantially with the lower court but disagrees with some particular point, it might modify or amend the decision. Usually, in the case of a complete or partial reversal, the case is sent back to the lower court to take further action consistent with the intermediate appellate or supreme court's opinion. This is called a "remand."

4. **Discussion.** This section explains why the court made the ruling. It's the court's reasoning or rationale. The court's reasoning is usually the longest part of the case and the most difficult to understand.

Many court opinions present these four components—facts, issues, decision, and reasoning—in this order. Others don't. For instance, one format used by some courts is a summary of the issue and the decision in the first couple of paragraphs, followed by a statement of the facts and the reasoning.

The actual opinion issued in a case called *Deason v. Metropolitan Property & Liability Insurance Co.* is shown below. The four elements described above are labeled.

Courts Where Appeals Are Normally Filed				
Courts Cases Appealed From	U.S. Supreme Court	U.S. Court of Appeals	State Supreme Court	State Court of Appeal
U.S. Courts of Appeals	✓			
U.S. District Courts	If issued by a 3-judge panel OR when the U.S., its agent, or its employee is a party, and an act of Congress is held unconstitutional on its face (not as applied)	✓		
State Supreme Courts	If a federal question is involved	✓		
State Courts of Appeal	If a federal question is involved and the State Supreme Court has denied relief OR declined to hear the case		✓	
State Trial Courts			If there's no court of appeal OR it is a special case (appeal of death penalty case)	✓

DEASON v. METRO. PROP. & LIABILITY INS. CO.   Ill. **783**
Cite as 474 N.E.2d 783 (Ill.App. 5 Dist. 1985)

130 Ill.App.3d 620
85 Ill.Dec. 823

Mary Kaye **DEASON**, Administratrix of the Estate of David A. Deason, Deceased, and Mary Kaye Deason, Plaintiff-Appellee,

and

Florence Petro, Administrator of the Estate of George Petro, deceased; Sherrill Josephson, Administratrix of the Estate of Mathew Josephson, deceased; and Michael Petro, Counter-Plaintiffs-Appellees,

v.

METROPOLITAN PROPERTY & LIABILITY INSURANCE COMPANY, a Corporation, Defendant-Appellant,

and

Auto-Owners Insurance Company, a Corporation, et al., Defendants.

No. 5–84–0073.

Appellate Court of Illinois,
Fifth District.

Jan. 10, 1985.

Action was brought against automobile insurer seeking a judgment declaring that policy issued to driver's parents afforded secondary coverage in connection with an accident which occurred while insureds' son was driving his grandmother's automobile. The Circuit Court, St. Clair County, Richard P. Goldenhersh, J., entered judgment in favor of plaintiffs, and insurer appealed. The Appellate Court, Harrison, J., held that automobile operated by driver was not a "temporary substitute vehicle" under terms of automobile policy issued to parents so as to afford secondary coverage in connection with driver's accident.

Reversed.

1. **Declaratory Judgment** ⊂=168
Case involving question whether coverage existed under terms of automobile insurer's policy was proper subject for declaratory judgment action.

2. **Insurance** ⊂=435.2(4)
Where driver's use of his grandmother's automobile was not to be temporary, but regular and permanent, and the automobile was not intended by driver's parents to be a substitute for either of two automobiles owned by driver's father, under terms of automobile policy issued to parents, the automobile operated by driver was not a "temporary substitute vehicle" so as to afford secondary coverage in connection with driver's accident.

See publication Words and Phrases for other judicial constructions and definitions.

3. **Evidence** ⊂=200
In action brought against automobile insurer seeking a judgment declaring that policy issued to driver's parents afforded secondary coverage in connection with an accident which occurred while insureds' son was driving his grandmother's automobile, trial court correctly noted in its judgment that statements by certain employees of insurer to the effect that they believed driver's parents' policy afforded coverage were merely opinions and were not binding on a court in its consideration of the legal question presented.

———

Feirich, Schoen, Mager, Green & Associates, Carbondale, for defendant-appellant.

C.E. Heiligenstein, Brad L. Badgley, Belleville, for Mary Kaye Deason.

H. Carl Runge, Jr., Runge & Gumbel, P.C., Collinsville, for Beth Martell, a minor, by her father and next friend, John Martell, John Martell and Patsie Gott, Administratrix of the Estate of Lisa J. Gott, Deceased.

Michael P. Casey, Edward R. Vrdolyak, Ltd., Chicago, for Florence Petro & Sherrill Josephson & Michael Petro.

HARRISON, Justice:

[1] Metropolitan Property & Liability Insurance Company (hereinafter referred to as Metropolitan) appeals from a judgment of the circuit court of St. Clair Coun-

Opinion in *Deason v. Metropolitan*

784 Ill.   **474 NORTH EASTERN REPORTER, 2d SERIES**

ty declaring that a policy of insurance issued by Metropolitan afforded secondary
coverage in connection with a November
30, 1980, accident involving a 1975 Mercury
Comet driven by Christopher Warner. The
primary issue for our consideration is
whether the trial court properly concluded
that, under the terms of the policy issued
by Metropolitan to Christopher Warner's
parents, the Comet operated by Christopher Warner was a "temporary substitute
automobile". Because this case involves
the question of whether or not coverage
exists under the terms of Metropolitan's
policy, it is a proper subject for a declaratory judgment action. *Reagor v. Travelers
Insurance Co.* (1980), 92 Ill.App.3d 99,
102–03, 47 Ill.Dec. 507, 415 N.E.2d 512.

The policy in question provides coverage
to the insured for accidents arising out of
the ownership, maintenance or use of an
owned or non-owned automobile. The
terms "non-owned automobile" and "owned
automobile" are defined in the policy as
follows:

"'[N]on-owned automobile'* means an
automobile which is neither owned by
nor furnished nor available for the regular use of either the *named insured* or
any *relative*, other than a *temporary
substitute automobile*, and includes a
utility trailer while used with any such
automobile:

    •   •   •   •   •   •

'[O]wned automobile' means

(a) a *private passenger automobile* or
utility automobile owned by the
named insured and described in the
Declarations to which the Automobile
Liability Coverage of the policy applies and for which a specific premi-
um for such insurance is charged, or

(b) a *private passenger automobile* or
utility automobile ownership of
which is newly acquired by the
named insured, provided (i) it re-
places an *owned automobile* as defined in (a) above, or (ii) METROPOL-
ITAN insures all *automobiles* owned
by the *named insured* on the date of
such acquisition and the *named in-*

sured notifies METROPOLITAN
within thirty (30) days of such acquisition of his election to make this and
no other policy issued by METRO-
POLITAN applicable to such *automobile* and pays any additional pre-
mium required therefor, or

(c) a *temporary substitute automobile:*"

The policy defines "temporary substitute
automobile" in this manner:

"'[T]emporary substitute automobile'
means an *automobile* not owned by the
named insured or any resident of the
same household, while temporarily used
with the permission of the owner as a
substitute for an *owned automobile*
when withdrawn from normal use for
servicing or repair or because of breakdown, loss or destruction:"

The facts relevant to a determination of
whether the 1975 Comet was a temporary
substitute automobile are not in significant
dispute. Christopher Warner spent the
summer of 1980 in Ohio with his grandmother, Vera Fry. Ms. Fry, an Ohio resident, owned the 1975 Comet, which was
insured by a company other than Metropolitan. During that summer, arrangements
were made whereby Christopher would
take the Comet with him when he returned
to his parents' Cobden, Illinois home at the
end of the summer. It was further agreed
that Christopher would return to Ohio at
Christmas time and pay Vera Fry $100
after which she would have the title to the
Comet transferred to Christopher and one
of his parents. Christopher did in fact
bring the Comet back to Cobden in August,
1980, and he and his parents used it regularly. On November 30, 1980, before
Christopher had paid any money to Vera
Fry, and before title to the Comet had been
transferred, the accident in question occurred.

On the date of the accident, Andrew
Warner, Christopher's father, owned a
1973 Mercury and a 1974 Dodge pickup
truck. Both of these vehicles were insured
by Metropolitan. Neither was operable at

Issue

Facts

Opinion in *Deason v. Metropolitan* (continued)

DEASON v. METRO. PROP. & LIABILITY INS. CO. Ill. 78!
Cite as 474 N.E.2d 783 (Ill.App. 5 Dist. 1985)

the time of the accident; the Mercury had a defective transmission and the Dodge had a twisted drive shaft. Both vehicles were put back into operation shortly after the accident involving the Comet. During his deposition, Andrew Warner testified as follows:

"Q. Did you have any intention if the Comet hadn't been wrecked, did you have any intention to dispose of either of these other two cars just because you got the Comet?

A. Oh, no."

Lower court's decision

[2] In ruling that Metropolitan's policy afforded secondary coverage in connection with the accident involving the 1975 Comet, the court found that Christopher Warner was "a relative operating a temporary substitute" automobile. Metropolitan contends that this conclusion is incorrect, and we are compelled to agree. Under the terms of the policy, a temporary substitute automobile is defined as one "temporarily used with the permission of the owner as a substitute for an owned automobile when withdrawn from normal use for servicing or repair or because of breakdown, loss, or destruction." Here, the unequivocal deposition testimony of all concerned establishes that Christopher Warner's use of the Comet was not to be temporary, but regular and permanent, as it was the intention of both Vera Fry and Christopher Warner that he would pay $100 for the car at Christmas time, and would not return it to her. Moreover, the Comet was not intended by the Warners to be a substitute for either the Mercury or the Dodge; rather, it was to be kept as a third car, and the fact that the Dodge and Mercury broke down during the Warners' use of the Comet was entirely coincidental. Under these circumstances, the "temporary substitute" provision of the policy issued by Metropolitan did not encompass Christopher Warner's use of the Comet on the date of the accident. (See *Sturgeon v. Automobile Club Inter-Insurance Exchange* (1979), 77 Ill. App.3d 997, 1000, 34 Ill.Dec. 66, 397 N.E.2d 522.) This conclusion is buttressed by the holding of *Nationwide Insurance Compa-*

Rationale

ny v. Ervin (1967), 87 Ill.App.2d 432, 436-87, 231 N.E.2d 112, wherein it was recognized that a "temporary substitute" provision of the type under consideration here is to be applied to those situations where an insured automobile is withdrawn from use for a short period, and not where, as here coverage is sought to be extended to an additional automobile for a significan' length of time.

[3] *Providence Mutual Casualty Company v. Sturms* (1962), 37 Ill.App.2d 304 185 N.E.2d 366, relied on by appellees, is not on point. *Sturms* addresses the question of whether coverage afforded on a temporary substitute automobile expires immediately upon repair of the insured's regular automobile (37 Ill.App.2d 304, 306 185 N.E.2d 366), and does not discuss the more fundamental issue of when a vehicle is considered to be a temporary substitute in the first place. While appellees also suggest that portions of Metropolitan's claim file show that certain Metropolitan employees believe that the policy in question afforded coverage, the trial court correctly noted in its judgment that these statements are merely opinions, and are not binding on a court in its consideration of the legal question presented. 31A C.J.S *Evidence* § 272(b) (1964).

For the foregoing reasons, the judgment of the circuit court of St. Clair County is reversed.

Reversed.

Decision

JONES, P.J., and KARNS, J., concur.

Opinion in *Deason v. Metropolitan* (continued)

How Appellate Courts Decide Cases

Appellate courts are comprised of anywhere from three to nine justices. For example, the California Supreme Court and the New York Court of Appeals have seven justices, the Vermont Supreme Court has five, and the U.S. Supreme Court has nine. In New York (and in Texas for criminal cases), the highest state court is called the "Court of Appeals" rather than the "Supreme Court."

Only the actual decision of the majority (or plurality) of justices and the principles of law necessary to that decision serve as precedent that other courts must follow. Other discussions in the opinion might help you understand the decision, but the opinions aren't binding on other courts. The court's decision and the law necessary to arrive at it are called the "holding." The rest of the decision is called "dicta."

An appellate court justice who disagrees with the majority's decision on a case might issue a "dissenting" opinion, which is published along with the majority's opinion. No matter how passionate a dissent happens to be, it doesn't affect the particular case. However, it might persuade judges in future court decisions.

A justice who agrees with the majority decision but disagrees with the reasons given might issue a "concurring opinion." A concurring opinion is published with the majority's opinion and can have a persuasive influence on future court decisions.

If the main opinion in the case is supported by less than a majority—called a "plurality" opinion—the concurring opinion can operate as a weak type of authority for future cases. For instance, in a 1985 case, the U.S. Supreme Court issued an opinion in which only four justices joined. A fifth justice, Chief Justice Burger, concurred and swung the court's holding to the plurality's view; if Chief Justice Burger had sided with the other four justices, they might have been the majority (or plurality, if he only concurred with and didn't join their opinion).

For a fascinating account of how the U.S. Supreme Court decides its cases, read *The Brethren: Inside the Supreme Court*, by Woodward and Armstrong (Simon and Schuster, 1979).

Using Synopses and Headnotes to Read and Understand a Case

In addition to the court opinions, the publishers of case reports also publish a one-paragraph synopsis of the case and some helpful one-sentence summaries of the legal issues discussed in it. The synopsis and headnotes come just before the opinion itself. Below are the headnotes from *Deason v. Metropolitan Property & Liability Insurance Co.*

The headnotes are numbered in the order in which the legal issues they summarize appear in the opinion. The part of the opinion covered by each headnote is marked off in the opinion with a number in brackets. See the *Deason* opinion, above, for an example.

Headnotes can be very useful in several ways. They serve as a table of contents to the opinion, so that if you are only interested in one of the many issues raised in a case, you can skim the headnotes, find the relevant issue, and then turn to the corresponding bracketed number in the opinion. As discussed in Chapter 6, headnotes also allow discussions of legal issues in one case to be cross-indexed to similar discussions in other cases using "digests." Finally, headnotes are helpful when you are "Shepardizing" a case. We'll cover that in Chapter 9.

 CAUTION

Headnotes are prepared by the publisher. They aren't part of the case. Because the editors who prepare the headnotes are human, don't rely on the headnotes to accurately state the issue or principle of law as it appears in the opinion. Headnotes tend to simplify issues, so beware—what might seem like a helpful case holding might not be what the case stands for. Also, never quote a headnote in any argument you submit to a court because you will likely misrepresent what the case stands for. Instead, you must read the pertinent opinion section and cite the appropriate page if the case is helpful.

DEASON v. METRO. PROP. & LIABILITY INS. CO.   Ill.   783
Cite as 474 N.E.2d 783 (Ill.App. 5 Dist. 1985)

130 Ill.App.3d 620
85 Ill.Dec. 823

Mary Kaye DEASON, Administratrix of the Estate of David A. Deason, Deceased, and Mary Kaye Deason, Plaintiff-Appellee,

and

Florence Petro, Administrator of the Estate of George Petro, deceased; Sherrill Josephson, Administratrix of the Estate of Mathew Josephson, deceased; and Michael Petro, Counter-Plaintiffs-Appellees,

v.

METROPOLITAN PROPERTY & LIABILITY INSURANCE COMPANY, a Corporation, Defendant-Appellant,

and

Auto-Owners Insurance Company, a Corporation, et al., Defendants.

No. 5-84-0073.

Appellate Court of Illinois,
Fifth District.

Jan. 10, 1985.

Action was brought against automobile insurer seeking a judgment declaring that policy issued to driver's parents afforded secondary coverage in connection with an accident which occurred while insureds' son was driving his grandmother's automobile. The Circuit Court, St. Clair County, Richard P. Goldenhersh, J., entered judgment in favor of plaintiffs, and insurer appealed. The Appellate Court, Harrison, J., held that automobile operated by driver was not a "temporary substitute vehicle" under terms of automobile policy issued to parents so as to afford secondary coverage in connection with driver's accident.

Reversed.

1. Declaratory Judgment ⟞168

Case involving question whether coverage existed under terms of automobile insurer's policy was proper subject for declaratory judgment action.

2. Insurance ⟞435.2(4)

Where driver's use of his grandmother's automobile was not to be temporary, but regular and permanent, and the automobile was not intended by driver's parents to be a substitute for either of two automobiles owned by driver's father, under terms of automobile policy issued to parents, the automobile operated by driver was not a "temporary substitute vehicle" so as to afford secondary coverage in connection with driver's accident.

See publication Words and Phrases for other judicial constructions and definitions.

3. Evidence ⟞200

In action brought against automobile insurer seeking a judgment declaring that policy issued to driver's parents afforded secondary coverage in connection with an accident which occurred while insureds' son was driving his grandmother's automobile, trial court correctly noted in its judgment that statements by certain employees of insurer to the effect that they believed driver's parents' policy afforded coverage were merely opinions and were not binding on a court in its consideration of the legal question presented.

Headnotes From *Deason v. Metropolitan Property & Liability Insurance Co.*

How Cases Are Published

In Chapter 6, we explained that cases are published in volumes called "reporters." There are many separate reporters for different courts and geographical areas, and an opinion might be published in more than one. For example, New York Court of Appeals cases are found in a publication titled *New York Appeals* and in a regional reporter called the *North Eastern Reporter,* which contains state court cases from New York, Illinois, Indiana, Massachusetts, and Ohio.

Federal Cases

Federal court cases are published according to the court they are decided by.

U.S. District Court Cases

Only a very small percentage of U.S. District Court cases are published. All published U.S. District Court cases are collected in the *Federal Supplement* (F.Supp.) or *Federal Rules Decisions* (F.R.D.).

Bankruptcy Court Cases

Decisions of the U.S. bankruptcy courts are reported in the *Bankruptcy Reporter* (B.R.), published by West.

U.S. Court of Appeals Cases

All published decisions by the U.S. Courts of Appeals are collected in the *Federal Reporter.* It's currently in its fourth series and is abbreviated as "F." or "F.2d" or "F.3d" or "F.4th" (*Federal Reporter, Fourth Series*).

The U.S. Court of Appeals (the intermediate federal appellate court) is divided into 12 circuits and a special court called the Federal Circuit that hears appeals relating to patents and customs. Below is a table of the states in each circuit.

Circuits of the U.S. Court of Appeals

First Circuit
  Maine
  Massachusetts
  New Hampshire
  Puerto Rico
  Rhode Island

Second Circuit
  Connecticut
  New York
  Vermont

Third Circuit
  Delaware
  New Jersey
  Pennsylvania
  Virgin Islands

Fourth Circuit
  Maryland
  North Carolina
  South Carolina
  Virginia
  West Virginia

Fifth Circuit
  Louisiana
  Mississippi
  Texas

Sixth Circuit
  Kentucky
  Michigan
  Ohio
  Tennessee

Seventh Circuit
  Illinois
  Indiana
  Wisconsin

Eighth Circuit
  Arkansas
  Iowa
  Minnesota
  Missouri
  Nebraska
  North Dakota
  South Dakota

Ninth Circuit
  Alaska
  Arizona
  California
  Guam
  Hawaii
  Idaho
  Montana
  Nevada
  Oregon
  Washington

Tenth Circuit
  Colorado
  Kansas
  New Mexico
  Oklahoma
  Utah
  Wyoming

Eleventh Circuit
  Alabama
  Florida
  Georgia

District of Columbia Circuit
  Washington, D.C.

Federal Circuit
  Patent and Customs Cases

U.S. Supreme Court Cases

Last, but certainly not least, U.S. Supreme Court cases have three separate reporters. Each of them contains the same cases but different editorial enhancements as described below:

- *United States Supreme Court Reports (U.S.).* This reporter is the so-called "official" reporter, commissioned by Congress. Other reports that cover these cases are "unofficial" reports. The opinions collected in the official reporter aren't more accurate or authoritative. For legal research purposes, there is little difference among them. However, most courts require a citation to the official reporter when referring to a U.S. Supreme Court case in court documents.
- *Supreme Court Reporter (S.Ct.).* This reporter is part of the West Group series of reporters. It is part of an elaborate cross-reference system known as the "key system" (explained in Chapter 6). If you are using the West research system, using this reporter is a good idea.
- *United States Supreme Court Reports, Lawyers' Edition (L.Ed.).* LexisNexis publishes this reporter, which is handy if you use that company's research system. This reporter contains the U.S. Supreme Court cases (as do the other two reporters) and considerable editorial comment about the case's impact, including an annotation relating the case to other cases on the same subject.

You might wonder why having three reporters for a single court is necessary. It's not. Many small law libraries buy one or two at the most.

State Court Cases

Each state arranges for its appellate court cases to be published in official state reporters. In the larger states, there are usually two official reporters: one for the highest court cases and another for the intermediate appellate court cases. If you are interested in using the official reporters for your state while researching, ask your law librarian where to find the official state reporter.

In addition to these official reporters, the cases of each state—both supreme court and appellate—are published by West in a series of reporters called "regional reporters." West has divided the country into seven regions. Cases produced by the state courts of an area are published together. For example, Alabama, Florida, Louisiana, and Mississippi cases are all published in the *Southern Reporter*.

West also publishes state-specific versions of its regional reporters. For this reason, the *Southern Reporter* found in an Alabama library might contain only Alabama cases.

Most academic law libraries carry official reporters for their state and the regional reporters for the entire country. However, they probably won't have state-specific reporters from other states. So, if you are in New Hampshire and want to look up a New Hampshire case, you will have a choice between the New Hampshire official reports and the *Atlantic Reporter* (the regional reporter for the Northeast). However, you will most likely need to use the *Southern Reporter* to find a Florida case.

Keeping Case Reporters Up to Date

A significant time lag usually exists between the date a case is decided and the publication of a new hardcover reporter. To make new cases available during the interim, reporters have weekly update pamphlets called "advance sheets." The chances are great that if a case was decided within several months (or even years for some Supreme Court cases) of when you are doing your research, it will be found in an advance sheet rather than in the latest hardcover volumes. This won't be nearly so problematic if you research online.

The National Reporter System

Full Name of Reporter	Abbreviation	State Courts Included
Atlantic Reporter (First, Second, and Third Series)	A., A.2d, and A.3d	Supreme and intermediate appellate courts in D.C., Connecticut, Delaware, Maine, Maryland, New Hampshire, New Jersey, Pennsylvania, Rhode Island, and Vermont
North Eastern Reporter (First, Second, and Third Series)	N.E., N.E.2d, and N.E.3d	Court of Appeals in New York and supreme and intermediate appellate courts in Illinois, Indiana, Massachusetts, and Ohio
North Western Reporter (First and Second Series)	N.W. and N.W.2d	Supreme and intermediate appellate courts in Iowa, Michigan, Minnesota, Nebraska, North Dakota, South Dakota, and Wisconsin
Pacific Reporter (First, Second, and Third Series)	P., P.2d, and P.3d	Supreme and intermediate appellate courts in Alaska, Arizona, California (Sup. Ct. only since 1960), Colorado, Hawaii, Idaho, Kansas, Montana, Nevada, New Mexico, Oklahoma, Oregon, Utah, Washington, and Wyoming
South Eastern Reporter (First and Second Series)	S.E. and S.E.2d	Supreme and intermediate appellate courts in Georgia, North Carolina, South Carolina, Virginia, and West Virginia
Southern Reporter (First, Second, and Third Series)	So., So.2d, and So.3d	Supreme and intermediate appellate courts in Alabama, Florida, Louisiana, and Mississippi
South Western Reporter (First, Second, and Third Series)	S.W., S.W.2d, and S.W.3d	Supreme and intermediate appellate courts in Arkansas, Kentucky, Missouri, Tennessee, and Texas
New York Supplement (First, Second, and Third Series)	N.Y.S., N.Y.S. 2d, and N.Y.S. 3d	All New York supreme and intermediate appellate courts
California Reporter (First, Second, and Third Series)	Cal.Rptr., Cal. Rptr. 2d, and Cal.Rptr. 3d	All California supreme and intermediate appellate courts

It is important to remember that all appellate opinions (and some at the trial level) are followed by a period during which the parties can request a rehearing before the same court. Also, most decisions are appealable by filing a petition for a hearing or a writ of *certiorari* to the next higher court. Opinions might appear in the advance sheets during this period. If either rehearing or a petition for hearing or *certiorari* is granted, the underlying opinion is rendered null and void, and it can't be cited. For this reason, the advance sheets have subsequent case history tables that you should consult whenever you cite a case that is still in the advance sheets.

Most law libraries shelve advance sheets next to the hardcover volumes. Sometimes, however, they are kept behind the reference desk.

The Newest Cases

When a judge issues an opinion, it has a life of its own before it appears in the weekly advance sheets. Typically, the opinion is signed by the judge(s) and then sent to the clerk's office for distribution to the public. Copies go to the parties, the general press, the local legal newspapers, the case reporter services (for inclusion in the next advance sheet booklet), and *Shepard's*.

During this time, it is referred to as a "slip opinion," and it is identified by its docket number—the court number the case received when it was first filed. It will get a regular citation when it appears in the next week's advance sheets. But before that time, it might be picked up by *Shepard's* if it cites other cases, and *Shepard's* will refer to the case by its docket number. If you need to see an opinion identified only by its docket number, your best bet is to go to an online site or use one of the computerized research services (LexisNexis or Westlaw).

It is risky to cite a slip opinion. As with opinions in the advance sheets, slip opinions can be wiped off the books if a rehearing is ordered or a higher court decides to take the case. Slip opinions don't become "final" and citable until the time for filing these motions has passed.

If you cite a slip opinion, be sure to thereafter track its course through the advance sheets, by checking to see if it appears and whether it shows up in the subsequent case history table.

Researching California Cases

In California, unlike most other states, there is a good reason to use the official reporters—*California Reports* for California Supreme Court cases and *California Appellate Reports* for California Court of Appeal cases. The California Supreme Court frequently depublishes published Court of Appeal opinions. Depublished opinions can no longer be relied on as correct statements of California law. When a case is depublished, its conclusion remains intact as far as the case's parties are concerned, but it is taken out of the official reports and replaced with a notation to that effect. It usually remains in the unofficial reports. By using the unofficial reports, you run a small risk of relying on a case that appears helpful but no longer exists from a legal standpoint.

In California, the advance sheets for the official case reports published by LexisNexis contain a section at the back that tells you what has happened to cases since they were published in the reports. Cases are sometimes reheard, taken for hearing by the Supreme Court, or ordered depublished. A table in the advance sheets—the cumulative Subsequent History Table or Case History Table—informs you when this happens. You might also use *Shepard's* (discussed in Chapter 8) to determine whether a case has been depublished.

Depublication allows the Supreme Court to administratively weed out misstatements of the law without having to handle the errant case on appeal. Also, it enables a weak or divided Court to render impotent a decision by a lower court that creates new law or is controversial. Depublication allows the appellate court decision to operate as far as the parties to that case are concerned, but its decision doesn't become a precedent upon which others can rely.

Publishing Cases Online

Cases have been available electronically for many years. However, the two large legal databases—LexisNexis and Westlaw—charge substantial fees for their use and are largely inaccessible to the individual legal researcher for home use.

However, many law libraries now subscribe to one or both of these services and make them available to their patrons. So, if you have access to a law library that gives you access to Westlaw or LexisNexis, the law librarian can get you started on your case research. After a few minutes, you'll have the hang of it.

As we explained in Chapter 2, you can access cases online for no cost on websites like Google Scholar (www.scholar.google.com) or Justia (www.justia.com). While this allows you to see the actual text of the cases and will give you the citation to the official reporter, online cases don't always have "pincites"—the ability to tell you on what page of an official reporter particular text appears. This isn't generally a problem unless you're drafting a document you will submit to a court. In that case, you will typically need a pincite from the official reporter.

You might need to go to the library, or you might want to utilize an online service like Westlaw on a short-term basis.

How Cases Affect Later Disputes

Past decisions in appellate cases are powerful predictors of what the courts will do in future cases, given similar facts. Most judges try hard to be consistent with decisions that either they or a higher court have made. This consistency is essential to a just legal system and is the essence of the common law tradition. (Common law— the decisions of courts over the years—is discussed in Chapter 3.) For this reason, if you can find a previous court decision that rules your way on facts similar to your situation, you can persuade a judge to follow that case and decide in your favor.

There are two basic principles to understand when you intend to use cases to persuade a judge to rule your way. One is called "precedent," the other "persuasive authority."

Precedent

In the legal sense, a precedent is an earlier case that is relevant to a case to be decided. If there is nothing to distinguish the circumstances of the current case from the already-decided one, the earlier holding is considered binding on the court.

The idea of a precedent comes from a basic American common law system principle: *stare decisis*, Latin for "Let the decision stand." Once a high court decides how to apply the law to a particular set of facts, this decision controls later decisions by that and other courts.

A case is only a precedent for its particular decision and the law necessary to arrive at that decision. If, in passing, a judge deals with a legal question that isn't essential to the decision, the reasoning and opinion regarding this tangential question are not precedent but nonbinding "dicta."

> EXAMPLE: A Court of Appeals rules that the lesser dung beetle is protected under the Endangered Species Act. As part of his reasoning, the judge's opinion states that as he reads the statute, even mosquitoes are entitled to protection. Because the court was asked to rule on the lesser dung beetle, the judge's comments on mosquitoes are dicta—language unnecessary to decide the case before the court—and not binding as to any future dispute on that point.

It is common for courts to avoid overruling earlier decisions by distinguishing the earlier one from the present one based on some insignificant factual difference or small legal issue. Getting a court to "distinguish" an old case is much easier than openly overruling it. It is sometimes difficult to tell whether an earlier case has been overruled and is no longer precedent or if it has been distinguished and is still operative as precedent.

On the other hand, prior decisions are sometimes expressly overruled as inconsistent with the times. When the U.S. Supreme Court decided *Brown v. Board of Education* in 1954, it held that separate educational facilities for black and white students were unconstitutional. That overruled a 19th-century case called *Plessy v. Ferguson*, which had held that such "separate but equal" facilities were constitutional.

The precedential value of the earlier case is affected by which court decided it. Here are some guidelines for determining the effect that one court's decisions has on another's:

- Appellate court cases (including supreme court cases) operate as precedent for future decisions by the same courts.

  EXAMPLE: In 2020, the Indiana Supreme Court rules that county general relief grants can't be terminated without first providing the recipient with a hearing. In 2021, a fiscally strapped county cuts everyone off general assistance without hearings. A group of recipients seeks court relief. In 2021, the issue gets to the Indiana Supreme Court, which orders the recipients reinstated on the grounds of its earlier ruling.

- U.S. Supreme Court cases are precedent for all courts regarding decisions involving the U.S. Constitution or any aspect of federal law.

  EXAMPLE: In 2020, the U.S. Supreme Court ruled that under the First Amendment to the U.S. Constitution, nonlawyers may help the public use self-help law books without being charged with the unauthorized practice of law. In 2021, the Nebraska Bar Association sued a nonlawyer to stop him from telling people how to use a self-help divorce book. He claimed a violation of his First Amendment rights and won based on the U.S. Supreme Court case.

- U.S. Courts of Appeals cases are precedent for U.S. District Courts within their circuits (that is, the states covered by the circuit) and for state courts in this area with respect to issues concerning the U.S. Constitution and any aspect of federal law. (The country is divided into 12 circuits—see "Circuits of the U.S. Court of Appeals," above.)

> **EXAMPLE:** Let's say the U.S. Court of Appeals for the First Circuit rules that the Eighth Amendment to the U.S. Constitution requires that bail in a criminal case be set in an amount that the defendant can reasonably afford to raise. A few years later, Perry is charged in the U.S. District Court for New Hampshire with the crime of assault against a federal officer. Because the U.S. District Court for New Hampshire is within the First Circuit, it must follow the rule for bail laid down by the Court of Appeals for that circuit. However, if Perry were charged with the crime in the U.S. District Court in Vermont— which is in the Second Circuit—the First Circuit case wouldn't be binding.
>
> If Perry were charged with a crime in a New Hampshire state court, he would still be entitled to the new bail rule, because it is based on the U.S. Constitution and New Hampshire is within the First Circuit.

- U.S. District Court case opinions are never precedent for other courts. (They might be persuasive authority; see "Persuasive Authority," below.)

> **EXAMPLE:** A U.S. District Court in Hawaii rules that the Federal Endangered Species Act applies to mosquitoes. A U.S. District Court in Houston is asked to stop a local development because it threatens an endangered mosquito species. The U.S. District Court in Houston can follow the Hawaii case or reach a different conclusion.

- State supreme court cases are precedent with respect to all courts within the state.

> **EXAMPLE:** The Nevada Supreme Court rules that casinos may not require female employees to wear revealing outfits. This ruling is binding on all Nevada courts that are later faced with this issue.

• State intermediate appellate court cases are precedent with respect to the trial courts in the state. In larger states (for example, California), where the intermediate appellate courts are divided into districts (for instance, the fifth appellate district or the second appellate district), any particular intermediate appellate court's decision is sometimes regarded as precedent only by the trial courts within that district.

> EXAMPLE: The intermediate appellate court for the Fifth Appellate District in California rules that preparing an uncontested divorce petition for another isn't the practice of law. As long as this is the only intermediate appellate court ruling on this issue in the state, it is binding on all California trial courts. The following year, the intermediate appellate court for the Second Appellate District rules that preparing an uncontested divorce petition is the practice of law and can be done only by attorneys. The first ruling, from the Fifth Appellate District, is binding on the trial courts in that district—for example, those in Fresno. The second ruling is binding on trial courts in the Second Appellate District—for instance, Los Angeles. Trial courts in other appellate districts may follow either precedent until their intermediate appellate courts issue their own rulings.

Persuasive Authority

If a case is not precedent (binding on later courts) but contains an excellent analysis of the legal issues and provides guidance for any court that reads it, it is persuasive authority. For example, the landmark California Supreme Court case of *Marvin v. Marvin*, the first major case establishing the principle of "palimony," was considered persuasive authority by many other states when considering the same issue. However, the *Marvin* decision wasn't binding on courts outside California.

364 Colo.   **697 PACIFIC REPORTER, 2d SERIES**

must inevitably result in suppressing protected speech." *Id.* at 526, 528, 78 S.Ct. at 1342, 1343.

Presumptions similar or identical to the one at issue here have been invalidated as unconstitutional by various courts. In *State v. Bumanglag*, 63 Hawaii 596, 634 P.2d 80 (1981), for example, the court held that such a presumption [18] impermissibly inhibited free expression: "Its application would tend to limit public access to protected material because booksellers may then restrict what they offer to works they are familiar with and consider 'safe.' The distribution of protected, as well as obscene, matter may be affected by this self-censorship." [19] 634 P.2d at 96.

In *Davis v. State*, 658 S.W.2d 572 (Tex. Crim.App.1983), the court perceived a similar danger to the guarantees of the first amendment, noting that, especially in the case of a large establishment, "[t]he risk of suppressing freedom of expression is not negligible; ... it rises to astronomical proportions." 658 S.W.2d at 579. In addition to observing that the presumption cannot survive due process analysis, *see Leary v. United States*, 395 U.S. 6, 89 S.Ct. 1532, 23 L.Ed.2d 57 (1969), the Texas court concluded that "[f]reedom of expression is too important a right to allow it to be seriously impeded or impaired by a presumption such as the one implicated in this case." 658 S.W.2d at 580. *See also Grove Press, Inc. v. Evans*, 306 F.Supp. 1084 (E.D.Va.1969); *Skinner v. State*, 647 S.W.2d 686 (Tex.App. 1982) (presumption impermissibly shifts burden of proof and eliminates element of

scienter); Model Penal Code § 251.4(2), comment 11 (1980) ("A presumption that one who disseminates or possesses obscene material in the course of his business does so knowingly or recklessly places a severe burden of prior examination and screening on legitimate business. It seems unlikely today that such a presumption would pass constitutional scrutiny."); Note, *The Scienter Requirement in Criminal Obscenity Prosecutions*, 41 N.Y.U.L.Rev. 791, 797–99 (1966) (evidentiary presumptions similar to the one at issue here are invalid after *Smith v. California*).

The Supreme Court has, on one occasion, expressly declined to reach the issue of the constitutionality of such presumptions. *Ginsberg v. New York*, 390 U.S. 629, 632 n. 1, 88 S.Ct. 1274, 1276 n. 1, 20 L.Ed.2d 195 (1968). More recently, however, in a case in which the same issue was raised, the Supreme Court dismissed an appeal for want of a substantial federal question in *People v. Kirkpatrick*, 32 N.Y.2d 17, 343 N.Y.S.2d 70, 295 N.E.2d 753 (1973), *appeal dismissed*, 414 U.S. 948, 94 S.Ct. 283, 38 L.Ed.2d 204 (1973). In *Kirkpatrick*, the state courts upheld the constitutionality of a statutory presumption that the seller of obscene materials knows the contents of that material, and also held that there was sufficient independent evidence of scienter to support the conviction.

[23] This dismissal, in its procedural context, was equivalent to an adjudication of the federal issue on its merits.[20] *Hicks*

---

18. HRS § 712–1214 provided that:
  (1) A person commits the offense of promoting pornography if, knowing its content and character, he:
  (a) Disseminates for monetary consideration any pornographic material....
The presumption at issue, contained in HRS § 712–1216, provided that:
  (1) The fact that a person engaged in the conduct specified by sections 712–1214 or 712–1215 is prima facie evidence that he engaged in that conduct with knowledge of the character and content of the material disseminated or the performance produced, presented, directed, participated in, exhibited, or to be exhibited....

19. Additionally, the court in *Bumanglag* implied that the challenged presumption violated due process. The court agreed that salespeople generally were less likely than not to know the contents of their entire stock: "We find this difficult to discount, for a conclusion that a person who sold a book also was familiar with its character and content does not comport with what common sense and experience tell us about booksellers, salesclerks and their knowledge of the contents of books." 634 P.2d at 96.

20. We are aware that summary affirmances have sometimes been accorded less than full precedential weight by the Supreme Court. *See Edelman v. Jordan*, 415 U.S. 651, 671, 94 S.Ct. 1347, 1359, 39 L.Ed.2d 662 (1974); *Richardson*

Colorado Case

Generally, the higher the court, the more persuasive its opinion. Every word (even dicta) of a U.S. Supreme Court opinion is considered important in assessing the state of the law. However, opinions written by an intermediate appellate court in a small state aren't nearly so influential on other courts.

> EXAMPLE: In the case partially set out above, a Colorado court used cases from Hawaii, Texas, and Virginia as guidance in arriving at its own decision.

How to Analyze the Effect of an Earlier Case on Your Issue

Reading cases and understanding how they apply to your issue can be challenging. Most law and paralegal schools offer an entire course on case analysis, and this book can't replace that training. But the steps below provide a possible approach:

Step 1. Identify the precise issues decided in the case—that is, what issues of law the court had to decide to make its ruling.

Step 2. Compare the issues in the case to those you are interested in and decide whether the case addresses one or more of them. If so, move to Step 3. If not, the case is probably not helpful.

Step 3. Carefully read and understand the facts underlying the case and compare them to the facts of your situation. Does the case's decision on the relevant issues logically stand up when applied to your facts? If so, move to Step 4. If not, go to Step 5.

Step 4. Determine whether the court that decided the case you are reading creates precedent for the trial or appellate courts in your area. If so, the case might serve as precedent. If not, move to Step 5.

Step 5. Carefully read and understand the legal reasoning employed by the court when deciding the relevant issues and determine whether it logically would help another court resolve your issues. If so, the case might be persuasive authority.

Validating Your Research

Once you've found the relevant statutes and cases you've been looking for, you'll probably feel like you're in the home stretch. But wait—there's a final step to take before completing your research. You must ensure that any primary sources remain "good law" and haven't been overruled, reversed, repealed, or otherwise invalidated. As unlikely as it might seem, it happens somewhat frequently.

This chapter explains how to check the validity of a law using a process informally known as "Shepardizing," a shorthand term that references *Shepard's* books and the original service's publisher (LexisNexis is the current provider). You'll also learn to use LexisNexis's online and print versions, along with similar resources like Westlaw's online Key-Cite feature.

Making Sure It's "Good Law"

"Shepardizing" refers to the process used by legal researchers to ensure a case or statute remains good law. Shepardizing can also streamline the research process by providing highly focused subject matter search results. This section focuses on the first function—checking that you're relying on current law.

What Is "Shepardizing"?

Although the law changes regularly, people who appear in court must use current law to support their arguments. Shepardizing services track and catalog references made in legal cases and statutes to help people quickly determine the status of a particular law. The services verify legal authorities are current before being relied on in court.

Why You Must Shepardize

Shepardizing is as crucial as finding a case or statute, if not more so because every successful legal case relies on valid law. Imagine you are a plaintiff in a lawsuit. You write a legal brief to the court explaining that you found a case that says a person in your position is entitled to compensation. But before the hearing, the judge reads your brief, pulls up your authorities, and discovers the appellate court overruled the primary case on which you based your entire argument.

Not only is your argument out the window but so is your credibility. The judge will doubt your work's thoroughness and quality because you didn't take the time to validate your sources. The bottom line is that crafting an entire legal argument based on a legal proposition that no longer exists is every lawyer's worst nightmare. Fortunately, it's also avoidable.

Understanding Your Results

Before learning how to Shepardize, you'll want to understand the type of information you can expect to find. Shepardizing cases and statutes will tell you more than whether your authority remains good law. You'll also learn how other courts have reacted to it since its publication and how they have dealt with similar issues.

The list will usually start with federal courts (the Supreme Court, if applicable, then by circuit) followed by individual states' courts. At the bottom of the list are references to the *A.L.R.*, a secondary source discussed in Chapter 4.

These citations give you information using a set of letter codes. The codes will differ depending on whether you Shepardize online—which you likely will because many libraries no longer carry the hard copy form of *Shepard's*—or use books and pamphlets in the law library.

How to Shepardize a Case

Once you locate a case addressing your research issues, you'll use a Shepardizing service to get a list of subsequent cases referencing it. The list will tell you whether the case was affirmed, modified, or reversed by a higher court and more. In many instances, you also find other cases that better support your argument or answer your question.

Shepardizing services work when the case you are interested in has been referred to in another case by name. If a later case deals with the same subject but doesn't mention your case, Shepardizing won't help. Fortunately, attorneys arguing appeals usually present every possibly relevant case to the court, so many get included in the court's opinion. Shepardizing services reliably document how these subsequent courts have handled a case.

As discussed earlier, most law libraries will provide users free access to LexisNexis and Westlaw on library computers. Each provider includes Shepardizing services you can use to validate your research. You'll likely choose this avenue when available because most find Shepardizing online easier than the old-school book approach.

Also, there's a reasonable chance you won't have the opportunity to use *Shepard's* in print. Although *Shepard's* books and pamphlets are still published, many law libraries have canceled their subscriptions because they already have convenient access as part of their LexisNexis or Westlaw service.

Shepardizing Cases Online

Validating cases online has distinct benefits over using the law library stacks. First of all, it's much quicker. Simply typing the citation into Westlaw or LexisNexis allows you to pull up all subsequent citations simultaneously. If you want to read a search result, you can click it and be taken to it immediately.

Second, citations are marked using systems that show how each subsequent case affects your original citation. For instance, Westlaw includes graphical depictions that make it easy to understand how subsequent cases relate to your original citation and a flag indicating whether your case is at risk of being overruled.

Third, unlike print copies, citations are updated electronically almost immediately. When dealing with print copies, you would have to check several sources to be as up to date as possible, and even then, you wouldn't be able to rival that timeliness.

However, validating your research online is expensive, so unless your local law library provides free access to LexisNexis or Westlaw, you could end up paying some serious cash. Luckily, many law libraries offer access to LexisNexis, Westlaw, or both.

> **RESOURCE**
>
> **Look up your cases for free.** We recommend you look up cases for free on a website like CourtListener (www.courtlistener.com) or the Caselaw Access Project (https://case.law) or use a lower-cost service like Fastcase (www.fastcase.com) and see if you can validate your cases online at your local law library using Westlaw or LexisNexis.

Shepardizing Cases in the Law Library

Before online legal databases like LexisNexis and Westlaw made it easy to validate research, people had to spend significant time Shepardizing cases in the law library. Even though you'll likely use an online service, we think it's important to understand how to use the print version of *Shepard's* if you don't have online access or want to learn the Shepardizing process yourself. Below, you'll find detailed instructions explaining how to Shepardize using physical books and pamphlets.

> **TIP**
>
> **Read first, practice second.** As you read the following pages, you might feel the information is dry and technical and have difficulty absorbing it all at once. Don't try to. Just get a feel for how the system works. You can always bring this book along for reference when using *Shepard's*. After a few times, you'll surely get the hang of it.

Shepard's: The Basics

Before learning how to use the print version of *Shepard's*, it helps to
know the basics:

- Separate *Shepard's* series are published for each state, for federal
  court cases, and for U.S. Supreme Court cases. Sometimes the
  Shepard's is in a separate volume; sometimes it is combined in the
  same volume with *Shepard's Citations for Statutes* for a state.

- The outside of each *Shepard's* volume tells whether it covers statutes,
  cases, or both.

SHEPARD'S
NORTHEASTERN REPORTER
CITATIONS

A COMPILATION OF CITATIONS TO
ALL CASES REPORTED IN THE NORTHEASTERN REPORTER

THE CITATIONS
which include affirmances, reversals and dismissals by higher state courts
and by the United States Supreme Court

APPEAR IN

NORTHEASTERN REPORTER
UNITED STATES SUPREME COURT REPORTS
LAWYERS' EDITION, UNITED STATES SUPREME COURT
   REPORTS
SUPREME COURT REPORTER
FEDERAL CASES
FEDERAL REPORTER
FEDERAL SUPPLEMENT
FEDERAL RULES DECISIONS
ATLANTIC REPORTER
CALIFORNIA REPORTER
NEW YORK SUPPLEMENT
NORTHWESTERN REPORTER
PACIFIC REPORTER
SOUTHEASTERN REPORTER
SOUTHERN REPORTER
SOUTHWESTERN REPORTER
AMERICAN BAR ASSOCIATION JOURNAL

and in annotations of

LAWYERS' EDITION, UNITED STATES SUPREME COURT REPORTS
AMERICAN LAW REPORTS

also in Vols. 1–283 Illinois Appellate Court Reports, Vols. 1–19 Ohio
Appellate Reports and Vols. 1–101 Pennsylvania Superior Court Reports

SECOND EDITION - - - - - - - - - - - - - VOLUME 2 (1974)

SHEPARD'S CITATIONS, Inc.
COLORADO SPRINGS
COLORADO 80901

- *Shepard's* is organized according to the case reporters that publish cases. Each *Shepard's* volume has a box in the first couple of pages telling you the specific publications covered by that volume. Above is a sample taken from the *Shepard's* that correlates to the *North Eastern Reporter.*
- To use *Shepard's*, you need a case citation—the name of the case reporter your case appears in, its volume number, and the first page on which the case appears.
- *Shepard's* hardcover volumes for the cases of a particular state's courts, or the federal courts, cover different time periods. For example, one hardcover volume might contain all references made by cases decided before 1980, another might contain all references made by cases decided between 1980 and 1985, and a third might contain all references made by cases decided between 1985 and 1990.
- *Shepard's* uses its own citation system. Every *Shepard's* volume has a table of abbreviations in case you get confused.

Shepard's, Step by Step

Now, let's walk through how to use *Shepard's*. Remember, it's challenging to understand without being in the law library, so even if it doesn't make sense now, you'll probably be fine when you have the books in front of you. Just bring these instructions along.

Step 1. Identify the citation of the case you want to Shepardize. Most cases are published in at least two reporters—the official reporter and a West regional reporter. You can use *Shepard's* for either. The only parts of the citation you need are the volume, reporter abbreviation, and page number— for instance, 112 Cal.Rptr. 456.

Step 2. Find the *Shepard's* volumes that cover the reporter in the citation. If you chose the *North Western Reporter* citation, for example, select the *Shepard's* for the *North Western Reporter.*

Step 3. If a *Shepard's* volume contains citations for more than one reporter (for example, for both the official reporter and for the West regional reporter), find the part that covers citations for the reporter named in the citation you have selected. For instance, if your citation is for the *North Western Reporter,* locate the pages that cover this series rather than the pages that pertain to your state's official reporter.

Step 4. Note the year of the case you are Shepardizing. Select the volume or volumes that contain citations for cases decided after the case you are Shepardizing. Remember to check the update pamphlets if you have started with a hardcover volume. Some researchers prefer to work backwards, checking the pamphlets first and then working back to the earliest relevant hardcover volume. Either way is fine.

Step 5. Find the volume number (in boldface) that corresponds to the volume number in the citation to the case being Shepardized. For example, if you are Shepardizing a case with the citation "874 F.2d 1035," search for Vol. 874 in bold print at the top of or on the page. (Each volume of *Shepard's* will cover multiple volumes of the case reporter.)

Step 6. Under the correct volume number, find the page number of the citation for the cited case. To continue the example from Step 5, search for the page number ("-1035-") in bold print.

Step 7. Under the bold page number, review the citations given for the citing cases.

Step 8. Use the letters to the left of the citation to decide whether any subsequent citation is worth reviewing.

Step 9. Use the numbers to the right of the citation to decide whether the citing case is referring to the cited case for issues you might be interested in.

Step 10. After you write down all potentially useful citations, go on to more recent *Shepard's* volumes and update pamphlets, and repeat these steps.

How *Shepard's* Works: An Example

This example shows how Steps 1 through 7 work. Steps 8 and 9 are covered above. We are searching for cases referring to *Nationwide Insurance v. Ervin*, 231 N.E.2d 112 (1967). We call *Ervin* the "cited case," and any case referring to *Ervin* is a "citing" case.

Step 1. Identify the citation for the *Ervin* case. We will use the West regional reporter citation, 231 N.E.2d 112 (1967).

Step 2. Find the volume that contains citations to cases published by the *North Eastern Reporter.*

Step 3. Use the part of the volume that contains *North Eastern Reporter* citations. The volume that contains citations for *North Eastern Reporter* cases also contains citations for the official case reporter (*Illinois Appellate Reports*).

Step 4. Find the volume for the correct period. We only want to use volumes with citations for cases decided after 1967, the year *Ervin* was decided. In this example, all volumes of *Shepard's* that contain *North Eastern Reporter* citations have at least some citations to cases that have been decided after 1967, so we must check them all, including the pamphlets.

Step 5. Find the volume number in the *North Eastern Reporter* citation for *Ervin*—Vol. 231.

Step 6. Find the page number. The *Ervin* page number appears as "-112-."

Step 7. Review the citations. The citations to every case referring to the *Ervin* decision appear under the page number ("-112-").

See the illustration of this example on the following page.

323FS⁸344
596FS⁴784
650FS437
64R506s

—70—
(120S26)
(41⊕p159)
231NE²332
370NE²458
371NE²843
381NE²972
414NE⁴438
453NE⁴664
454NE²1389
488NE927

—71—
(120A68)
(41⊕p122)
p166NE808
c484NE²220
j484NE²221
18R813s

—81—
(120A87)
(41⊕p163)
432NE²212
Cir. 6
577FS⁴1131
Md
513A2d938

—85—
(120A59)
(41⊕p117)

—91—
(120A83)
(41⊕p160)
521NE⁴1153
521NE²1153
31R585n

—94—
(120hM127)
(41⊕p131)

—97—
(87IIR411)
Cert Den
269NE²355
269NE²356
273NE¹162
280NE¹²46
283NE¹⁵43
318NE¹²122
326NE²468
363NE²625
363NE²2626
369NE¹295
369NE²295
447NE²441
458NE²1069
f502NE²478
18R633s

—103—
(87IIR181)
Cert Den
323NE²809
323NE²809
374NE⁴1140

—107—
(87IIR139)
cc257NE233
317NE¹631
347NE¹70
360NE²¹1197
378NE¹¹1157

—109—
(87IIR82)
Cert Den
262NE¹797
281NE¹388
378NE²606
412NE¹629

—112—
(87IIR432)
241NE¹120
241NE²120
272NE¹761
274NE²879
287NE¹530
289NE²703
293NE²704
305NE²417
379NE²66
d412NE⁸632
d412NE⁷632
e427NE⁷130
474NE⁶785
474NE⁷785
481NE¹45
497NE²479
502NE²¹295
510NE²¹183
Ga
221SE482
Iowa
174NW383
N C
198SE56
39R333n

—115—
(87IIR159)
m243NE225
231NE¹³713
367NE²395

—120—
(20NY417)
(284NYS2d
[441]
j437NE1095
437NE⁴1095
287NYS2d
[467]
298NYS2d
[645]
300NYS2d
[397]
f304NYS2d
[263]
318NYS2d
[653]
335NYS2d
[749]
387NYS2d
[718]
e388NYS2d
[472]
j452NYS2d
[338]
452NYS2d⁴
[338]

453NYS2d
[597]
513NYS2d72
Cir. 2
d282FS⁴73
j282FS⁴82
f292FS⁴115
439FS⁴975
439FS⁴977
Cir. 4
339FS⁴499
Cir. 6
311FS⁴1191
Calif
90CaR921
94CaR604
484P2d580
Colo
509P2d1272
Iowa
247NW271
Mich
164NW37
N H
400A2d53
Wash
496P2d516
W Va
279SE408
34R155s
65R1069n

—126—
Case 1
(20NY792)
(284NYS2d
[449]
s282NYS2d
[664]
242NE395
295NYS2d
[163]

—126—
Case 2
(20NY793)
(284NYS2d
[449]
s238NE502
s278NYS2d
[770]
s291NYS2d12

—127—
Case 1
(20NY793)
(284NYS2d
[450]
s275NYS2d
[960]
s282NYS2d
[973]

—127—
Case 2
(20NY794)
(284NYS2d
[450]
s272NYS2d
[446]
294NYS2d77

—128—
Case 1
(20NY794)
(284NYS2d
[451]
s274NYS2d
[392]
s281NYS2d
[974]

—128—
Case 2
(20NY795)
(284NYS2d
[451]
s281NYS2d
[985]

—128—
Case 3
(20NY796)
(284NYS2d
[452]
s281NYS2d
[864]
468NYS2d
[161]

—129—
Case 1
(20NY796)
(284NYS2d
[452]
s282NYS2d
[438]

—129—
Case 2
(20NY797)
(284NYS2d
[453]
292NYS2d45
j292NYS2d47
307NYS2d
[191]
321NYS2d
[842]
426NYS2d
[843]
432NYS2d
[156]

—130—
Case 1
(20NY798)
(284NYS2d
[454]

—130—
Case 2
(20NY798)
(284NYS2d
[454]
s282NYS2d
[934]

—130—
Case 3
(20NY798)
(284NYS2d
[455]
s242NE486
s280NYS2d
[952]

—131—
(20NY799)
(284NYS2d
[455]
s232NE652
s234NE840
s261NYS2d
[336]
s271NYS2d
[523]
s285NYS2d
[621]
s287NYS2d
[886]
Cir. 2
9BRW824

—132—
Case 1
(20NY801)
(284NYS2d
[456]
s219NE295
s269NYS2d
[368]
s272NYS2d
[782]
s388US41
s18LE1040
s87SC1873
59LE962n
37R630n
57R178n
57R201n
82R376n
60RF710n

—132—
Case 2
(20NY801)
(284NYS2d
[457]
s229NE192
s245NYS2d
[353]
s272NYS2d
[974]
s282NYS2d
[497]
385NYS2d
[681]
39R497n
65R512n
44R888n
44R893n
68RF957n

—133—
(20NY801)
(284NYS2d
[458]
Cert Den
US cert den
in390US971
s229NE220
s282NYS2d
[538]
495NYS2d
[539]
33R1132n

—134—
Case 1
(20NY802)
(284NYS2d
[459]
s189NE620
s239NYS2d
[124]

—134—
Case 2
(20NY802)
(284NYS2d
[459]

—134—
Case 3
(20NY802)
(284NYS2d
[460]
s205NE879
s257NYS2d
[960]
s282NYS2d
[174]

—135—
Case 1
(20NY803)
(284NYS2d
[460]
s273NYS2d
[572]
s282NYS2d
[639]
250NE582
265NE924
288NYS2d
[246]
j288NYS2d
[247]
303NYS2d
[524]
317NYS2d
[629]
391NYS2d
[220]
392NYS2d28
433NYS2d
[657]
434NYS2d
[278]
497NYS2d
[530]
42R828n

—135—
Case 2
(20NY804)
(284NYS2d
[461]
s275NYS2d
[674]
527NYS2d
[585]

—136—
(20NY805)
(284NYS2d
[462]
s274NYS2d
[850]
268NE646
j295NYS2d
[970]
24R327n

24R363n

—138—
(249Ind173)
304NE⁴877
336NE692
339NE97
430NE¹787
452NE1006
526NE1229

—140—
(249Ind178)
242NE42
f363NE226
e400NE²¹1111

—145—
(249Ind141)
338NE¹262
j403NE811

—147—
(249Ind144)
360NE604
f408NE620
f408NE⁴621
f408NE⁵621
f408NE⁶621
409NE⁶1272
409NE⁴1274
j437NE113
441NE⁵22
471NE⁸731
471NE⁹731
486NE¹662
Mass
j440NE776
Calif
140CaR294
Conn
261A2d296
Tex
547SW624
61R1210n
61R1219n
1R75n

—151—
(249Ind168)
241NE¹368
309NE²845
309NE⁹847
316NE²689
323NE¹239
e331NE¹780
399NE¹368
Me
318A2d498

—154—
(141InA649)
274NE⁵742
301NE¹243
310NE²279
348NE¹81
Ala
361So2d9
Minn
222NW80
4COA569§3
16R192n
17R494n

—157—
(142InA154)
241NE¹77
Nebr
421NW3

—159—
(141InA669)
d252NE2606
d252NE³606
254NE²219
255NE¹829
j275NE¹856
278NE¹336
278NE²336
280NE²865
316NE¹593
316NE⁸593
339NE¹112
340NE¹813
357NE¹256
387NE²1339
433NE²21

—161—
(141InA655)
233NE²805
256NE³923
322NE⁸103
323NE¹238
323NE²238
f355NE⁷438
f355NE⁸438
393NE⁸810
417NE⁷338
486NE⁸442
9R1044s

—165—
(141InA672)
231NE¹863
j235NE¹99
242NE⁴140
261NE⁶602
308NE878
Okla
541P2d861
40R342n
40R358n
40R375n

—169—
(141InA662)
f239NE¹173
249NE516
j249NE³517
j251NE³26
j251NE²26
251NE¹34
269NE³767
j269NE⁴770
270NE767
e272NE⁴629
e272NE³633
272NE⁴874
f273NE²553
f273NE³553
277NE606
280NE³303
284NE²735
286NE¹698
297NE¹471
307NE¹504
383NE1085

Continued

Cases That Cite _Nationwide Insurance v. Ervin_, 231 N.E.2d 112 (1967)

Reviewing Subsequent History

Once you have found a case, you first want to find out whether it has been appealed and, if so, whether the appeal affected the case as a source of law. *Shepard's* uses a code next to its citations that instantly gives you this information.

For example, suppose you read a case called *Jones v. Smith*, located at 500 F.Supp. 325. Because the case is published in the *Federal Supplement*, we know a U.S. District Court decided it. (See Chapter 7.) The District Court case might not have had the last word, however; the case quite possibly was appealed to a higher court—typically, a U.S. Circuit Court of Appeals, but in rare instances the U.S. Supreme Court.

Once a case is appealed, the published opinion of the lower or intermediate appellate court might or might not continue to be a valid expression of the law. When a higher appellate court reverses a lower court's published decision, it usually vacates the lower court's opinion. The opinion isn't to be considered as law for any purpose. The underlying case might also be affirmed or modified on appeal. In these situations, the lower court's opinion will usually remain to guide future courts, but sometimes also might be ordered vacated and replaced with the higher court's opinion.

When a case is directly affected by a higher court on appeal, *Shepard's* places a small letter just before the citation of the case. For instance, if the higher court vacated the cited case's opinion, a "v" will appear next to the citation, as shown below. You'll find the full list of abbreviations and their meanings in a table at the front of each *Shepard's* volume.

In addition, with laws constantly changing, a case you find in your research might not reflect the way current courts would decide the same issue. *Shepard's* provides a second set of abbreviations to explain why the citing case referred to the cited case. This set is used only when the citing case is unrelated to the cited case—that is, not reviewing the cited case on appeal. You'll also find a key to these abbreviations in the table at the front of each volume of *Shepard's*.

```
  —1243—
v463US1202
v77LE1383
v103SC3530
s710F2d566
 462US²675
 462US¹688
 77LE²297
j77LE105
 103SC²2627
 103SC¹2633
j103SC2633
 51USLW
        [4838
j51USLW
        [4842
   Cir. 5
 782F2d551
```

Citation Showing Vacating of Later Court

Abbreviations Showing Action by the Supreme Court

When an unsuccessful attempt was made to take the cited case before the U.S. Supreme Court, *Shepard's* uses notations to tell you what happened.

US cert den. The U.S. Supreme Court refused to issue a writ of certiorari. When this happens, the cited case is considered to be good law, since the Supreme Court declined to review it.

US cert dis. The petition for cert was dismissed, usually for procedural reasons. It's possible that the case might be taken by the Supreme Court at a later time.

US reh den. This only appears when the cited case is a U.S. Supreme Court case, and the U.S. Supreme Court refused to grant a rehearing in that case.

US reh dis. A request for a rehearing was dismissed.

Suppose you are using *Shepard's* primarily to check a case for its precedential or persuasive value. You can skim a list of the citations under the cited case and search for these abbreviations. If none appear, or the ones that do indicate that the cited case is still good law, you might stop there. But if the cited case was questioned, criticized, or overruled by the citing case, you would want to read that citing case. If there is no letter to the left of the citation, it usually means that the cited case was mentioned in passing and wasn't important to the decision in the citing case.

Summing Up ...
How to Shepardize State Court Cases

✓ Select one of the parallel citations of the case you wish to Shepardize.

✓ Note the year of the case you are Shepardizing.

✓ Find the *Shepard's* volumes that cover the reporter in the citation.

✓ Select the volume or volumes that contain citations for cases decided after the case you are Shepardizing.

✓ Find the volume number (in boldface) corresponding to the volume number of the case being Shepardized.

✓ Under this volume number, find the page number (in boldface) of the citation for the cited case.

✓ Under this page number, review the citations given for the citing cases.

✓ Use the letters to the left of the citation to decide whether the case has been directly affected by a higher court in an appeal.

✓ Use the numbers to the right of the citation to decide whether the citing case refers to the cited case for issues in which you might be interested.

✓ After you write down all potentially useful citations, repeat these steps with the more recent *Shepard's* volumes and update pamphlets.

Summing Up ...
How to Shepardize U.S. Supreme Court Cases

✓ Select one of the three parallel citations for the case you wish to Shepardize.

✓ Note the year of the case.

✓ Find the *Shepard's* labeled *United States Case Citations*.

✓ Select the volume or volumes that contain citations for cases decided after the date of the case you are Shepardizing.

✓ Select the part of the *Shepard's* volume that pertains to the citation you are using. For instance, if your citation is for the *U.S. Supreme Court Reporter* (S.Ct.), locate the pages that cover this reporter rather than the pages that pertain to the *United States Supreme Court Reports* (U.S.) or the *Supreme Court Reports, Lawyer's Edition* (L.Ed.).

✓ Find the boldface volume number corresponding to the volume number of the case being Shepardized.

✓ Under this volume number, find the page number of the cited case.

✓ Under the page number, review the citations of the citing cases.

✓ Use the letters to the left of each citation to decide whether the case has been directly affected by a higher court in an appeal.

✓ Use the numbers to the right of the citation to decide whether the citing case refers to the cited case for issues in which you might be interested.

✓ After you write down all potentially useful citations, repeat these steps with the more recent *Shepard's* volumes and update pamphlets.

Shepard's Abbreviations: Appeal of the Cited Case

Here are some of the most common *Shepard's* Signals codes you'll encounter using *Shepard's* Citations in LexisNexis.

Signal	Meaning
Red Stop Sign	**Warning - Negative treatment indicated** - indicates that citing references or history in the *Shepard's* Citations Service contain strong negative history or treatment of your case (*e.g.,* overruled by or reversed).
① **Red Exclamation Mark in a White Circle**	**Warning** - indicates that citing references for a statute in the *Shepard's* Citations Service contain strong negative treatment of the section (*e.g.,* the section may have been found to be unconstitutional or void).
[Q] **White Q in an Orange Square**	**Questioned: Validity questioned by citing reference** - indicates that the citing references or history in the *Shepard's* Citations Service contain treatment that questions the continuing validity or precedential value of your case because of intervening circumstances, including judicial or legislative overruling as mentioned in the citing reference.
△ **Yellow Triangle**	**Caution: Possible negative treatment indicated** - indicates that citing references or history in the *Shepard's* Citations Service contain history or treatment that may have a significant negative impact on your case (*e.g.,* limited or criticized by).
✚ **White Plus Sign in a Green Diamond**	**Positive treatment indicated** - indicates that citing references or history in the *Shepard's* Citations Service contain history or treatment that has a positive impact on your case (*e.g.,* affirmed or followed by).
White A in a Blue Circle	**Citing references with analysis available** - indicates that citing references or history in the *Shepard's* Citations Service contain treatment of your case that is neither positive nor negative (*e.g.,* explained).
White I in a Blue Circle	**Citation information available** - indicates that citing references or history are available in the *Shepard's* Citations Service for your case, but the references do not have history or treatment analysis (*e.g.,* the references are law review citations).

Source: www.lexisnexis.com

Westlaw's KeyCite has its own system.

Westlaw's KeyCite Abbreviations

Red Flag

In cases and administrative decisions, a red flag warns that the case or administrative decision is no longer good law for at least one of the points of law it contains. In statutes and regulations, a red flag indicates that the statute or regulation has been amended by a recent session law or rule, repealed, superseded, or held unconstitutional or preempted in whole or in part.

Yellow Flag

In cases and administrative decisions, a yellow flag warns that the case or administrative decision has some negative history but hasn't been reversed or overruled. In statutes and regulations, a yellow flag indicates that the statute has been renumbered or transferred by a recent session law; that an uncodified session law or pending legislation affecting the statute is available (statutes merely referenced, *i.e.*, mentioned, aren't marked with a yellow flag); that the regulation has been reinstated, corrected, or confirmed; that the statute or regulation was limited on constitutional or preemption grounds or its validity was otherwise called into doubt; or that a prior version of the statute or regulation received negative treatment from a court.

Blue-striped Flag

A blue-striped flag indicates that the case has been appealed to the U.S. Courts of Appeals or the U.S. Supreme Court (excluding appeals originating from agencies).

Over-ruling Risk Icon

The Overruling Risk icon warns that the case might have been undermined due to its reliance on another case that has been overruled.

The KeyCite "Depth" column lets you see how subsequent cases affect your current case. Four green bars ("Examined") means the subsequent case includes extended discussion of your case; three green bars ("Discussed") means the subsequent case includes substantial discussion of your case; two green bars ("Cited") means the subsequent case includes some discussion of your case; and one green bar ("Mentioned") indicates that the subsequent case makes brief reference to your case.

RESOURCE
Before you use either service, learn the basics online. This will ensure your research is as efficient as possible.

To learn more about *Shepard's* Citations Service, check out www. lexisnexis.com/en-us/products/lexis/shepards.page.

For KeyCite, find out more at https://legal.thomsonreuters.com/en/products/westlaw/keycite.

An Alternative to Online Shepardizing

If you can't access a law library, you have an alternative. However, we're hesitant to recommend it because it's time-consuming and prone to human error.

A few websites, like CourtListener (www.courtlistener.com), offer an alternative to Shepardizing. The website provides the user with a list of all subsequent case citations for the case in question. The downsides are that CourtListener does this only for cases, not statutes, and the subsequent citations don't tell you how the cases handled the cited case. For instance, you won't know if the subsequent case overruled your case without reading it.

Because you must read all the cited cases, this system might work if you're dealing with a fairly new case that hasn't been cited extensively. But if you're checking a case that has been around a long time or that many courts have discussed at a great length, you could find yourself overwhelmed by the volume of cases.

Not only will you risk missing a critical case that overrules or reverses your case, but you won't have access to statutory citations, which could have the same effect. Also, it's not always clear how often these services are updated.

For these reasons, we recommend you don't rely on this shortcut. It won't necessarily save time and opens you up to a greater possibility for error.

Validating Statutes

You can and should make sure statutes are still current, too. As with case law, the quickest way to do this is online using Westlaw or LexisNexis. However, if you Shepardize in the law library stacks, here are the basics for using *Shepard's Citations for Statutes*:

- *Shepard's Citations for Statutes* are thick hardcover volumes with separate update pamphlets.
- A separate *Shepard's* exists for state and federal statutes.
- *Shepard's* hardcover volumes for the statutes of a state or the federal government cover different periods. For example, one hardcover volume might contain all references made by court decisions before 1980; another might contain all references made between 1980 and 1990; a third might contain all references made between 1990 and 1998, and so on.
- To use *Shepard's*, you need the exact citation number of the statute. It is also helpful to know the approximate year the law was passed.
- Each *Shepard's* volume is organized in the same way as the statutes in the codes of each state or the federal government. So, if you want to know whether a court has interpreted a particular New York criminal statute, you would first locate the place in the New York *Shepard's Citations for Statutes* covering New York criminal laws and look for the specific statute by number. In other states, where statutes are not grouped by topic but by sequential number, you would only need to find the statute by its number.
- Once you find the statute you are Shepardizing, you will see whether any court decisions have referred to it. If so, the citations tell you the reporter, the volume, and the page where the reference appears.

- *Shepard's Citations for Statutes* has its own set of abbreviations for codes (similar to those used for cases) listed in the front of the *Shepard's* volume.

 CAUTION

Four warnings when you're using *Shepard's Citations for Statutes*:

- Make sure you use the *Shepard's* for the correct state.

- When you look up a statute in *Shepard's*, use the part that deals with statutes (marked clearly on the front of the volume and the top of the page) and not with the part dealing with cases, regulations, or the constitution.

- Use the *Shepard's* volumes for the appropriate years. A hardcover volume that contains citations from 1980 through 1985 won't do you any good for a statute enacted in 1986. Only use volumes containing citations to cases decided after the statute was passed.

- Look in all hardbound volumes and paperback supplements that might contain citations.

 Summing Up ...
How to Shepardize Federal Statutes

✓ Note the year the statute you wish to Shepardize was passed.

✓ Find *Shepard's Citations for Statutes*.

✓ Select the volumes covering the years since the statute was passed.

✓ Find the title of the citation as it appears in boldface at the top of the page (for example, Title 25 U.S.C.).

✓ Under the appropriate title number, find the section number of the statute (for example, Title 25 U.S.C. § 863).

✓ Copy the citations listed under the section number. The citations refer to the exact page in the case where the statute is referred to.

✓ Follow this procedure for all volumes and pamphlets up to the most recent.

> **Summing Up ...**
> ## How to Shepardize State Statutes
>
> ✓ Find the *Shepard's* volume for your state's statutes.
>
> ✓ Select the volumes covering the years since the statute was passed.
>
> ✓ If your state statutes are organized into codes, find the title of the code in the upper margin in boldface (for example, *Penal Code*). If your state goes by a title system, find the title number at the top of the page. If your state's statutes are consecutively numbered without reference to a code or title, find the place in *Shepard's* where the number appears in boldface.
>
> ✓ If you are dealing with a code or title, find the section number of the statute (for example, Title 19, § 863).
>
> ✓ Note the citations under the section number. These citations are to the book and pages where the statute is referred to.
>
> ✓ Follow this process for all volumes and pamphlets up to the most recent.

Sheparding for Research

Shepard's was designed primarily as an updating tool. However, as we've pointed out, it can be used for much more than updating. Once you've found a relevant case or statute, you can use *Shepard's* (or Westlaw's KeyCite) to find other cases addressing the same issue. Every citing case is potentially relevant; thus, if you start with one cited case, you might find other useful cases that have referred to it. Then, each of these citing cases can itself be validated.

Suppose, for example, *Shepard's* lists five cases that have referred to your initial case. Then, you check these five cases and find two more citing cases for each one. In very little time, you will have a list of more than 10 cases that could be relevant to your situation.

There is a catch, though. We have seen that *Shepard's* gives you a list of every case that has referred to the cited case. But most cited cases deal with several legal issues, and a citing case will usually only mention the cited case in connection with one (or perhaps several) of those issues.

For example, a cited case might refer to 3 of the 20 issues involved in the cited case. It won't be helpful unless one of the three issues is also the issue you're dealing with. A discussion of irrelevant issues won't do you any good.

To help you separate the wheat from the chaff and avoid this time trap, *Shepard's* identifies the specific issues the citing case was interested in when it referred to the cited case. It does this by:

- identifying the issue from the cited case that is being discussed by the citing case
- selecting the headnote in the cited case that most closely states the issue being discussed in the citing case, and
- placing that headnote number just to the right of the citation to the citing case.

EXAMPLE: *Nationwide Insurance v. Ervin*, 231 N.E.2d 112 (1967) is referred to (cited) in *Deason v. Metropolitan Property & Liability Insurance Co.*, 474 N.E.2d 783 (1985).

Therefore, in this example, *Ervin* is the cited case and *Deason* is the citing case. If you Shepardize *Ervin*, you will find the citation to the page in *Deason* where the *Deason* court cited *Ervin*.

The little numbers (6 and 7) between the N.E.2d and the page number (785) are the numbers of the headnotes in *Ervin* that, in the opinion of *Shepard's*, best describe the issues which the case is being cited for in *Deason*.

Thus, *Deason* used *Ervin* to discuss the issues summarized in these two headnotes. If the issues in these two headnotes were why you were Shepardizing *Ervin*, you would want to read *Deason*. However, if you weren't interested in the issues discussed in headnotes 6 and 7, you might wisely choose not to read *Deason*.

If there is no headnote number next to the citation—that is, the citation doesn't identify the issue for which the cited case is being mentioned—it means that the reference to the cited case appeared, to the *Shepard's* editors, to be general rather than about a specific legal issue. The citing case might or might not interest you, but you should at least skim it to find out.

DEASON v. METRO. PROP. & LIABILITY INS. CO.
Cite as 474 N.E.2d 783 (Ill.App. 5 Dist. 1985)
Ill. **785**

the time of the accident; the Mercury had a defective transmission and the Dodge had a twisted drive shaft. Both vehicles were put back into operation shortly after the accident involving the Comet. During his deposition, Andrew Warner testified as follows:

"Q. Did you have any intention if the Comet hadn't been wrecked, did you have any intention to dispose of either of these other two cars just because you got the Comet?

A. Oh, no."

[2] In ruling that Metropolitan's policy afforded secondary coverage in connection with the accident involving the 1975 Comet, the court found that Christopher Warner was "a relative operating a temporary substitute" automobile. Metropolitan contends that this conclusion is incorrect, and we are compelled to agree. Under the terms of the policy, a temporary substitute automobile is defined as one "temporarily used with the permission of the owner as a substitute for an owned automobile when withdrawn from normal use for servicing or repair or because of breakdown, loss, or destruction." Here, the unequivocal deposition testimony of all concerned establishes that Christopher Warner's use of the Comet was not to be temporary, but regular and permanent, as it was the intention of both Vera Fry and Christopher Warner that he would pay $100 for the car at Christmas time, and would not return it to her. Moreover, the Comet was not intended by the Warners to be a substitute for either the Mercury or the Dodge; rather, it was to be kept as a third car, and the fact that the Dodge and Mercury broke down during the Warners' use of the Comet was entirely coincidental. Under these circumstances, the "temporary substitute" provision of the policy issued by Metropolitan did not encompass Christopher Warner's use of the Comet on the date of the accident. (See *Sturgeon v. Automobile Club Inter-Insurance Exchange* (1979), 77 Ill. App.3d 997, 1000, 34 Ill.Dec. 66, 397 N.E.2d 522.) This conclusion is buttressed by the holding of *Nationwide Insurance Compa-*

ny v. Ervin (1967), 87 Ill.App.2d 432, 436–37, 231 N.E.2d 112, wherein it was recognized that a "temporary substitute" provision of the type under consideration here is to be applied to those situations where an insured automobile is withdrawn from use for a short period, and not where, as here, coverage is sought to be extended to an additional automobile for a significant length of time.

[3] *Providence Mutual Casualty Company v. Sturms* (1962), 37 Ill.App.2d 304, 185 N.E.2d 366, relied on by appellees, is not on point. *Sturms* addresses the question of whether coverage afforded on a temporary substitute automobile expires immediately upon repair of the insured's regular automobile (37 Ill.App.2d 304, 306, 185 N.E.2d 366), and does not discuss the more fundamental issue of when a vehicle is considered to be a temporary substitute in the first place. While appellees also suggest that portions of Metropolitan's claim file show that certain Metropolitan employees believe that the policy in question afforded coverage, the trial court correctly noted in its judgment that these statements are merely opinions, and are not binding on a court in its consideration of the legal question presented. 31A C.J.S. *Evidence* § 272(b) (1964).

For the foregoing reasons, the judgment of the circuit court of St. Clair County is reversed.

Reversed.

JONES, P.J., and KARNS, J., concur.

Page From Deason v. Metropolitan Property & Liability Insurance Co.

NORTHEASTERN REPORTER, 2d SERIES

Vol. 231

Deason

```
323FS⁴344        —107—        453NYS2d      —128—        —131—        —134—        24Æ363n       —157—
596FS⁸784        (87Il𝕬139)     [597        Case 1       (20NY799)    Case 1                     (142InA154)
650FS437        cc257N𝕰233    513NYS2d72   (20NY794)    (284NYS2d    (20NY802)    —138—        241N𝕰¹77
64Æ506s         317N𝕰'631     Cir. 2       (284NYS2d    [455)       (284NYS2d    (249Ind173)   Nebr
                 347N𝕰¹70     d282FS⁴73    [451)       s232N𝕰652    [459)       304N𝕰⁴877     421NW3
—70—            360N𝕰²1197   j242FS⁴82    s274NYS2d    s234N𝕰840   s189N𝕰620    336N𝕰692
(12⊘S26)        378N𝕰¹1157   f292FS⁴115   [392        s261NYS2d    s239NYS2d    339N𝕰97       —159—
(41⊕p159)                    439FS⁴975    s281NYS2d    [336        [124        430N𝕰¹787     (141InA669)
231N𝕰³332       —109—        439FS⁴977    [974        s271NYS2d                452N𝕰1006     d252N𝕰²606
370N𝕰²458       (87Il𝕬82)    Cir. 4                    s285NYS2d    —134—        526N𝕰1229     d252N𝕰²606
371N𝕰²843       Cert Den     339FS⁴499    —128—        [621        Case 2                     254N𝕰²219
381N𝕰²972       262N𝕰¹797    Cir. 6       Case 2       s287NYS2d    (20NY802)    —140—        255N𝕰¹829
414N𝕰⁴438       281N𝕰¹388    311FS⁴1191   (20NY795)    [886        (284NYS2d    (249Ind178)   j275N𝕰¹856
453N𝕰⁴664       378N𝕰³606    Calif       (284NYS2d    Cir. 2       [459)       242N𝕰42       278N𝕰¹336
454N𝕰²1389      412N𝕰¹629    90CaR921     [451)       9BRW824                   f363N𝕰226     278N𝕰²336
488N𝕰927                     94CaR604     s281NYS2d                 —134—        e400N𝕰²1111   280N𝕰²865
                —112—        484P2d580    [985        —132—        Case 3                     316N𝕰¹593
—71—            (87Il𝕬432)   Colo                     Case 1       (20NY802)    —145—        316N𝕰⁸593
(12⊘A68)        241N𝕰¹120    509P2d1272   —128—        (20NY801)    (284NYS2d    (249Ind141)   339N𝕰¹112
(41⊕p122)       241N𝕰³120    Iowa        Case 3       (284NYS2d    [460)       338N𝕰¹262     340N𝕰¹813
p166N𝕰808       272N𝕰⁷61     247NW271     (20NY796)    [456)       s205N𝕰879    j403N𝕰811     357N𝕰¹256
c484N𝕰220       274N𝕰³879    Mich        (284NYS2d    s219N𝕰295    s257NYS2d                 387N𝕰²1339
j484N𝕰221       287N𝕰¹530    164NW37      [452)       s269NYS2d    [960        —147—        433N𝕰²21
18Æ813s         289N𝕰³703    N H         s281NYS2d    [368        s282NYS2d    (249Ind144)
                293N𝕰³704    400A2d53     [864        s272NYS2d    [174        360N𝕰604     —161—
—81—            305N𝕰³417    Wash        468NYS2d     [782                    f408N𝕰620     (141InA655)
(12⊘A87)        379N𝕰²66     496P2d516    [161                    —135—        f408N𝕰⁴621    233N𝕰²805
(41⊕p163)       d412N𝕰⁵632   W Va                     s388US41     Case 1       f408N𝕰³621    256N𝕰³923
432N𝕰⁸212       d412N𝕰⁷632   279S𝕰408     —129—        s18L𝕰1040   (20NY803)    f408N𝕰¹621    322N𝕰¹610
Cir. 6          e427N𝕰⁷130   34Æ155s      Case 1       s87SC1873   (284NYS2d    409N𝕰⁴1272    323N𝕰¹238
577FS⁴1131      474N𝕰⁶785    65Æ31069n   (20NY796)    59L𝕰962n    [460)       409N𝕰⁴1274    323N𝕰²238
Md              474N𝕰⁸785                 (284NYS2d    37Æ3630n    s273NYS2d    j437N𝕰113     f355N𝕰⁷438
513A2d938       481N𝕰⁴45     —126—        [452)       57Æ3178n     [572        441N𝕰⁵22      f355N𝕰⁸438
                497N𝕰³479    Case 1       s282NYS2d    57Æ3201n    s282NYS2d    471N𝕰⁴731     393N𝕰⁸810
—85—            502N𝕰²1295   (20NY792)    [438        82Æ376n      [639        471N𝕰⁶731     417N𝕰⁷338
(12⊘A59)        510N𝕰²1183   (284NYS2d               60ÆRF710n    250N𝕰582     486N𝕰¹662     486N𝕰⁴442
(41⊕p117)       Ga           [449)       —129—                    265N𝕰924     Mass        9Æ1044s
                221S𝕰482     s282NYS2d    Case 2       —132—        288NYS2d     j440N𝕰776
—91—            Iowa         [664        (20NY797)    Case 2                    Calif       —165—
(12⊘A83)        174NW383     242N𝕰395     (284NYS2d    (20NY801)    [246        140CaR294     (141InA672)
(41⊕p160)       N C          295NYS2d     [453)       (284NYS2d    j288NYS2d    Conn        231N𝕰¹863
521N𝕰⁴1153      198S𝕰56                  292NYS2d45   [457)        [247        261A2d296     j235N𝕰¹99
521N𝕰⁶1153      39Æ4333n    —126—        j292NYS2d47  s229N𝕰192    303NYS2d     Tex        242N𝕰⁴140
31Æ3585n                    Case 2       307NYS2d     s245NYS2d     [524        547SW624     261N𝕰⁸602
                —115—        (87Il𝕬159)    [191        [353        317NYS2d     61Æ31210n    308N𝕰878
—94—            (87Il𝕬159)   m243N𝕰225   321NYS2d     s272NYS2d     [629        61Æ31219n    Okla
(12OhM127)      m243N𝕰225    231N𝕰¹³713   [842        [974        391N𝕰²4      1Æ475n       541P2d861
(41⊕p131)       231N𝕰¹³713   367N𝕰²395   426NYS2d     s282NYS2d    392NYS2d28               40Æ342n
                367N𝕰²395                 [843        [497        433NYS2d     —151—        40Æ358n
—97—                        —120—        432NYS2d    385NYS2d      [657        (249Ind168)   40Æ375n
(87Il𝕬411)      —120—        (20NY417)    [156        [681        434NYS2d     241N𝕰¹368
Cert Den        (20NY417)    (284NYS2d                39Æ3497n     [278        309N𝕰²845     —169—
269N𝕰²355       (284NYS2d    [441)       —130—        65Æ3512n    497NYS2d     309N𝕰⁸847     (141InA662)
269N𝕰⁸356       [441)       j437N𝕰1095   Case 1       44Æ4888n     [530        316N𝕰²689     f239N𝕰¹173
273N𝕰¹162       j437N𝕰1095   437N𝕰⁴1095   (20NY798)    44Æ4893n    42Æ4828n     323N𝕰¹239     249N𝕰516
280N𝕰¹246       437N𝕰⁴1095   287NYS2d     (284NYS2d    68ÆRF957n                e331N𝕰¹780    j249N𝕰³517
283N𝕰¹⁵43       287NYS2d     [467        [454)                   —135—        399N𝕰¹368     j251N𝕰³26
318N𝕰¹²122      [467        298NYS2d                 —133—        Case 2       Me          j251N𝕰⁴26
326N𝕰⁹468       298NYS2d     [645        —130—        (20NY801)    (20NY804)    318A2d498     251N𝕰¹34
363N𝕰⁸625       [645        300NYS2d     Case 2       (284NYS2d    (284NYS2d                269N𝕰³767
363N𝕰¹²626      300NYS2d     [397        (20NY798)    [458)       [461)       —154—        j269N𝕰⁴770
369N𝕰¹295       [397        f304NYS2d    (284NYS2d    Cert Den     s275NYS2d    (141InA649)   270N𝕰767
369N𝕰²295       f304NYS2d    [263        [454)       US cert den   [674        274N𝕰⁵742     e272N𝕰⁴629
447N𝕰⁶441       [263        318NYS2d     s282NYS2d    in390US971   527NYS2d     301N𝕰¹243     e272N𝕰³633
458N𝕰⁵1069      318NYS2d     [653        [934        s229N𝕰220     [585        310N𝕰²279     272N𝕰⁴874
f502N𝕰⁶478      [653        335NYS2d                s282NYS2d                 348N𝕰¹81      f273N𝕰²553
18Æ3633s        335NYS2d     [749        —130—        [538        —136—        Ala        f273N𝕰³553
                [749        387NYS2d     Case 3       495NYS2d     (20NY805)    361So2d9     277N𝕰606
—103—           387NYS2d     [718        (20NY798)    [539        (284NYS2d    Minn        280N𝕰³303
(87Il𝕬181)      [718        e388NYS2d    (284NYS2d    33Æ61132n    [462)       222NW80      284N𝕰³735
Cert Den        e388NYS2d    [472        [455)                   s274NYS2d     4COA569§3    286N𝕰¹698
323N𝕰²809       [472        j452NYS2d    s242N𝕰486                [850        16Æ4192n      297N𝕰¹471
323N𝕰⁴809       j452NYS2d    [338        s280NYS2d    268N𝕰646               17Æ4494n      307N𝕰¹504
374N𝕰⁴1140      [338        452NYS2d⁴    [952        j295NYS2d                              383N𝕰1085
                452NYS2d⁴    [338                    [970                                  Continued
                [338                                 24Æ3327n
```

Page From *Shepard's*

Organizing and Putting Your Legal Research to Use

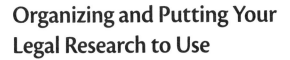

After spending hours in the law library or scouring countless websites, you're probably much more knowledgeable about your chosen legal topic than when you started. Congratulations! You've come a long way.

To ensure you don't lose the benefit of all your hard work, you'll want to organize your research in a usable way. How you do this largely depends on what you intend to do with the information. For instance, your approach will differ depending on whether you plan to file a court document, meet with a lawyer, write an academic paper, or explain research results to your boss.

Whatever the purpose, this chapter will help by providing tools you can use to get the most out of your research. By the end of this chapter, you'll know how to keep track of your findings and write them up in a clear and concise manner.

Organizing Your Research

If you're like many researchers, at some point, you'll find yourself surrounded by a stack of books and papers while collecting the information you need. At this stage, keeping track of what's in front of you is essential to avoid impending chaos. Disorganized researchers quickly lose track of that perfect case and find themselves repeating work.

Although organization styles can differ depending on the research, the plan we suggest will work for most projects. It's the same simple approach we encouraged in Chapter 3. You'll organize your research according to the legal questions you need answered.

Start with several folders or accordion files (sometimes called "redwells")—one folder for each legal question you have. This approach allows you to keep all documents answering a particular question in one place. Simply put the information in its corresponding folder or file.

When researching in a law library, consider making copies of critical documents, such as statutes, cases, and secondary sources, and storing them in your folders. Put documents that apply to more than one issue in the file dealing with the first or most important issue, along with a note reminding you that it's useful for another question.

It's also helpful to write notes directly on the documents. For example, Chapter 7 addressed the essential parts of an opinion—the issue, facts, decision, and rationale. Highlighting these points in each case ensures that the critical information is easy to find when referring to the case again.

You don't need to make copies of the things found online if you keep track of the URLs—but printing important pages and keeping track of them using the procedure above can be helpful. You'll probably want copies of *Shepard's* pages because it's often easier to have hard copies at hand when following up on the listed cases.

How to Write a Legal Memorandum

The words "legal memorandum" can undoubtedly be intimidating. If so, your first step is to relax because creating one isn't as complicated as it might seem. A legal memorandum can be a couple of paragraphs long, written in plain English, and, in many cases, relatively easy to prepare.

Why Prepare a Legal Memorandum?

Whether you are doing research for yourself or someone else, the primary purpose of a legal memo is to force you to put your search results in writing. Doing so is essential for three fundamental reasons.

The first consideration is that it isn't easy to know whether you've completed your research until you try to write it up. Ultimately, a legal memorandum conveys legal information to the reader and serves as a "checklist" for your research. The process forces you to answer all the tough questions the issue requires. You might think you've answered the legal question but find that the answer isn't clear once you put pen to paper. At this point, researchers often discover they must complete additional research.

A second important function of a legal memorandum is to create a research record before you forget how the cases, statutes, and other laws relate to your problem. It is common for people to put in a day or two of research in the law library, neglect to take an extra hour or two to write up the results, and later have to spend another day researching because they can't reconstruct what they found.

Finally, a legal memorandum helps you communicate your research results to someone else. If you're a paralegal researching for a supervising lawyer, you'll likely present the memorandum to your superior to read. If you're preparing your case for court, you can refer to the memorandum when explaining the law to the judge—it will serve as a great backup if you forget a crucial point. In either instance, taking the time to summarize what you've learned in a legal memorandum won't be time wasted.

How to Prepare a Legal Memorandum

Before creating a legal memorandum, you'll want to learn how to organize your legal writing using the style accepted throughout the legal community. In Chapter 7, we stated that case opinions written by a judge almost always have four primary elements: a statement of the facts, a statement of the issue or issues, a decision or holding on the issue or issues (the court's conclusion), and a discussion of the reasoning underlying the holding.

This organizational system is referred to by the acronym "I.R.A.C." (pronounced "I-Rack"). It stands for "issue, rule, analysis, conclusion"— the most common ordering of each section. It's called "F.I.R.A.C." when it includes a section for the case's facts.

Lawyers developed the approach of using specific sections in legal writing for several reasons. It makes legal research more manageable and helps lawyers organize their thoughts. It also makes reading legal documents more straightforward for all involved. Law students learn to use the system in law school students, and you can—and should—use it, too. Here's what you'll include in each I.R.A.C. section:

- **Issue.** Start by identifying the issue you are addressing. What is the problem before you that the case will answer? For example, "In this case, we must determine whether a Louisiana employer is liable for injuries sustained by a pedestrian hit by an employee driving negligently while talking on a cell phone about work-related matters." If written as a question, it would be, "Is a Louisiana employer liable for injuries sustained by a pedestrian hit by an employee driving negligently while talking on a cell phone about work-related matters?"

- **Rule.** Next, lay out the rule the case or cases you've found provides. For example, "In *Ellender v. Neff Rental, Inc.*, a Louisiana appellate court determined that an employee who was found 100% responsible for a car accident was acting in the course and scope of his employment because he was on work-related business, took a work-related call at the time of the accident on a cell phone provided by his employer and that this contributed to or caused the accident. The court explained that because the employee acted in the course and scope of employment, the employer could be held 'vicariously liable' for the employee's actions."

- **Analysis.** Next, take the rule from the case you are citing and apply it to the facts of your situation. While the situations might not be the same, it's up to you to show how they are similar. "Here, as in the *Ellender* case, the employee admitted he didn't see the pedestrian and caused the accident. At the time of the accident, he acted in the course and scope of his employment because he dialed a phone number to make a work-related call on his work-provided phone."

- **Conclusion.** In the conclusion, you sum up the logical outcome that would be reached when applying the law to the facts in your case. For example, "Applying *Ellender*, the employer in this case could be held vicariously liable for hitting the pedestrian because the employee who caused the accident when making a work-related call was acting within the course and scope of his employment."

All legal writing uses the same organizational system, except that the section order could change depending on the document. For instance, law students typically write up case briefs for class discussion using the F.I.R.A.C. method. Similarly, legal memoranda should include a statement of the facts, a statement of the issue or issues, a conclusion about what the law is (equivalent to the holding), and a brief discussion of why you reached your conclusion.

The memo format switches the analysis and conclusion sections, creating "F.I.R.C.A."—primarily because knowing the final result before the analysis can help a reader grasp a memorandum's contents more quickly. Some law firms even ask associates to list the conclusion first. Logically laying out the sections will help you summarize critical points effectively, regardless of order.

A final tip before you start preparing your memorandum: Keep emotions out of the analysis. Although you might be furious that the pizza delivery guy ran over the bike your son left in the driveway, your feelings won't be relevant when determining whether the pizza business must pay for the ruined bike. Instead, focus on the elements of your claim and the evidence needed to prove that the pizza delivery guy was responsible for the damage.

CAUTION

A memorandum isn't the same as a brief. In this discussion, we are talking about internal memoranda or "briefs" intended solely for your personal use (law students create briefs regularly) or your employer's use. We aren't referring to legal documents prepared for the court, commonly called "memoranda of points and authorities," or a publicly dispersed brief written by an interested group hoping to influence the outcome of a case. The purpose of creating an internal memo or brief is to objectively set forth the facts and law. In contrast, although documents written for the court or public consumption use the same organizational format, they are intended to convince someone that a particular argument should prevail.

The Statement of Facts

Many label the statement of facts section "Facts" or "Statement of Facts." In that section, you will lay out the most critical and relevant facts needed to answer your legal questions—that is, the legally relevant facts. For example, if your issue is whether a new owner of an apartment house can evict a tenant for having pets even though the prior landlord allowed them, your statement of facts would include the following:

- the pets in question
- the date apartment ownership was transferred, and
- information about any rental agreement or lease signed by the tenant.

If you recall or recognize additional important facts when writing other parts of the memo, amend your statement of facts to ensure you capture all relevant information.

The Statement of Issues

In a legal memorandum, the statement of issues is often called the "question presented" or simply the "issue" of the case. The general idea is that you want to summarize, in as concise a way as possible, the legal problem central to your case. It's common to have multiple issues and subissues within a memorandum.

When written as a question, the issue can usually be answered with "yes" or "no," even though the answer might not be a simple "yes" or "no" (for instance, the answer might be "yes, in certain instances"). Issues also tend to incorporate essential facts of the case. An example of a well-written issue might be, "Can a new owner of an apartment house in California evict a tenant for having pets even though a prior landlord allowed them?"

The Decision or Holding

The decision—sometimes labeled "conclusion" or "answer"—is like a court's holding. The idea is that the decision answers whatever question or questions you're researching and is the conclusion you anticipate the court would reach if presented with the issue. You'll explain how you arrived at the conclusion in the discussion section, which is covered next.

Continuing the example above, the decision might read, "Probably not. The new owner takes ownership subject to the written and oral agreements that the prior owner negotiated. If a tenant has a lease that allows pets, the new owner can't evict the tenant for having a pet."

A Discussion of the Reasoning

The most important part of your memo is the discussion of the reasoning used to reach your conclusion. It is where you will take what you've learned when reading the law and applying it to the facts of your case. This section is often the most challenging for new researchers, but doing it will help you identify, understand, and forward potential arguments.

If more than one case or statute is relevant to your issue and they reach different conclusions or go to other points, you might repeat this structure several times in your legal memo.

Preparing a Memo for Someone Else

If you are preparing a legal memorandum for someone else—for example, you're a paralegal, and you are putting it together for a supervising attorney, a student writing a paper, or an employee writing for an employer—three additional points might be helpful. First, it is usually a good idea to list the resources you've checked, even if some or many didn't pan out. This approach helps the reader feel secure, knowing you've covered everything out there. For example, in any research project, you might check *A.L.R., Am. Jur.*, a local digest or two, some treatises, and a local encyclopedia. Even if you don't find any useful information in the local encyclopedia, the reader will feel better knowing you've thoroughly checked each available resource.

Second, you might also want to insert citations throughout your legal memorandum. As we explained in Chapter 6, citations are the roadmap to finding a relevant resource. In the example above, the citation for the *Ellender* case is 965 So.2d 898. Some people even like to see the "pincites"—the exact page number on which a legal principle or factual information is found. For instance, the rule in the *Ellender* case is found on page 902, so the pincite would look like this: 965 So.2d 898, 902. Recall that a standard format for citing cases can be found in *The Bluebook* (www.legalbluebook.com). Also, remember that if you print a case online, it might not include the page citations to the official reporter. If you want or need the pincite, you might have to look up the case in the law library or pay to obtain it using an online service like Westlaw.

Finally, all statements about the law should be supported by primary legal authority, such as statutes, regulations, cases, or ordinances. Other legal materials generally comprise somebody else's opinion about the law. Including references to these secondary or background sources is okay and desirable, but they can't replace primary authority.

Going to Court

Today, many individuals conduct legal research when representing themselves in small claims court or other legal actions. Initially, you might have researched your case when determining whether you wanted to proceed. If so, your next step is likely filing a legal action.

 CAUTION

In most cases, we anticipate that if you are a self-represented litigant, it will be for a simple matter only. If you're planning on representing yourself in a criminal matter or a civil matter involving more than a few thousand dollars, we recommend you at least talk to an attorney first because the matter is likely to be complex. As we'll explain below, you might be able to reach a mutually agreeable solution to allow the attorney to represent or advise you at a low cost.

The Court Process

When someone new to the law—whether a law student, paralegal, or citizen interested in a personal case—thinks of "going to court," the images that come to mind are often movie-like scenes with argumentative attorneys, stern judges, and courtrooms filled with spectators and the press. The complexity of it all can seem too much to deal with.

In fact, most court matters are handled quite straightforwardly—but it would be unreasonable to say that you'll be able to avoid the parts of litigation that bring on stress, such as preparing for and appearing in court. A few cases move forward without fanfare, such as asking a judge to appoint a guardian or conservator, approve an adoption or name change, allow the probate of a simple estate, grant an uncontested divorce, discharge certain debts in bankruptcy, or seal a criminal record. On the other hand, criminal cases are usually no picnic, and any case can get messy when a genuine dispute exists, or lawyers have a financial incentive to string the matter out, as can happen in complicated business disputes for which attorneys bill by the hour. (In such cases, consulting with an attorney is likely in your best interests.)

Also, keep in mind that whatever the matter, filing a case and pushing it through court always involves carefully following several technical court rules. The trick is to know these procedural rules in minute detail. Fortunately, these rules are, for the most part, available to all—but to be frank, they aren't always easy to master in the amount of time available to most litigants.

CAUTION

This isn't a practice guide. This section talks in general terms about the steps in civil litigation. It isn't intended as a guide for the aspiring lawyer, paralegal, or reader who wants to self-represent in court. To learn more about civil and criminal procedure, start with a good background resource (discussed in Chapter 4). You can get information about how to represent yourself in a civil court proceeding in *Represent Yourself in Court*, by Paul Bergman and Sara J. Berman (Nolo).

Court procedures and rules are substantially similar in all state and federal courts. Details vary, however, and different names often refer to similar procedures. For example, an eviction action is called "unlawful detainer" in California and "summary process" in Massachusetts. Yet the proceedings are basically the same.

In Chapter 6, we explained that you can learn more about how courts where you live do things by looking at any court or local rules. If you can't find such rules, contact the court to find out if they exist and, if so, how you can access them. These rules might cover anything from how the legal papers you submit must look to how much it costs to file and serve papers, and it's important to know when they apply.

The sections below describe the typical course of a civil case. Because most charged with a criminal offense will have a lawyer, we don't cover the usual course of a criminal case (for details, see *The Criminal Law Handbook*, by Paul Bergman and Sara J. Berman (Nolo)).

Small Claims Court

All states have small claims courts with simplified rules that are relatively easy to follow. Small claims court clerks are usually required by statute to help people with all procedural details. If you are the plaintiff (the one bringing the case) and can squeeze the amount of your monetary claim within the small claim limits for your state (usually from $2,000 to $15,000), you might find that small claims court is an excellent alternative to the formal legal system.

One of the nicest aspects of small claims court is that in many states, litigants aren't allowed to be represented by lawyers (there's no rule against consulting with a lawyer beforehand, however). By learning to do your own research and writing, you can present a solid case without being overwhelmed by an experienced hired gun on the other side. Unfortunately, most small claims courts aren't designed to handle problems other than those where one person has a monetary claim against the other. (For more information, see *Everybody's Guide to Small Claims Court*, by Cara O'Neill (Nolo).)

The Pretrial Process

The first phase of a contested civil case is called the "pretrial" phase. Here, we'll outline the typical steps you'll go through in this phase.

The Plaintiff Files a Complaint

A case begins when the plaintiff (the party who sues) files a document called a "complaint" with the court. This document tells what allegedly happened and what the plaintiff wants the court to do, such as asking for a monetary award, court order, or another remedy. It also tells the court the legal basis for the litigation, and the plaintiff must file the lawsuit in the correct jurisdiction (see "Jurisdiction and Venue," below.)

Part of the plaintiff's responsibility will be to "serve" the complaint. That means making sure the defendant (the party sued) gets a copy according to the rules set out by the court. Most often, the plaintiff must arrange for "personal service"—that is, to have a copy of the complaint personally handed to the defendant by a neutral third party (a person not involved in the suit). The proof of service, signed by the person who made the delivery, gets filed with the court to show the defendant received the document. Many courts have a standard form for this purpose.

The Defendant Responds

After the plaintiff serves the defendant with a copy of the complaint, the defendant must respond in writing within a specific time—usually 30 days or less, depending on state law. If the defendant doesn't respond, the plaintiff can obtain a "default" judgment and win the case without proceeding to trial. At the default hearing, the plaintiff presents the judge with evidence proving the amount of money lost.

There are a variety of ways the defendant might respond, including:

- **The Answer.** Most commonly, the defendant files an "answer," a statement stating which parts of the complaint the defendant agrees and disagrees with. Under the procedural rules of most states, the defendant's answer must also contain any affirmative defenses (factual statements of the reasons or excuses for the defendant's actions) and counterclaims (claims that the plaintiff is legally responsible and owes the defendant something) that the defendant has. The defendant can also deny the allegations based on a lack of knowledge.

- **Motion to Dismiss Case.** This document—also called a "demurrer" in some states—asks the court to dismiss the suit instead of requiring an answer from the defendant. There are many reasons why you'd want to file a motion to dismiss instead of an answer. For instance, the plaintiff has only a certain amount of time to file the action. The judge will dismiss the lawsuit if the case wasn't filed within this "statute of limitations" period. You'd also file this motion if the plaintiff doesn't plead all the elements necessary to prove a case against you within the complaint. Usually, the basis for this request boils down to this: Even if the facts in the plaintiff's complaint are true, so what?

The defendant is essentially saying that even if everything the plaintiff says is true, the plaintiff's claims don't add up to a legal violation—you simply didn't do anything wrong. To make the decision, the judge assumes that the factual allegations in the complaint are true and then decides whether the law supports the claim for relief. This is the first "dispositive motion" a party can file because it has the potential to end the case entirely. If the judge grants the motion but allows the plaintiff a chance to fix the problem ("granted with leave to amend"), the plaintiff rewrites the complaint, and the process starts all over again. If the judge grants the motion without leave to amend, the case ends unless the plaintiff appeals the decision. On the other hand, if the judge overrules (denies) the motion or demurrer, the defendant must file an answer.

Both Sides Engage in Discovery

When the pleadings in a case are filed, the parties begin to exchange information about the case in each other's possession through a process called "discovery." While it might seem strange to ask the other side to give up information that helps your case willingly, there's often no other way to get it—and the law favors the open exchange of information.

Jurisdiction and Venue

As you know from reading this book, there are courts nationwide in all 50 states. But you can't simply file a lawsuit anywhere you wish. Rules about the proper location for filing suit limit what you can do. The general idea is that it isn't fair to sue someone in a location that doesn't relate to where the problems that led to the suit occurred or where the person being sued can reasonably be expected to go. For example, if you live in New York and, while vacationing in Hawaii, get hit by a motorist who lives in Hawaii, is it fair to expect that you can sue that person in California because you think the law in California favors your case? Should you be able to sue that Hawaiian in New York?

Jurisdiction and venue rules prevent both choices. Jurisdiction rules decide whether a court has the authority to hear the case, while venue rules determine the most convenient location for a lawsuit based on the parties' position. Venue rules can be waived—for example, a defendant in a lawsuit can agree to have the case heard in a neighboring county where the plaintiff resides, even if he'd usually be entitled to have the case heard in his home county, where the accident occurred.

In many cases, jurisdiction and venue won't be an issue. However, suppose you are planning on initiating a lawsuit against someone who lives outside your state or county and the incident giving rise to the lawsuit occurred outside your state or county. In that case, we suggest you check your court and local rules or speak with a lawyer to determine the proper jurisdiction and venue.

Of course, that doesn't mean it's always willingly surrendered. For this reason, discovery often adds considerably to the time and expense of litigation. Disputes can arise over what information must be turned over—for example, one side might assert that the requested documents are protected from disclosure by the attorney-client privilege or that a request for information isn't relevant (doesn't have anything to do with the issue being resolved), or that what's being asked for isn't clear. Often, the parties try to resolve these disputes on their own, which takes time as they go back and forth (usually writing letters to each other).

If the dispute can't be resolved informally, the parties can file a motion asking the court to decide. If a party doesn't like the result, it is usually possible to take the matter to a higher court before the underlying case proceeds further; however, this rarely happens.

Typically, discovery consists of the following devices:

- **Depositions.** Witnesses or parties must go to one of the attorneys' offices and answer questions about their knowledge of the dispute under oath. A court reporter usually takes down the testimony, but sometimes, it's recorded on tape or using a video recorder.
- **Interrogatories.** One party sends another written questions to be answered under oath by a certain date. Interrogatories are also used to ask the other party to identify the source and validity of documents that might be introduced as evidence at trial. Most courts limit the number of interrogatories either side can ask.
- **Admissions of Facts.** Factual statements are sent that the other side must admit or deny. Anything that isn't denied is considered admitted. Parties are often reluctant to admit to facts and often object to the language instead of responding directly.
- **Production of Documents.** One party asks another to produce specified documents. In a complicated case, the documents exchanged can be extensive.

One or More Sides File Motions

At any time after the pleadings have been filed, but before trial, the plaintiff or defendant might ask the court to order the other side to do something or to refrain from doing something. Sometimes these motions preserve the status quo until the case can be tried. For example, suppose the circumstances are genuinely urgent. In that case, a party can request the court to issue a "temporary restraining order" (TRO) or "preliminary injunction," stopping the defendant from taking some action before trial. This often occurs when the plaintiff fears that the defendant will liquidate assets or make other changes that will defeat the purpose of the litigation. As mentioned, motions might also be filed to enforce discovery (requiring a party to answer questions or produce documents when appropriate) or to protect a party against abusive discovery (for example, requiring attendance at a weeklong deposition).

In some cases, one of the parties will file a summary judgment motion. Like a demurrer, this is a dispositive motion, because it potentially ends the entire case. With this motion, a party tries to show that there isn't a dispute about any important facts in the case (called "triable issues of material fact"). Trials determine facts, so there's no reason to have a trial if there are no disputed facts. The judge can apply the relevant law to the undisputed facts, resolving the case entirely before it ever goes to trial, saving everyone time and money. Preparing a summary judgment motion can be costly, too, however, and it rarely occurs without the parties first engaging in extensive discovery. Why? The motion is essentially like trying the case on paper. The party bringing the motion will need to spell out all of the relevant issues and provide evidence—or demonstrate a lack of evidence—that supports the facts that make up the factual scenario claimed by the person bringing the motion. The opposing side will also present evidence in an opposition brief that supports a different version of the facts. Once the briefing is complete, the parties will argue their position before the judge deciding the matter.

One Side Requests a Trial Date

In some court systems, a case is never set for trial unless one of the parties requests it. Accordingly, a party who feels adequately prepared can file a document with the court requesting a trial and specifying whether it should be held in front of a jury. These documents are titled differently in different courts, such as "memorandum to set," "at issue memorandum," and "motion to set for trial." Whatever their titles, they might be opposed by the other party (for various reasons) or agreed to.

Alternative Dispute Resolution

Most courts require the parties to try to resolve the dispute before going to trial. For instance, it's common for litigants to submit the case to a volunteer attorney in an informal nonbinding arbitration. Either side can reject the arbitration award and continue toward trial. Additionally, most courts require the parties to appear at a settlement conference shortly before the trial date. Again, a volunteer attorney will likely encourage resolution by helping each side see the weaknesses of the case.

A Pretrial Conference Is Held

Usually, once a case is set for trial, a pretrial conference between the parties, their lawyers, and the judge is scheduled. At the pretrial conference, the judge ensures that everyone understands the remaining issues in the case and knows how long the trial will take. Many judges use these conferences—often quite successfully—to pressure the parties to settle the case. If no settlement is reached, the trial moves forward.

The Trial

Most lawsuits never go to trial. The parties usually settle their dispute beforehand—likely because trying a case is extremely expensive, and the stakes can be high.

The parties can opt for a trial by jury or a trial by judge (either side can demand a jury; otherwise, the case will be tried by the judge). A jury trial is more advantageous for a defendant who believes an emotional issue might pull the jury's heartstrings favorably. By contrast, a trial by judge might be the better choice for a defendant worried that irrelevant evidence might negatively sway the jury in some way (judges are presumed to be able to act impartially and tell reliable evidence from unreliable evidence).

Jury Trials

Jury trials begin with the selection of the jury. The judge and lawyers for both sides question potential jurors about their knowledge of the case and possible biases relating to their clients and the important issues in the case. This process is called "*voir dire.*"

Once a jury is selected, the attorneys address the jury in opening statements that outline what they expect to show in the upcoming trial. Then, the plaintiff begins, offering testimony from witnesses and information in documents to establish a version of events. The testimony and documents are then subject to challenge by the defendant through a process called "cross-examination."

Motions *in Limine*

Before the trial begins, each side can ask the judge to handle evidence (allow it or refuse to admit it) in a certain way. For instance, the plaintiff might want to prevent the defendant from trying to prove a certain point, believing that to do so would hopelessly prejudice the jury against the plaintiff. These requests are called "motions *in limine*" (that is, motions on the verge of trial). They are considered by the judge in a meeting outside the hearing of the jury, usually in the judge's office.

Once the plaintiff's case is presented, the defendant has the opportunity to present a defense, subject to the plaintiff's cross-examination. Commonly, the plaintiff gets the last shot (called a "rebuttal") in an opportunity to answer the defendant's case.

RESOURCE

Represent Yourself in Court, **by Paul Bergman and Sara J. Berman (Nolo), is an excellent guide to what goes on in a trial.** It is based on the Federal Rules of Civil Procedure, which many states follow, and is a good place to start if you are facing or involved in a trial. *How to Win Your Personal Injury Claim*, by Joseph Matthews (Nolo), provides a straightforward discussion on how to file, process, and settle a personal injury claim.

When the parties finish presenting their cases, both sides get to make closing arguments summarizing what they think they've proved and imploring the jury to see it their way. The judge then explains to the jurors that it is their job to decide the facts in the case and apply those facts to the law. Next, the judge reads the jury specially written versions of the law called "jury instructions." (As discussed in Chapter 3, these are the streamlined summaries of law designed to be easily understood by people who aren't legal professionals. They're invaluable when researching a case because they set forth the legal elements a plaintiff must prove to win the case.)

Although it is the judge's responsibility to give the instructions, the plaintiff and defendant are first invited to give the judge a set of proposed instructions that they believe apply to the case (and will be most favorable to their side). The judge and attorneys review the proposed instructions together, but the judge makes the final decision.

The judge assembles the final instructions and reads them verbatim to the jury. On average, it takes the judge approximately 45 minutes to complete the reading.

Researching Jury Instructions

A judge who refuses to instruct the jurors on the appropriate law creates an appealable issue that could result in the case being tried a second time. So, a judge will carefully review the jury instructions offered by each side. (See "Appeals," below.)

Compilations of acceptable jury instructions are available in most states for common types of cases—for instance, auto accident cases (and many more). To find jury instructions online, try searching for "jury instructions" and the name of your state. For instance, searching for "jury instructions New York" brings up the New York State Unified Court System page (www.nycourts.gov) and you'll find New York's jury instructions at www.nycourts.gov/judges/cji/index.shtml.

In California, civil jury instructions are published in *California Civil Jury Instructions for Judges and Attorneys* (C.A.C.I.) and criminal instructions are in *California Criminal Jury Instructions for Judges and Attorneys* (C.A.L.C.R.I.M.). You can find copies of both sets on the California Court website at www. courts.ca.gov/partners/juryinstructions.htm.

Federal jury instructions are located in either *Federal Jury Practice and Instructions* (West) or *Modern Federal Jury Instructions: Civil and Criminal* (LexisNexis). Try searching for the titles or visit Marquette University Law School at https://law.marquette.edu/law-library/model-jury-instructions-research-guide to access them online.

Once the jury has heard the instructions, they retire to a room to decide the case. In civil cases, the plaintiff must prove its case by a "preponderance of evidence"—that is, it must be more probable than not that the plaintiff is right. The jury needn't be unanimous; the standard requirement is a three-quarters vote in favor of either party (check your state's requirements). Most civil juries have 12 jurors, but some states are experimenting with smaller juries.

When the jury has reached a verdict, they report it to the judge, who announces it in open court with the parties present. Any party dissatisfied with the verdict can ask the judge to set it aside or modify it. Usually, the judge upholds the verdict and issues a judgment for the winner.

Judge Trials

Judge trials are a lot easier than jury trials. There are fewer disputes about evidence and no jury instructions to prepare. When all the evidence is in, and parties have made final arguments to the judge, the judge decides the case and issues a judgment, usually accompanied by a document termed "Findings of Facts and Conclusions of Law." This document tells the parties why the judge reached the decision and gives them a basis for deciding whether to appeal.

Researching the Rules of Evidence

Any source of information a party offers as proof of a fact is called "evidence." There is admissible evidence and inadmissible evidence, and the rules that determine what is allowed to be introduced at trial are quite complex.

Many of the disputes during a trial revolve around what evidence is admissible and what isn't, and the many bench conferences (when the attorneys and the judge huddle and whisper out of the jury's hearing) that occur during the typical trial involve whether a bit of testimony or a particular document should or shouldn't be allowed "into evidence." Decisions by the judge on these disputes are often the subject of an appeal by the losing party.

The rules of evidence for each state are usually published as part of that state's statutes. Most states also have secondary sources designed to help you understand the rules of evidence. (See Chapter 3.)

Appeals

Any party dissatisfied with the judgment can appeal the issue to a higher court (but you'll need to demonstrate that a mistake occurred at the trial level). As we've explained, in most cases an appeal doesn't start the whole process over. Instead, the appellate court only looks to see if the trial court made any errors, such as failing to allow the jury to hear relevant evidence, allowing in evidence overly prejudicial to the defendant, failing to provide the jury with the appropriate law, and so on. The appellate court won't usually hear new evidence or conduct a new trial.

Appeals are usually allowed from final decisions in a case, such as a judgment of dismissal, summary judgment, or judgment after trial. However, sometimes decisions by the court before final judgment is entered can be reviewed by an appellate court before the trial continues. These are termed "interlocutory appeals." These interlocutory appeals are the exception to the rule; appellate courts prefer to refrain from reviewing lower court decisions until the trial is over and decide all questions at once.

In an appeal, "briefs"—typewritten statements of the parties' views of the facts and law—are submitted to the appellate court. The appellate court also has a copy of the entire written "record" of the trial court. This record usually consists of all documents submitted by the parties to the trial court, exhibits and documents introduced in the trial, a transcript of exactly what was said at the trial (produced by a court reporter or a tape recorder), and all judgments and orders entered by the trial court.

In addition to considering the briefs and the trial court record, the appellate court usually hears oral arguments from the attorneys on each side. After the oral arguments, the justices (judges on courts of appeal are typically called "justices") discuss the case and arrive at a decision. A justice representing the majority (sometimes the justices who hear the case won't agree on how it should be decided) is assigned to write the opinion.

If a party disagrees with the outcome of an appeal in the appellate court, another appeal can usually be made—to a state supreme court or the U.S. Supreme Court. That requires filing a "Petition for Hearing" in a state court or a "Petition for Writ of Certiorari" (usually called "Petition for Cert") asking the Supreme Court to consider the case. If the court grants a hearing or issues a Writ of Certiorari to the court that decided the case being appealed, it will consider the case. If it denies a hearing or "cert," then it won't.

Supreme courts grant hearings or cert only in a very small percentage of cases presented to them. They usually choose cases that present interesting or important questions of law or an issue that two or more lower appellate courts have disagreed on. For example, suppose the federal Court of Appeals for the Sixth Circuit decides that the military registration system is unconstitutional because it doesn't include women. The Court of Appeals for the Seventh Circuit decides that the system is constitutional. The U.S. Supreme Court might grant cert in these cases and resolve the conflict.

When the U.S. Supreme Court or a state's highest court decides a case, it almost always issues a published opinion. U.S. Supreme Court cases serve as precedent and binding authority for all federal courts, and cases from a state's highest court serve as precedent and authority for all state courts in that state.

Filing Cases Directly in Appellate and Supreme Courts

Occasionally, cases can be brought directly in the intermediate appellate courts or supreme courts, but only when there are significant issues of law in the case and little factual dispute. Also, under federal and state constitutions, certain disputes go directly to the supreme courts; this is called "original jurisdiction," as opposed to their usual appellate jurisdiction. For example, if one state sues another, the suit is brought in the U.S. Supreme Court, not a U.S. district court.

Writing and Filing Court Documents

If you are involved in a civil suit, you will follow most or all of the abovementioned steps. In virtually all cases, you'll submit documents to the court and provide copies to your opponent.

Fortunately, many courts have standard forms for this purpose. For example, your state court might have a complaint form you can use to initiate the lawsuit. An attorney might prefer to write a new complaint without a form's limiting language in complex matters. But for your purposes, these forms can be invaluable. Instead of figuring out the exact format of any legal document you file, you can spend your time and energy filling out the form accurately, following any instructions provided.

Check your state court website or call the local clerk for standard forms. Or, if none exist, the clerk can tell you the format you should use. Pay special attention to the court's rules—you might need to use a specific font size and style. If you get it wrong, the court might reject your papers, which can be particularly stressful if you're up against a deadline.

If you are going to write a legal brief or even fill out a form explaining your case's facts to the court, we encourage you to look back at your legal memorandum. You will have already laid out the most important facts, which you can copy onto other documents.

We can't tell you how to write a legal brief here—it's too complicated and varies depending on the type of motion you're making and the court. As we've explained, if you get to that level of complexity in a lawsuit, we recommend you at least talk to a lawyer. However, if you're determined to do it yourself or are working with a lawyer to draft such a document, your legal memorandum will be a good starting point for preparing a well-reasoned argument. Just remember that the purpose of the brief is different. While in a legal memorandum, you're laying out the basics of the law objectively, in a brief, you're persuading a court that your position is correct. For this reason, the same material in your legal memorandum can look very different in a brief.

Finding and Working With a Lawyer

Perhaps the issue of filing documents doesn't apply to you because you already have or plan to hire an attorney. Or, even after doing a lot of legal research on your own, you might find you need an expert's help. Here are some tips for finding and working with a lawyer.

Finding a Lawyer

The best way to find a lawyer is to get a recommendation from someone you know who has worked with that person. Keep in mind that lawyers often specialize by subject area and limit practice to a particular geographic area. For instance, if your parents have a great estate planning lawyer in Denver, Colorado, that won't do you any good if you're looking for a family law expert in Louisville, Kentucky. The general idea is that you want to look for someone local with skills in the area of law at issue. Usually, that means finding someone with at least several years of experience.

If you can't get a recommendation, consider whether any local professional organizations can help. If you're a new landlord looking for advice on how to deal with a problematic tenant, for example, a local apartment association might know local lawyers with the experience and knowledge you are looking for.

Finally, if these two methods don't work, you might want to use a lawyer referral system. For example, Nolo's Lawyer Directory provides detailed profiles of attorney advertisers, including information about each lawyer's education, experience, practice areas, and fee schedule. Go to www.nolo.com/lawyers or Nolo's main website at www.nolo.com.

With a few names, you can make some phone calls to set up appointments with prospective lawyers. Be sure to determine whether you'll be charged for this initial consultation; some lawyers charge, while others don't. You'll want to know about the lawyer's education and experience, any history of professional discipline, and so forth. You shouldn't be shy about asking for recommendations, either—former clients have just the kind of perspective you'll need.

When you choose a lawyer, you'll have to decide how payment will be structured. Some lawyers are willing to work on a contingency basis. They won't get paid unless you win or settle your case. The amount you'll pay the lawyer depends on what you agree to; in a case that settles, 25% of the recovery is typical, and in a case that the attorney wins at trial, 33% isn't uncommon.

Other lawyers might work for a flat fee, while some will charge you an hourly rate. If you have an attorney charging you by the hour, we suggest you set a time limit, after which the lawyer must call before doing additional work. This approach will prevent your costs from going sky-high without your input.

As we'll explain in the next section, you and the lawyer might be able to work out a more flexible work arrangement, with you utilizing some of the knowledge you've gained through the legal research you've already done.

Working With a Lawyer

Hopefully, after reading this book, the world of legal research no longer feels like a foreign place that only lawyers ever visit. Instead, you should be well-versed in the resources available to you. And if you've already researched your legal topic, you might be an expert in that as well.

These resources can be used if you are working with an attorney. First, as we've already discussed, they help you establish a list of questions you can ask your attorney. Second, understanding important legal concepts will help you focus on the most important facts and information you must convey to your attorney to help make your legal case. Not only will your attorney appreciate your ability to recognize important issues, but you'll save money because you won't waste time talking to your lawyer about facts the court won't consider.

And third, knowing the law will allow you to assure yourself that your attorney is strongly advocating on your behalf or, if necessary, recognize when it's time to find a lawyer who is a better fit.

Glossary

abstract of title

A short history of a piece of land that lists any transfers in ownership and any liabilities attached to it, such as mortgages, easements, liens, or property taxes. It is usually prepared by an abstracter or title insurance agent.

admissible evidence

The evidence that a trial judge can allow the judge or jury to consider when reaching a trial decision. Evidence is admitted or deemed inadmissible based on the applicable rules of evidence in the place where the case is being heard. The basic rules of evidence are the same in almost all jurisdictions. See *evidence, inadmissible evidence.*

admission

One side's statement that certain facts are true, or failure to respond to certain allegations, in response to a request from the other side during pretrial discovery. An out-of-court statement by an adverse party that is against the interest of the party who said it, offered into evidence as an exception to the hearsay rule.

adverse possession

Adverse possession is a means by which one can legally take another's property without paying for it. The requirements for adversely possessing property vary between states but usually include continuous and open use for a number of years and paying taxes on the property in question.

age of majority

Adulthood in the eyes of the law. After reaching the age of majority, a person can vote, make a valid will, enter into binding contracts, enlist in the armed forces, and purchase alcohol. Also, parents can stop making child support payments when a child reaches the age of majority. In most states, the age of majority is 18, but this varies depending on the activity. For example, people are allowed to vote when they reach the age of 18 but can't purchase alcohol until they're 21.

agent

A person authorized to act for and under the direction of another person when dealing with third parties. The person who appoints an agent is called the "principal." An agent can enter into binding agreements on the principal's behalf and might even create liability for the principal if the agent causes harm while carrying out their duties. See also *attorney-in-fact*.

aggravate

To make more serious or severe.

aggravating circumstances

Circumstances that increase the seriousness or outrageousness of a crime, which will increase the wrongdoer's penalty or punishment. For example, the crime of aggravated assault is a physical attack made worse because it is committed with a dangerous weapon, results in severe bodily injury, or is made in conjunction with another serious crime. Aggravated assault is usually considered a felony, punishable by a prison sentence.

alternate beneficiary

A person, organization, or institution that receives property through a will, trust, or insurance policy when the first named beneficiary is unable or refuses to take the property. For example, Jake leaves his sheet music collection to his daughter, Mia, in his will and names the local symphony as an alternate beneficiary. If Mia dies before Jake or if Mia decides to disclaim the gift, the manuscripts will pass directly to the symphony. In insurance law, the alternate beneficiary, usually the person who receives the insurance proceeds because the initial or primary beneficiary has died, is sometimes called the "secondary" or "contingent" beneficiary.

alternative dispute resolution (ADR)

A catchall term describing methods parties can use to resolve disputes outside of court, including negotiation, conciliation, mediation, collaborative practice, and the many types of arbitration. The common denominator of all ADR methods is that they are faster, less formalistic, less expensive, and often less adversarial than a court trial.

amicus curiae

Latin for "friend of the court," a person or organization that is not a party to a lawsuit but that has a strong interest in the case and wants to participate, usually by filing a brief in support of one party's position. *Amicus curiae* must be invited by the court or obtain permission from the court before participating.

ancillary jurisdiction

A term used in federal courts that applies when the court takes control of matters not typically under federal jurisdiction to allow adjudication of the entire controversy, part of which is a federal matter authorized by law to determine.

annuity

A purchased policy that pays a fixed amount of benefits each year—although most annuities actually pay monthly—for the life of the person entitled to those benefits. In a simple life annuity, when the person receiving the annuity dies, the benefits stop; there is no final lump sum payment and no provision to pay benefits to a spouse or another survivor. A continuous annuity pays monthly installments for the life of the retired worker and provides a smaller continuing annuity for the worker's spouse or another survivor after the worker's death. A joint and survivor annuity pays monthly benefits as long as the retired worker is alive and then continues to pay the worker's spouse for life.

annulment

A court procedure that dissolves a marriage and treats it as if it never happened. Annulments are rare since the advent of no-fault divorce, but could be obtained in most states for one of the following reasons: misrepresentation, concealment (for example, of an addiction or criminal record), misunderstanding, and refusal to consummate the marriage.

answer

A defendant's written response to a plaintiff's initial court filing (called a "complaint" or "petition"). An answer typically denies some or all of the facts the complaint asserts. It sometimes seeks to turn the tables on the plaintiff by making allegations or charges against the plaintiff (called "counterclaims") or providing justification for the defendant's behavior (called "affirmative defenses"). Usually, a defendant has 30 days to file an answer after being served with the plaintiff's complaint. In some courts, an answer is called a "response."

appeal

A written request made after a trial, asking another court (usually the court of appeals) to review the trial court's decisions. The party filing the appeal is called the "appellant" or "petitioner." The other party is called the "appellee" or "respondent." Appellate courts typically decide whether a legal mistake was made in the trial court and whether the mistake changed the case's outcome.

appellant

A party to a lawsuit who appeals a losing decision to a higher court to have it modified or reversed.

appellate court

A higher court that reviews the decision of a lower court when a losing party files for an appeal.

appellee

A party to a lawsuit who wins in the trial court—or sometimes on a first appeal—only to have the other party (called the "appellant") file for an appeal. An appellee files a written brief and often makes an oral argument before the appellate court, asking that the lower court's judgment be upheld. In some courts, an appellee is called a "respondent."

arbitration

An out-of-court procedure for resolving disputes in which one or more people—the arbitrator(s)—hear evidence and make a decision. Arbitration is like a trial in some ways, but typically proceeds much more quickly and with less formality.

arraignment

A court appearance in which the defendant is formally charged with a crime and asked to respond by entering a plea. Other matters often handled at the arraignment are arranging for the appointment of a lawyer to represent the defendant and the setting of bail.

arrearages

Overdue alimony or child support payments. Child support arrearages can't be discharged in bankruptcy, and courts usually won't retroactively cancel them. A spouse or parent who falls on tough times and is unable to make payments should request a temporary modification of the payments before the arrearages build up.

arrest

Being detained by the police in a manner that, to any reasonable person, makes it clear they aren't free to leave. A person can be "under arrest" even though the police haven't announced it. Handcuffs or physical restraints aren't necessary. Questioning an arrested person about involvement in or knowledge of a crime must be preceded by *Miranda* warnings.

arrest warrant

A document issued by a judge or magistrate authorizing the police to arrest someone. Warrants are issued when law enforcement personnel present convincing evidence to a judge or magistrate of the reasonable likelihood that a crime has taken place and that the person named in the warrant is criminally responsible for that crime.

articles of incorporation

A document filed with state authorities (usually the secretary of state or corporations commissioner, depending on the state) to form a corporation. As required by the general incorporation law of the state, the articles typically include the purpose of the corporation, its principal place of business, the names of its initial controlling directors, and the amounts and types of stock it is authorized to issue.

assault

An intentional act that causes another person to reasonably fear imminent harmful or offensive contact. Actual physical contact isn't necessary. Threatening gestures that would alarm any reasonable person can constitute an assault. An assault can be both a crime and an intentional tort.

assignee

A person to whom a property right is transferred. For example, an assignee takes over a lease from a tenant who wants to permanently move out before the lease expires. The assignee takes control of the property and assumes all the tenant's legal rights and responsibilities, including rent payment. However, the original tenant remains legally responsible if the assignee fails to pay the rent.

assignment

A transfer of property rights from one person to another, called the "assignee."

attestation

The act of watching someone sign a legal document, such as a will or power of attorney, and then signing your own name as a witness. When you witness a document in this way, you are attesting—that is, stating and confirming—that the person you watched sign the document in fact did so. Attesting a document doesn't mean you are vouching for its accuracy or truthfulness. You are only acknowledging that you watched it being signed by the person whose name is on the signature line.

attorneys' fees

The payment made to a lawyer for legal services. These fees can take several forms, including hourly, per job or service, contingency, or retainer. Attorneys' fees must usually be paid by the client who hires a lawyer, though occasionally a law or contract will require the losing party of a lawsuit to pay the winner's court costs and attorneys' fees.

attorney general

Head of the U.S. Department of Justice and chief law officer of the federal government. The attorney general represents the United States in legal matters, oversees federal prosecutors, and provides legal advice to the president and to heads of executive governmental departments. Each state also has an attorney general responsible for advising the governor and state agencies and departments about legal issues, and overseeing state prosecuting attorneys.

attorney work product privilege

A rule that protects materials prepared by a lawyer in preparation for trial from being seen and used by the adversary during discovery or trial.

attorney-client privilege

A rule that keeps communications between an attorney and client confidential and protects everything said between attorney and client from being discovered by the opposing party during pretrial investigation, or used as evidence in a trial. The same type of privilege exists between physician and patient, clergy and parishioner, and spouses.

attorney-in-fact

A person named in a written power of attorney document to act on behalf of the person who signs the document, called the "principal." The attorney-in-fact has only the powers and responsibilities that are granted in the specific power of attorney document. An attorney-in-fact is an agent of the principal.

attractive nuisance

Something on a piece of property that attracts children but also endangers their safety. For example, unfenced swimming pools, open pits, farm equipment, and abandoned refrigerators, have all qualified as attractive nuisances. Landowners have a duty to keep their property free of attractive nuisances.

authenticate

To offer testimony that tells the judge what an item of evidence is and its connection to the case. The purpose of authentication is usually to establish that the evidence can be admitted for purposes of making a decision in the case.

avowal

A direct statement or declaration. Often refers to a sworn statement a witness makes after the judge rules that their testimony won't be admitted at trial. The avowal creates a record of what the witness would have said, which may be considered by a higher court if a party appeals the judge's refusal to allow the testimony.

bail

The money paid to the court, usually at arraignment or shortly thereafter, to ensure that an arrested person who is released from jail will show up at all required court appearances. The amount of bail is determined by the local bail schedule, which is based on the seriousness of the offense. The judge can increase the bail if the prosecutor convinces them that the defendant is likely to flee (for example, if he has failed to show up for court in the past), or they can decrease it if the defense attorney shows that the defendant is unlikely to run (for example, he has strong ties to the community by way of a steady job and a family).

bailiff

A court official, usually a peace officer or deputy sheriff, who keeps order in the courtroom and handles errands for the judge and clerk.

In some jurisdictions, a person appointed by the court to handle the affairs of an incompetent person or to be a keeper of goods or money pending further order of the court.

bailor

Someone who delivers an item of personal property to another person for a specific purpose. For example, a person who leaves a broken computer with a repairperson in order to get it fixed would be a bailor.

bankruptcy

A federal legal process for debtors seeking to eliminate or repay their debts. There are two types of bankruptcies for consumers: Chapter 7, which allows debtors to wipe out many debts in exchange for giving up nonexempt property to be sold to repay creditors, and Chapter 13, which allows debtors to keep all of their property and repay all or a portion of their debts over three to five years. Businesses can file for Chapter 7 or Chapter 11 bankruptcy. Chapter 11 lets companies reorganize their debt load to stay in business.

bankruptcy trustee

A person appointed by the court to oversee the case of a person or business that has filed for bankruptcy. In a consumer Chapter 7 case, the trustee's role is to gather, liquidate, and distribute the debtor's nonexempt property proportionally to creditors. In a Chapter 13 case, the trustee's role is to receive the debtor's monthly payments and distribute them proportionally to creditors.

battery

An intentional, harmful, or offensive touching of another person. A battery can be both an intentional tort and a crime. Unintentional harmful contact isn't battery, no matter how careless the behavior or how severe the injury, though it might be negligence. A fistfight is a common battery. Being hit by a wild pitch in a baseball game isn't.

bench

The seat (usually a chair rather than a bench) where a judge sits in the courtroom. Sometimes the word "bench" is used in place of the word "judge"—for example, someone might say she wants a bench trial, meaning a trial by a judge without a jury.

bench trial

A trial before a judge with no jury. The term derives from the fact that the judge's stand is called the "bench."

beneficiary

A person or an organization legally entitled to receive benefits through a legal device, such as a will, trust, or life insurance policy.

bequeath

A legal term sometimes used in wills that means "leave." For example, "I bequeath my garden tools to my brother-in-law, Buster Jenkins."

bequest

The legal term for personal property (anything but real estate) left in a will.

best evidence rule

A rule of evidence that demands that the original of any document, photograph, or recording be used as evidence at trial, rather than a copy. A copy will be allowed into evidence only if the original is unavailable.

beyond a reasonable doubt

The burden of proof that the prosecution must carry in a criminal trial to obtain a guilty verdict. Reasonable doubt is sometimes explained as being convinced "to a moral certainty." The prosecutor must convince the jury that the defendant committed each element of the crime before returning a guilty verdict.

bifurcate

To separate the issues in a case so that one issue or set of issues can be tried and resolved before the others. For example, death penalty cases are always bifurcated: The court first hears the evidence of guilt and reaches a verdict, then second hears evidence about and decides which punishment to impose (death or life in prison without parole). Bifurcated trials are also common in product liability class action lawsuits in which many people claim that they were injured by the same defective product: The issue of liability is tried first, followed by the question of damages. Bifurcation is authorized by Rule 42(b) of the Federal Rules of Civil Procedure.

binding precedent

The decisions of higher courts that set the legal standards for similar cases in lower courts within the same jurisdiction.

blue law

A statute that forbids or regulates an activity, such as the sale of liquor on Sundays.

blue-sky laws

The laws that aim to protect people from investing in sham companies that consist of nothing but "blue sky." Blue-sky laws require that companies seeking to sell stock to the public submit information to and obtain the approval of a state or federal official who oversees corporate activity.

bond

1. A written agreement purchased from a bonding company that guarantees a person will properly carry out a specific act, such as managing funds, showing up in court, providing good title to a piece of real estate, or completing a construction project. If the person who purchased the bond fails at their task, the bonding company will pay the aggrieved party an amount up to the value of the bond.

2. An interest-bearing document issued by a government or company as evidence of a debt. A bond provides predetermined payments at a set date to the bondholder. Bonds can be "registered" bonds, which provide payment to the bondholder whose name is recorded with the issuer and appears on the bond certificate, or "bearer" bonds, which provide payments to whoever holds the bond in hand.

breach

A failure or violation of a legal obligation.

breach of contract

A legal claim that one party failed to perform as required under a valid agreement with the other party. For example, you might say, "The roofer breached our contract by using substandard supplies when repairing my roof."

brief

A document used to submit a legal contention or argument to a court. A brief typically sets out the facts of the case and a party's argument as to why they should prevail. These arguments must be supported by legal authority and precedent, such as statutes, regulations, and previous court decisions. Although it is usually possible to submit a brief to a trial court (called a "trial brief"), briefs are most commonly used as a central part of the appeal process (an "appellate brief"). But don't be fooled by the name—briefs are usually anything but brief, as pointed out by writer Franz Kafka, who defined a lawyer as "a person who writes a 10,000-word document and calls it a 'brief.'"

burden of proof

A party's job of convincing the trial judge or jury that the party's version of the facts is true. In a civil trial, the plaintiff must convince the judge or jury "by a preponderance of the evidence" that the plaintiff's version is true—that is, more than 50% of the believable evidence is in the plaintiff's favor. In a criminal case, because a person's liberty is at stake, the government must convince the judge or jury that the defendant is guilty beyond a reasonable doubt.

burglary

The offense of illegally entering a building with the intent to commit a crime inside. In the past, most states defined burglary as using force to break into a residence at night. Modern burglary statutes tend to be much broader. Today, burglary is generally defined as simply entering any building without permission at any time of day in order to steal something or commit a felony inside.

business records exception

An exception to the evidence rule prohibiting hearsay. The business records exception allows a business document to be admitted into evidence if a proper foundation is laid to show the document is reliable.

bylaws

The rules governing the internal affairs or actions of a corporation. Bylaws are adopted by the shareholders or the board of directors of a corporation. They generally include procedures for holding meetings and electing the board of directors and officers. The bylaws also set out the duties and powers of a corporation's officers.

capital case

A prosecution for murder wherein the jury must decide if the death penalty is an appropriate punishment for a defendant found guilty. The federal government and each state have a list of "special circumstances" the prosecutor must prove before imposing the death penalty. Typical requirements include a finding of multiple murders, the use of a bomb, or a finding that the murder was especially heinous, atrocious, or cruel.

caption

A heading on all pleadings submitted to the court. It states basic information such as the parties' names, the court, and the case number.

case

A term referring to a lawsuit at any stage of litigation or review. For example, a "case" can refer to an action filed with the court or a written decision by a trial judge or appellate panel. "I have made my case" implies the party presented sufficient evidence to win the lawsuit. Similarly, a litigant might say, "My case-in-chief has been completed" after presenting all evidence.

cause of action

A specific legal claim, such as negligence, breach of contract, or medical malpractice, for which a plaintiff seeks compensation. A cause of action has discrete elements, each of which the litigant must prove with evidence before winning the case.

certified copy

A copy of a document issued by a court or government agency that is guaranteed to be a true and exact copy of the original. Many agencies and institutions require certified copies of legal documents before permitting certain transactions. For example, a certified copy of a death certificate is required before a bank will release the funds in a deceased person's payable-on-death account to the person who has inherited them.

challenge for cause

A party's request that the judge dismiss a potential juror from serving on a trial jury by providing a valid legal reason why they shouldn't serve. Potential bias is a common reason potential jurors are challenged for cause—for example, the potential juror is a relative of a party or one of the lawyers, or admits to prejudice against one party's race or religion. Judges can also dismiss a potential juror for cause. There is no limit on the number of successful challenges for cause. Compare *peremptory challenge*.

chambers

A fancy word for a judge's office. Trial court judges often schedule pretrial settlement conferences and informal meetings in chambers.

Chapter 7 bankruptcy

The most common type of bankruptcy, in which qualifying debts are wiped out completely in exchange for giving up nonexempt property.

Chapter 13 bankruptcy

A type of consumer bankruptcy designed to help debtors reorganize their debts and pay all or a portion of them over three to five years. In Chapter 13 bankruptcy, debtors keep their property and use their income to repay creditors according to a monthly repayment plan. At the end of the three-to-five-year period, the balance of what the debtor owes on many types of debts is erased.

charge

A formal accusation of criminal activity. The prosecuting attorney decides on the charges, after reviewing police reports, witness statements, and any other evidence of wrongdoing. Formal charges are announced at an arrested person's arraignment.

circuit court

The name used for the principal trial court in many states. In the federal system, appellate courts are organized into 13 circuits. Eleven of these cover different geographical areas of the country—for example, the U.S. Court of Appeal for the Ninth Circuit covers Alaska, Arizona, California, Hawaii, Idaho, Montana, Nevada, Oregon, and Washington. The remaining circuits are the District of Columbia Circuit and the Federal Circuit, (which hears patent, customs, and other specialized cases, based on subject matter). The term derives from an age before mechanized transit, when judges and lawyers rode "the circuit" of their territory to hold court in various places.

circumstantial evidence

Evidence that proves a fact by means of an inference. For example, from the evidence that a person was seen running away from the scene of a crime, a judge or jury might infer that the person committed the crime.

civil case

A noncriminal lawsuit, usually involving private property rights. For example, lawsuits involving breach of contract, probate, divorce, negligence, and copyright violations are just a few of the many hundreds of varieties of civil lawsuits.

civil procedure

The rules used to handle a civil case from the time the initial complaint is filed through pretrial discovery, the trial itself, and any subsequent appeal. Each state adopts its own rules of civil procedure (often set out in a separate Code of Civil Procedure), but many are influenced by or modeled on the Federal Rules of Civil Procedure.

class action

A lawsuit in which the interests of a large number of unnamed people with similar legal claims join together in a group (the class) and are represented by named plaintiffs who have been similarly affected by the wrongdoing alleged in the lawsuit. Common class actions involve cases in which a product has injured many people, or in which a group of people has suffered discrimination at the hands of an organization.

clear and present danger

A legal standard courts sometimes used in the past to determine when speech or expression could be banned for encouraging others to break the law. Today, the Supreme Court (and as a result, lower courts) use the "incitement test" to decide when speech can be punished for encouraging others to act lawlessly.

close corporation

A corporation owned and operated by a few individuals, often members of the same family, rather than by public shareholders. State laws permit close corporations to function more informally than regular corporations. For example, shareholders can make decisions without holding meetings of the board of directors, and can fill vacancies on the board without a vote of the shareholders.

closing argument

At trial, a speech made by each party after all the evidence has been presented. The purpose is to review the testimony and evidence presented during the trial to convince the trier of fact that your side should win. In trials before a judge (without a jury), it is common for both parties to waive closing argument on the theory that the judge has almost surely already arrived at a decision.

codicil

A supplement or addition to a will. A codicil can explain, modify, add to, subtract from, qualify, alter, or revoke existing provisions in a will. Because a codicil changes a will, it must be signed before witnesses.

collateral

Property that someone promises or gives to a creditor to guarantee payment of a debt, creating what's called a "secured debt." If the borrower defaults on the loan, the creditor can seize the property and sell it to cover the debt.

collateral estoppel

A legal doctrine that says that a judgment in one case prevents (estops) a party to that suit from trying to litigate the same issue in another legal action.

common law marriage

In some states, a type of marriage in which couples can become legally married by living together for a long period, representing themselves as a married couple, and intending to be married. Contrary to popular belief, the couple must intend to be married and act as though they are for a common law marriage to take effect—merely living together for a long time won't do it.

community property

A method of defining the ownership of property acquired during marriage, in which all earnings during marriage and all property acquired with those earnings are owned in common, and all debts incurred during marriage are the responsibility of both spouses. Typically, community property consists of all property and profits acquired during marriage, except property received by inheritance, gift, or the profits from property owned before marriage. Community property laws exist in Arizona, California, Idaho, Louisiana, Nevada, New Mexico, Texas, Washington, and Wisconsin. In Alaska, couples can create community property by written agreement. In Kentucky, South Dakota, and Tennessee, couples can create special community property trusts.

community property with right of survivorship

A way for married couples to hold title to property, available in some community property states. It allows one spouse's half-interest in community property to pass to the surviving spouse without probate.

comparable rectitude

A doctrine that grants the spouse least at fault a divorce when both spouses have shown grounds for divorce. It is a response to an old common law rule that prevented a divorce when both spouses were at fault.

competent evidence

Legally admissible evidence. Competent evidence tends to prove the matter in dispute. In a murder trial, for example, competent evidence might include the murder weapon with the defendant's fingerprints on it.

complaint

A document filed in court that starts a lawsuit. The party who files the complaint is the plaintiff. The party sued is the defendant. A complaint filing must be accompanied by a filing fee payable to the court clerk unless the plaintiff asks a judge to waive the fee based on inability to pay. The complaint describes the parties involved, why the case is before the court, the facts, and the requested relief. The plaintiff must serve the complaint on the defendant, who then must file a responsive pleading, such as a demurrer, motion to dismiss, or answer. However, a written response isn't required in criminal actions and some small claims courts.

confidential communication

Information exchanged between two people who have a relationship in which private communications are protected by law, and intend that the information be kept in confidence. The law recognizes certain parties whose communications will be considered confidential and protected, including spouses, doctor and patient, attorney and client, and priest and confessor. Communications between these individuals can't be disclosed in court unless the protected party waives that protection. The intention that the communication be confidential is critical. For example, if an attorney and his client are discussing a matter in the presence of an unnecessary third party— for instance, in an elevator with others present—the discussion won't be considered confidential and might be admitted at trial. Also known as "privileged communication."

conformed copy

An exact copy of a document filed with a court. To conform a copy, the court clerk will stamp the document with the filing date and add any handwritten notations to the document that exist on the original, including dates and the judge's signature.

consanguinity

An old-fashioned term referring to the relationship of "blood relatives"— people who have a common ancestor. Consanguinity exists, for example, between brothers and sisters but not between husbands and wives.

conservator

Someone appointed by a judge to oversee the affairs of an incapacitated person. A conservator who manages financial affairs is often called a "conservator of the estate." One who takes care of personal matters, such as health care and living arrangements, is known as a "conservator of the person." Sometimes, one conservator is appointed to handle all these tasks. Depending on where you live, a conservator might also be called a "guardian," "committee," or "curator."

consideration

A benefit or right for which the parties to a contract must bargain. In order to be valid, a contract must be founded on an exchange of one form of consideration for another. Consideration can be a promise to perform a certain act—for example, a promise to fix a leaky roof in return for a payment of $1,000—or a promise not to do something, such as build a second story on a house that will block the neighbor's view. Whatever its particulars, consideration must be something of value to the people who are making the contract.

constructive eviction

A housing provision so substandard that, for all intents and purposes, a landlord has evicted the tenant. For example, this could occur if the landlord refused to provide light, heat, water, or other essential services, destroyed part of the premises, or refused to clean up an environmental health hazard, such as lead paint dust. Because the premises are unlivable, the tenant has the right to move out and stop paying rent without incurring legal liability for breaking the lease. Usually, the tenant must first bring the problem to the landlord's attention and allow a reasonable amount of time for the landlord to make repairs.

contempt of court

Behavior in or out of court that violates a court order, or otherwise disrupts or shows disregard for the court. Refusing to answer a proper question, file court papers on time, or follow local court rules can expose witnesses, lawyers, and litigants to contempt findings. Contempt of court is punishable by fine or imprisonment.

contest [as in "to contest a will"]

To oppose, dispute, or challenge through formal or legal procedures. For example, the defendant in a lawsuit almost always contests the case made by the plaintiff. Or, a disgruntled relative might formally contest the provisions of a will.

contingency

A provision in a contract stating that some or all of the terms of the contract will be altered or voided by the occurrence of a specific event. For example, a contingency in a contract for the purchase of a house might state that if the buyer doesn't approve the inspection report of the physical condition of the property, the buyer doesn't have to complete the purchase.

contingency fee

A method of paying a lawyer for legal representation by which, instead of an hourly or per-job fee, the lawyer receives a percentage of the money their client obtains after settling or winning the case. Often, contingency fee agreements—which are most commonly used in personal injury cases—award the successful lawyer between 20% and 50% of the amount recovered. Lawyers representing defendants charged with crimes can't charge contingency fees. In most states, contingency fee agreements must be in writing.

contingent beneficiary

1. An alternate beneficiary named in a will, trust, or another document.
2. Any person entitled to property under a will if one or more prior conditions are satisfied. For example, if Fred is entitled to take property under a will only if he's married at the time of the willmaker's death, Fred is a contingent beneficiary. Similarly, if Ellen is named to receive a house only in the event her mother, who has been named to live in the house, moves out of it, Ellen is a contingent beneficiary.

continuance

The postponement of a hearing, a trial, or another scheduled court proceeding, at the request of one or both parties, or by the judge without consulting the parties. Unhappiness with long trial court delays has resulted in most states adopting "fast track" rules that sharply limit the ability of judges to grant continuances.

contract

A legally binding agreement involving two or more people or businesses (called "parties") that sets forth what the parties will or won't do. Most contracts that can be carried out within one year can be either oral or written. Major exceptions include contracts involving the ownership of real estate and commercial contracts for goods worth $500 or more, which must be in writing to be enforceable. A contract is formed when competent parties—usually adults of sound mind, or business entities—mutually agree to provide each other some benefit (called "consideration"), such as a promise to pay money, in exchange for a promise to deliver specified goods or services or the actual delivery of those goods and services. A contract typically requires one party to make a reasonably detailed offer to do something—including, typically, the price, time for performance, and other essential terms and conditions—and the other to accept without significant change. For example, if I offer to sell you 10 roses for $5 to be delivered next Thursday and you say "It's a deal," we've made a valid contract. On the other hand, if one party fails to offer something of benefit to the other, there is no contract. For example, if Maria promises to fix Josh's car, there is no contract unless Josh promises something in return for Maria's services.

conviction

A finding by a judge or jury that the defendant is guilty of a crime.

copyright

A legal device that provides the owner the right to control how a creative work is used. A copyright comprises a number of exclusive rights, including the right to make copies, authorize others to make copies, make derivative works, sell and market the work, and perform the work. Any one of these rights can be sold separately through transfers of copyright ownership.

corporation

A legal structure authorized by state law that allows a business to organize as a separate legal entity from its owners. A corporation is often referred to as an "artificial legal person," meaning that, like an individual, it can enter into contracts, sue and be sued, and do the many other things necessary to carry on a business. One advantage of incorporating is that a corporation's owners (shareholders) are legally shielded from personal liability for the corporation's liabilities and debts (unpaid taxes are often an exception). Theoretically, a corporation can be organized for profit-making or nonprofit purposes.

Most profit-making corporations are known as "C corporations" and are taxed separately from their owners, but those organized under Subchapter S of the Internal Revenue Code are pass-through tax entities, meaning that all profits are federally taxed on the personal income tax returns of their owners.

corpus delicti

Latin for the "body of the crime." Used to describe physical evidence, such as the corpse of a murder victim or the charred frame of a torched building.

cosigner

A person who signs a loan agreement, lease, or credit application. If the primary debtor doesn't pay, the cosigner is fully responsible for the loan or debt. Many people use cosigners to qualify for a loan or credit card. A landlord might require a cosigner when renting to a student or someone with a poor credit history.

counterclaim

A defendant's court papers that seek to reverse the thrust of the lawsuit by claiming that it was the plaintiff—not the defendant—who committed legal wrongs, and that the defendant is entitled to money damages or other relief. Usually filed as part of the defendant's answer—which also denies the plaintiff's claims—a counterclaim is commonly, but not always, based on the same events that form the basis of the plaintiff's complaint. For example, a defendant in an auto accident lawsuit might file a counterclaim alleging that the plaintiff caused the accident. In some states, the counterclaim has been replaced by a similar legal pleading called a "cross-complaint." In other states and in federal court, where counterclaims are still used, a defendant must file any counterclaim that stems from the same events covered by the plaintiff's complaint or forever lose the right to do so. In other states where counterclaims are still used, they aren't mandatory, meaning a defendant is free to raise a claim that it was really the plaintiff who was at fault, either in a counterclaim or later as part of a separate lawsuit.

counteroffer

The rejection of an offer to buy or sell that simultaneously makes a different offer, changing the terms in some way. For example, if a buyer offers $5,000 for a used car, and the seller replies that he wants $5,500, the seller has rejected the buyer's offer of $5,000 and made a counteroffer to sell at $5,500. The legal significance of a counteroffer is that it completely voids the original offer, so that if the seller decided to sell for $5,000 the next day, the buyer would be under no legal obligation to buy the car.

court calendar

A list of the cases and hearings a court will hold on a particular day, week, or month. A court calendar is sometimes called a "docket," "trial schedule," or "trial list."

court costs

The fees charged for the use of a court, including the initial filing fee, fees for serving the summons, complaint, and other court papers, fees to pay a court reporter to transcribe deposition and in-court testimony, and, if a jury is involved, to pay the daily stipend of jurors. Court costs must be paid by both parties as the case progresses. In some cases, the losing party will be responsible for both parties' costs.

covenant

A restriction on the use of real estate that governs its use, such as a requirement that the property will be used only for residential purposes. Covenants are found in deeds or in documents that bind everyone who owns land in a particular development. See *covenants, conditions, and restrictions.*

covenants, conditions, and restrictions (CC&Rs)

The restrictions governing the use of real estate, usually enforced by a homeowners' association and passed on to the new property owners. For example, CC&Rs might tell you how big your house can be, how you must landscape your yard, or whether you can have pets. If property is subject to CC&Rs, buyers must be notified before the sale takes place.

creditor

A person or an entity to whom a debt is owed, such as a bank.

crime

A type of behavior that the state defines as deserving of punishment, which usually includes imprisonment. Crimes and their punishments are defined by Congress and state legislatures.

criminal case

A lawsuit brought by a prosecutor employed by the federal, state, or local government that charges a person with the commission of a crime.

criminal insanity

A mental defect or disease that makes it impossible for a person to understand the wrongfulness of acts or, even if understood, to distinguish right from wrong. Defendants who are criminally insane can't be convicted of a crime since criminal conduct involves the conscious intent to do wrong—a choice that the criminally insane can't meaningfully make.

criminal law

Laws written by Congress and state legislators that make certain behavior illegal and punishable by fines and imprisonment. By contrast, most civil laws aren't punishable by imprisonment. For a defendant to be found guilty of a criminal law, the prosecution must show that the defendant intended to act. Civil law sometimes holds people responsible for actions even though the consequences weren't intended. For example, civil law holds someone financially responsible for car accidents that weren't intentionally caused.

cross-complaint

Sometimes called a "cross-claim," legal paperwork that a defendant files to initiate a lawsuit against the original plaintiff, a co-defendant, or someone who isn't yet a party to the lawsuit. A cross-complaint must concern the same events that gave rise to the original lawsuit. For example, a defendant accused of causing an injury when she failed to stop at a red light might cross-complain against the mechanic who recently repaired her car, claiming that his negligence resulted in the brakes failing and, hence, that the accident was his fault. In some states where the defendant wishes to make a legal claim against the original plaintiff and no third party is claimed to be involved, a counterclaim, and not a cross-complaint, should be used.

cross-examination

At trial, the opportunity to question any witness, including your opponent, who testifies against you on direct examination. The chance to cross-examine usually occurs after a witness completes direct testimony—often the opposing lawyer or party, or sometimes the judge, signals that it is time to begin cross-examination by saying, "Your witness." Typically, there are two important reasons to engage in cross-examination: to attempt to get the witness to say something helpful to your side or to cast doubt on (impeach) the witness with a credibility-reducing admission—for example, that her eyesight is so poor that she might not have seen an event.

custodial interference

The taking of a child from a parent with the intent to interfere with that parent's physical custody of the child. This act is a crime in most states, even if the taker also has custody rights.

custodian

A term used by the Uniform Transfers to Minors Act for the person named to manage property left to a child. The custodian will manage the property if the gift-giver dies before the child has reached the age specified by state law—usually 21. When the child reaches the specified age, the child will receive the property, and the custodian will have no further role in its management.

custody (of a child)

The legal authority to make decisions affecting a child's interests (legal custody) and the responsibility of taking care of the child (physical custody). When parents separate or divorce, one of the hardest decisions they have to make is which parent will have custody. The most common arrangement is for one parent to have custody (both physical and legal) while the other parent has a right of visitation. However, it isn't uncommon for parents to share legal custody, even if one parent has physical custody. The most uncommon arrangement is for the parents to share legal and physical custody.

damages

In a lawsuit, money awarded to one party based on injury or loss caused by the other.

compensatory damages

Money awarded to compensate plaintiffs for harm they've suffered. Common categories of compensatory damages include medical expenses, lost wages, and the repair or replacement of property (also called "actual damages").

general damages

Sometimes called "non-economic damages," in a lawsuit or insurance claim, "general damages" refers to monetary recovery (compensation) for injuries or harm that can't be quantified with an exact dollar value—as opposed to "special" or "economic" damages like medical bills and lost income, which tend to translate to a monetary figure easily. In a personal injury case, for example, general damages can include compensation for the injured person's shortened life expectancy, loss of the companionship of a loved one, and, in defamation cases (libel and slander), loss of reputation.

nominal damages

A small amount of money awarded to the plaintiff in a civil lawsuit when a judge or jury finds that the plaintiff has suffered a legal wrong, but no compensatory damages. A dollar is a common nominal damages award. Nominal damages are often considered a moral victory for the plaintiff and can serve as a hook for punitive damages. For example, if one neighbor sues another for libel based on untrue things the second neighbor said about the first, a jury might conclude that—although libel technically occurred—no serious damage was done to the first neighbor's reputation and award nominal damages of $1.

punitive damages

Sometimes called "exemplary damages," punitive damages are awarded over and above special and general damages to punish a losing party's willful or malicious misconduct.

special damages

Damages that cover the winning party's out-of-pocket costs. For example, in a vehicle accident, special damages typically include medical expenses, car repair costs, rental car fees, and lost wages. Often called "specials."

statutory damages

Damages required by statutory law. For example, in many states, if a landlord doesn't return a tenant's security deposit in a timely fashion or give a reason why it is being withheld, the state statutes give the judge authority to order the landlord to pay damages of double or triple the amount of the deposit.

treble damages

Another way of saying triple damages. Some statutes occasionally give judges the power to award the winning party in a civil lawsuit the amount lost plus damages of three times that amount to penalize lawbreakers.

debenture

A type of bond (an interest-bearing document that serves as evidence of a debt) that doesn't require security in the form of a mortgage or lien on a specific piece of property. Repayment of a debenture is guaranteed only by the general credit of the issuer. For example, a corporation might issue a secured bond that gives the bondholder a lien on the corporation's factory. But if it issues a debenture, the loan isn't secured by any property. When a corporation issues debentures, the holders are considered creditors of the corporation and are entitled to payment before shareholders if the business folds.

debtor

A person or an entity who owes money.

decedent

A person who has died or "deceased."

decision

The outcome of a proceeding before a judge, an arbitrator, a government agency, or another legal tribunal. "Decision" is a general term often used interchangeably with the terms "judgment" or "opinion." To be precise, a judgment is the written form of the court's decision in the clerk's minutes or notes, and an opinion is a written document stating the reasons for reaching the decision.

declaration under penalty of perjury

A signed statement, sworn to be true by the signer that will make the signer guilty of the crime of perjury if the statement is materially false and relevant to the case.

declaratory judgment

A court decision in a civil case that tells the parties what their rights and responsibilities are, without awarding damages or ordering them to do anything. Unlike most court cases, where the plaintiff asks for damages or other court orders, the plaintiff in a declaratory judgment case wants the court to resolve an uncertainty to avoid serious legal trouble in the future. Courts are usually reluctant to hear declaratory judgment cases, preferring to wait until there has been a measurable loss. But especially in cases involving important constitutional rights, courts will step in to clarify the legal landscape. For example, many cities regulate the right to assemble by requiring permits to hold a parade. A disappointed applicant who thinks the decision-making process is unconstitutional might hold his parade anyway and challenge the ordinance after he's cited; or he might ask a court beforehand to rule on the constitutionality of the law. By going to court, the applicant can avoid a messy confrontation with the city— and perhaps a citation.

deed

A document that transfers ownership of real estate.

defamation

A false statement that injures someone's reputation and exposes them to public contempt, hatred, ridicule, or condemnation. If the false statement is published in print or through broadcast media, such as radio or TV, it is called "libel." If it is only spoken, it is called "slander." Libel is considered more serious than slander because the communication is permanently recorded in print or because it was broadcast to a large number of people. Defamation is a tort (a civil wrong) that entitles the injured party to compensation if they can prove that the statement damaged their reputation. For example, if a worker can show that she lost her job because a coworker started a false rumor that she came to work drunk, she might be able to recover monetary damages. In certain extreme cases, such as a false accusation that a person committed a crime or has a feared disease, the plaintiff needn't prove that she was damaged because the law presumes that damage was done. These cases are called "libel *per se*" or "slander *per se.*" Public officials or figures who want to prove defamation must meet a higher standard than the standard for private citizens; they must prove that the person who issued the false statements knew they were false or recklessly disregarded a substantial likelihood that they were false.

default

A failure to perform a legal duty. For example, a mortgage or car loan default happens when you fail to make the loan payments on time, maintain adequate insurance, or violate some other agreement provision. A default on a student loan occurs when you fail to repay a loan according to the terms you agreed to when you signed the promissory note, and the holder of your loan concludes that you don't intend to repay it.

default judgment

At trial, a decision awarded to the plaintiff when a defendant fails to contest the case. To appeal a default judgment, a defendant must first file a motion in the court that issued it to have the default vacated (set aside).

defeasance

A clause in a deed, lease, will, or another legal document that completely or partially negates the document if a particular condition occurs or fails to occur. Defeasance also means the act of rendering something null and void. For example, a will could provide that a gift of property is defeasable—that is, it will be void—if the beneficiary fails to marry before the willmaker's death.

defendant

The person against whom a lawsuit is filed. In certain states, and in certain types of lawsuits, the defendant is called the "respondent." Compare *plaintiff.*

demurrer

A request made to a court, asking it to dismiss a lawsuit on the grounds that no legal claim is asserted. For example, you might file a demurrer if your neighbor sued you for parking on the street in front of her house. Your parking habits might annoy your neighbor, but the curb is public property and parking there doesn't cause any harm recognized by the law. After a demurrer is filed, the judge holds a hearing at which both sides can make their arguments about the matter. The judge might dismiss all or part of the lawsuit, or allow the party who filed the lawsuit to amend its complaint. In some states and in federal court, the term "demurrer" has been replaced by "motion to dismiss for failure to state a claim" (called a "12(b)(6) motion" in federal court) or similar term.

deponent

Someone whose deposition is being taken.

deposition

An important tool used in pretrial discovery where one party questions the other party or a witness who is in the case. Often conducted in an attorney's office, a deposition requires that all questions be answered under oath and be recorded by a court reporter, who creates a deposition transcript. Increasingly, depositions are being videotaped. An attorney can represent any deponent. At trial, deposition testimony can be used to cast doubt on (impeach) a witness's contradictory testimony or to refresh the memory of a suddenly forgetful witness. If a deposed witness is unavailable when the trial takes place—for example, the person died—the deposition can be read to the jury in place of live testimony.

devise

An old legal term generally used to refer to real estate left to someone under the terms of a will or to the act of leaving such real estate. In some states, "devise" now applies to any property left by will, making it identical to the term bequest. Compare *legacy*.

dictum

A remark, a statement, or an observation of a judge that isn't a necessary part of the legal reasoning needed to decide a case. Although dictum can be cited in a legal argument, it isn't binding as legal precedent, meaning that other courts aren't required to accept it. For example, if a defendant ran a stop sign and caused a collision, the judge's comments about the mechanical reliability of the particular make of the defendant's car wouldn't be necessary to reach a decision in the case and would be considered dictum. In future cases, lower court judges are free to ignore the comments when reaching their decisions. Dictum is an abbreviation of the Latin phrase *"obiter dictum,"* which means a remark by the way or an aside.

direct examination

At trial, the initial questioning of a party or witness by the side that called the witness to testify. The major purpose of direct examination is to explain your version of events to the judge or jury and to undercut your adversary's version. Good direct examination seeks to prove all facts necessary to satisfy the plaintiff's legal claims or causes of action—for example, that the defendant breached a valid contract and, as a result, the plaintiff suffered a loss.

directed verdict

A ruling by a judge, typically made after the plaintiff has presented all of their evidence but before the defendant puts on their case, that awards judgment to the defendant. A directed verdict is usually made because the judge concludes the plaintiff has failed to offer the minimum amount of evidence to prove their case even if there were no opposition. In other words, the judge is saying that, as a matter of law, no reasonable jury could decide in the plaintiff's favor. In a criminal case, a directed verdict is a judgment of acquittal for the defendant.

discharge (of debts)

A bankruptcy court's erasure of the qualifying debts of a person or business that has filed for bankruptcy.

discharge (of probate administrator)

A court order releasing the administrator or executor from any further duties connected with the probate of an estate. This typically occurs when the duties have been completed but can happen sooner if the executor or administrator wishes to withdraw or is dismissed.

dischargeable debts

Debts that can be erased by going through bankruptcy. Most debts incurred before declaring bankruptcy are dischargeable, including back rent, credit card bills, and medical bills. Compare *nondischargeable debts.*

disclaim

1. To refuse or give away a claim or a right to something. For example, if your aunt leaves you a white elephant in her will and you don't want it, you can refuse the gift by disclaiming your ownership rights.
2. To deny responsibility for a claim or act. For example, a merchant that sells goods secondhand can disclaim responsibility for a product's defects by selling it "as is."

disclaimer

1. A refusal or renunciation of a claim or right.
2. A refusal or denial of responsibility for a claim or an act.
3. The written clause or document that sets out the disclaimer. See also *disclaim.*

disclosure

The making known of a fact that had previously been hidden; a revelation. For example, in many states you must disclose major physical defects in a house you are selling, such as a leaky roof or potential flooding problem.

discovery

A formal investigation—governed by court rules—that is conducted before trial. Discovery allows one party to question other parties, and sometimes witnesses. It also allows one party to force the others to produce requested documents or other physical evidence. The most common types of discovery are interrogatories, consisting of written questions the other party must answer under penalty of perjury, and depositions, which involve an in-person session at which one party to a lawsuit has the opportunity to ask oral questions of the other party or their witnesses under oath while a written transcript is made by a court reporter. Other types of pretrial discovery consist of written requests to produce documents and requests for admissions, by which one party asks the other to admit or deny key facts in the case. One major purpose of discovery is to assess the strength or weakness of an opponent's case, with the idea of opening settlement talks. Another is to gather information to use at trial. Discovery is also present in criminal cases, in which by law the prosecutor must turn over to the defense any witness statements and any evidence that might tend to exonerate the defendant. Depending on the rules of the court, the defendant might also be obliged to share evidence with the prosecutor.

disinherit

To deliberately prevent someone from inheriting something. This is usually done by a provision in a will stating that someone who would ordinarily inherit property—a close family member, for example—shouldn't receive it. In most states, you can't completely disinherit your spouse; a surviving spouse can claim a portion (usually one-third to one-half) of the deceased spouse's estate. With a few exceptions, however, you can expressly disinherit children.

dissolution

A term used instead of divorce in some states.

distributee

Anyone who receives something. Usually, the term refers to someone who inherits a deceased person's property. If the deceased person dies without a will (called "intestate"), state law determines what each distributee will receive. Also called a "beneficiary."

district attorney (D.A.)

A lawyer who is elected to represent a state government in criminal cases in a designated county or judicial district. A D.A.'s duties typically include reviewing police arrest reports, deciding whether to bring criminal charges against arrested people, and prosecuting criminal cases in court. The D.A. might also supervise other attorneys, called "deputy district attorneys" or "assistant district attorneys." In some states, a district attorney is called a "prosecuting attorney," "county attorney," or "state's attorney." In the federal system, the equivalent to the D.A. is a U.S. attorney. The country has many U.S. attorneys, each appointed by the president, who supervise regional offices staffed with prosecutors called "assistant U.S. attorneys."

district court

In federal court and some states, the name of the main trial court. Thus, if you file suit in federal court, your case will typically be heard in federal district court. States may also group their appellate courts into districts—for example, the First District Court of Appeal.

diversity jurisdiction

The power of the federal courts to decide cases between two citizens of different states provided the amount the plaintiff seeks in damages exceeds $75,000.

docket

See *court calendar.*

doing business as (DBA)

A situation in which a business owner operates a company under a name different from their real name. When starting a new business that is named in this way, the owner must file a "fictitious name statement" or similar document with the appropriate county or state agency—for example, the county clerk or secretary of state's office. Putting this document on file enables consumers to discover the names of the business owners, which will be important if a consumer needs to sue the business. It also allows the business owner to conduct transactions in the business's name, such as opening bank accounts and obtaining a taxpayer identification number, and to bring lawsuits under the business's name for business-related debts. Filing a fictitious name statement doesn't confer trademark protection for the name.

dominant tenement

Property that carries a right to use a portion of a neighboring property. For example, property that benefits from a beach access trail across another property is the dominant tenement.

dower and curtesy

A surviving spouse's right to receive a set portion of the deceased spouse's estate—usually one-third to one-half. "Dower" (not to be confused with a "dowry") refers to the portion to which a surviving wife is entitled, while "curtesy" refers to what a man can claim. Until recently, these amounts differed in several states. However, because discrimination based on sex is now illegal in most cases, most states have abolished dower and curtesy and generally provide the same benefits regardless of sex—and this amount is often known simply as the "statutory share." Under certain circumstances, a living spouse might be unable to sell or convey property subject to the other spouse's dower and curtesy or statutory share rights.

durable power of attorney

A power of attorney that remains in effect if the principal becomes incapacitated. If a power of attorney isn't explicitly made durable, it automatically expires if the principal becomes incapacitated. See *durable power of attorney for finances, durable power of attorney for health care.*

durable power of attorney for finances

A legal document that gives someone authority to manage your financial affairs if you become incapacitated. The person you name to represent you is called an "attorney-in-fact."

durable power of attorney for health care

A legal document that you can use to give someone permission to make medical decisions for you if you can't make those decisions yourself. Depending on where you live, the person you name to represent you might be called an "attorney-in-fact," "health care proxy," "agent," or "patient advocate."

dynamite charge

A judge's admonition to a deadlocked jury to go back to the jury room and try harder to reach a verdict. The judge might remind the jurors to consider the opinions of others respectfully and will often assure them that if the case has to be tried again, another jury won't necessarily do a better job than they're doing. Because of its coercive nature, some states prohibit using a dynamite charge as a violation of their state constitution, but the practice passed federal constitutional muster in the case of *Allen v. Gainer*. The instruction is also known as a "dynamite instruction," "shotgun instruction," "*Allen* charge," or "third-degree instruction."

easement

A right to use another person's real estate for a specific purpose. The most common type of easement is the right to travel over another person's land, known as a "right of way." In addition, property owners commonly grant easements for the placement of utility poles, utility trenches, water lines, or sewer lines. The owner of property that is subject to an easement is said to be "burdened" with the easement, because they aren't allowed to interfere with its use. For example, if the deed to John's property permits Sue to travel across John's main road to reach her home, John can't do anything to block the road. On the other hand, Sue can't do anything that exceeds the scope of her easement, such as widening the roadway.

easement by prescription

A right to use property, acquired by a long tradition of open and obvious use. For example, if hikers have been using a trail through your backyard for 10 years and you've never complained, they probably have an easement by prescription through your yard to the trail.

effluxion of time

The normal expiration of a lease due to the passage of time, rather than due to a specific event that might cause the lease to end, such as the destruction of the building.

emancipation

The act of freeing someone from restraint or bondage. For example, on January 1, 1863, slaves in the Confederate states were declared free by an executive order of President Lincoln, known as the "Emancipation Proclamation." After the Civil War, this emancipation was extended to the entire country and made law by the ratification of the Thirteenth Amendment to the Constitution. Nowadays, "emancipation" refers to the point at which a child is free from parental control. It occurs when the child's parents no longer perform their parental duties and surrender their rights to the care, custody, and earnings of their minor child. Emancipation can result from a voluntary agreement between the parents and child, or it might be implied from their acts and ongoing conduct. For example, a child who leaves her parents' home and becomes entirely self-supporting without their objection is considered emancipated, while a child who stays with a friend or relative and gets a part-time job isn't. Emancipation might also occur when a minor child marries or enters the military.

emergency protective order

Any court-issued order meant to protect a person from harm or harassment. An emergency protective order is issued by the police, when court is out of session, to prevent domestic violence. An emergency protective order is a stopgap measure, usually lasting only for a weekend or holiday, after which the abused person is expected to seek a temporary restraining order (TRO) from a court.

eminent domain

The power of the federal or state government to take private property for a public purpose, even if the property owner objects, provided that the property owner is compensated for the loss. The Fifth Amendment to the U.S. Constitution allows the government to take private property if the taking is for a public use and the owner is "justly compensated" (usually, paid fair market value) for their loss. A public use is virtually anything that is sanctioned by a federal or state legislative body, but such uses can include roads, parks, reservoirs, schools, hospitals, or other public buildings. Sometimes called "condemnation," "taking," or "expropriation."

encroachment

The building of a structure entirely or partly on a neighbor's property. Encroachment might occur due to faulty surveying or sheer obstreperousness on the part of the builder. Solutions range from paying the rightful property owner for the use of the property to the court-ordered removal of the structure.

equitable distribution

A legal principle, followed by most states, under which assets and earnings acquired during marriage are divided equitably (fairly) at divorce. Typically, this involves a 50/50 split, but not always. If a spouse obtains a fault divorce, the "guilty" spouse might receive less than their equitable share upon divorce.

escheat

The forfeit of all property to the state when a person dies without heirs.

estate

Generally, all the property you own when you die. The term is also used when referring to a person's "probate estate" (the property passing through the probate process) and "bankruptcy estate" (the property subject to the bankruptcy court's jurisdiction).

estoppel

A legal principle that prevents a person from asserting or denying something in court that contradicts what has already been established as the truth.

estoppel by deed

A type of estoppel that prevents a person from denying the truth of anything that they stated in a deed, especially regarding who has valid ownership of the property.

estoppel by silence

A type of estoppel that prevents someone from asserting something when that person had both the duty and the opportunity to speak up earlier, and their silence put another person at a disadvantage.

promissory estoppel

A type of estoppel that prevents a person who made a promise from reneging when someone else has reasonably relied on the promise and will suffer a loss if the promise is broken.

evidence

The many types of information presented to a judge or jury designed to convince them of the truth or falsity of key facts. Evidence typically includes testimony of witnesses, documents, photographs, items of damaged property, government records, videos, and laboratory reports. Strict rules limit what can be properly admitted as evidence, but dozens of exceptions often mean that creative lawyers find a way to introduce such testimony or other items into evidence.

exclusionary rule

A rule of evidence that disallows the use of illegally obtained evidence in criminal trials. For example, the exclusionary rule would prevent a prosecutor from introducing evidence seized during an illegal search at trial.

executive privilege

The privilege allows the president and other high officials of the executive branch to keep certain communications private if disclosing those communications would disrupt the executive branch's functions or decision-making processes. As demonstrated by the Watergate hearings, this privilege doesn't extend to information relating to a criminal investigation.

executor

The person named in a will to handle the property of someone who has died. The executor collects the property, pays debts and taxes, and then distributes what's left, as specified in the will. The executor also handles any probate court proceedings and notifies people and organizations of the death. Also called "personal representative."

express warranty

An assurance or promise made by a contracting party or a guarantee about the quality of goods or services made by a seller, such as, "This item is guaranteed against defects in construction for one year." Most express warranties come directly from the manufacturer or are included in the sales contract.

expunge

To intentionally destroy, obliterate, or strike out records or information in files, computers, and other depositories. For example, state law might allow the criminal records of a juvenile offender to be expunged when he reaches the age of majority to allow him to begin his adult life with a clean record. Or, a company or government agency might routinely expunge out-of-date records to save storage space.

failure of consideration

The refusal or inability of a contracting party to perform its side of a bargain.

failure of issue

A situation in which a person dies without children or other descendants who could have inherited property.

fair use rule

A copyright principle that excuses unauthorized uses of a work when used for a transformative purpose such as research, scholarship, parody, criticism, or journalism. When determining whether an infringement should be excused on the basis of fair use, a court will use several factors including the purpose and character of the use, amount and substantiality of the portion borrowed, and effect of the use on the market for the copyrighted material. Fair use is a defense rather than an affirmative right—that is, a particular use only gets established as a fair use if the copyright owner decides to file a lawsuit and the court upholds the fair use defense.

false imprisonment

The wrongful, intentional restraint of another person without the legal right to do so. False imprisonment can involve actual physical restraint, such as locking someone in a car or tying a person to a chair. But it's not necessary that physical force be used. Threats or a show of apparent authority are sufficient. False imprisonment can be both a misdemeanor (a crime that results in jail time) and a tort (a civil wrong that leads to damages liability). If the perpetrator confines the victim for a substantial period of time (or moves the victim a significant distance) in order to commit a felony, the false imprisonment may become a kidnapping. People who are arrested and get the charges dropped, or are later acquitted, often think that they can sue the arresting officer for false arrest, a kind of false imprisonment. These lawsuits rarely succeed: As long as the officer had probable cause to arrest the person, the officer won't be liable for a false arrest, even if it turns out later that the information the officer relied upon was incorrect.

family court

A separate court or a separate division of the regular state trial court that considers only cases involving family-related issues, which could include divorce, child custody and support, guardianship, adoption, and the issuance of restraining orders in domestic violence cases.

fault divorce

A tradition that required one spouse to prove that the other spouse was legally at fault, to obtain a divorce. The "innocent" spouse was then granted the divorce from the "guilty" spouse. The traditional fault grounds for divorce are adultery, cruelty, desertion, confinement in prison, physical incapacity, and incurable insanity. Today, all states offer no-fault divorce, but quite a few states also still allow a spouse to allege fault in obtaining a divorce, and some states also allow the court to consider fault in dividing property or awarding custody or visitation.

federal court

A branch of the U.S. government with power derived directly from the U.S. Constitution. Federal courts decide cases involving the U.S. Constitution, federal law—for example, patents, federal taxes, labor law, and federal crimes, such as robbing a federally chartered bank—and cases where the parties are from different states and are involved in a dispute for $75,000 or more.

felony

A serious crime (contrasted with misdemeanors and infractions, less serious crimes), usually punishable by a prison term of more than one year or, in some cases, by death. For example, murder, extortion, and kidnapping are felonies; a minor fistfight is usually charged as a misdemeanor, and a speeding ticket is generally an infraction. In some states, certain crimes (known as "wobblers") can be charged as both a misdemeanor and a felony, and the eventual designation depends on the defendant's ability to fulfill the conditions of his sentence.

Feres doctrine

A legal doctrine that prevents people who are injured as a result of military service from successfully suing the federal government under the Federal Tort Claims Act. The doctrine comes from the U.S. Supreme Court case *Feres v. United States*, in which service members who picked up highly radioactive weapons fragments from a crashed airplane weren't permitted to recover damages from the government. Also known as the "*Feres-Stencel* doctrine" or the "*Feres* rule."

fictitious name

Fictitious names are often used in conducting a business. They are also be used when filing a lawsuit against a party whose real name is unknown or when it is appropriate to conceal the true name of the party.

fieri facias

Latin for "that you cause to be done." This court document instructs a sheriff to seize and sell a defendant's property to satisfy a monetary judgment against the defendant.

final beneficiary

The person or institution designated to receive trust property upon the death of a life beneficiary. For example, Jim creates a trust through which his wife, Jane, receives income for the duration of her life. Their daughter, the final beneficiary, receives the trust principal after Jane's death.

forbearance

Voluntarily refraining from doing something, such as asserting a legal right. For example, a creditor might forbear on its right to collect a debt by temporarily postponing or reducing the borrower's payments.

foreclosure

The legal process by which a creditor with a claim (lien) on real estate forces a sale of the property to collect on the debt. Foreclosure typically begins when a homeowner falls behind on mortgage payments for several months.

forfeiture

The loss of property or a privilege due to breaking the law. For example, a landlord could forfeit property to the federal or state government if the landlord knows it is a drug-dealing site but fails to stop the illegal activity.

form interrogatories

Preprinted sets of questions that one party in a lawsuit asks an opposing party. Form interrogatories cover the issues commonly encountered in the kind of lawsuit at hand. For example, there are form interrogatories designed for contract disputes, landlord-tenant cases, personal injury cases, and others. Form interrogatories are often supplemented by questions written by the lawyers and designed for the particular issues in the case.

forum

Refers to the court in which a lawsuit is filed or in which a hearing or trial is conducted. The appropriate forum depends on which court has personal jurisdiction over the parties and the subject matter of the case.

forum nonconveniens

Latin for "inconvenient court." The idea that a court may change the venue of a lawsuit if that is more convenient for the parties. However, because strict written rules of jurisdiction and venue are used to decide where a case can and can't be properly filed, this term has largely lost any real meaning.

forum shopping

The process by which a plaintiff chooses among two or more courts that have the power—technically, the correct jurisdiction and venue—to consider their case. This decision is based on which court is likely to consider the case most favorably. In some instances, a case can properly be filed in two or more federal district courts as well as in the trial courts of several states—and this makes forum shopping a complicated business. It often involves weighing several factors, including proximity to the court, the judge's reputation in the particular legal area, the likely type of available jurors, and subtle differences in governing law and procedure.

fraud

Intentionally deceiving someone and causing that person to suffer a loss. Fraud includes lies and half-truths, such as selling a car that is a lemon and claiming "she runs like a dream." Fraud can be the basis of a civil lawsuit for damages and for prosecution as a crime.

future interest

A right to property that cannot be enforced in the present, but only at some time in the future. For example, John's will leaves his house to his sister Marian, but only after the death of his wife, Hillary. Marian has a future interest in the house.

garnishment

A court-ordered process for taking money from a person to satisfy a debt. For example, a debtor's wages might be garnished 25% or more to pay child support, back taxes, or a lawsuit judgment.

general partner

A person who joins with at least one other to own and operate a business for profit—and who is personally liable for all the business's debts (unlike the owners of a corporation). A general partner's actions can legally bind the entire business. For example, if one partner signs a contract on behalf of the partnership, it will be fully enforceable against the partnership and each individual partner, even if the other partners weren't consulted in advance. In contrast, a limited partner is liable only to the extent of the capital invested in the business. The term "general partner" can also refer to the managing partner of a limited partnership who is responsible for partnership debts over and above the individual partnership investment. See also *partnership, limited partnership.*

general power of attorney

See *power of attorney.*

grand jury

A group of people chosen at random that regularly hears evidence brought by a prosecutor. The prosecutor presents evidence against a person the prosecutor thinks will justify an indictment (formal charges) and a trial. Unlike petit juries, grand juries meet in secret, needn't reach unanimous decisions, and don't decide on a person's guilt. They only decide whether the person should stand trial.

grandfather clause

A provision in a new law that limits its application to individuals or businesses that are new to the system, while those already in the system are exempt from the new regulation. For example, when Washington, D.C., raised its drinking age from 18 to 21, people between those ages who could drink under the old law were allowed to retain the right to legally consume alcohol under a grandfather clause.

grant deed

A deed containing an implied promise that the person transferring the property has good title and that the property isn't encumbered in any way except as described in the deed. This is the most commonly used type of deed. Compare *quitclaim deed*.

gravamen

The essential element of a lawsuit. For example, the gravamen of a lawsuit involving a car accident might be the careless driving or "negligence" of the defendant.

gross lease

A commercial real estate lease in which the tenant pays a fixed amount of rent per month or year, regardless of the landlord's operating costs, such as maintenance, taxes, and insurance. A gross lease closely resembles a typical residential lease. The tenant can agree to a "gross lease with stops," meaning that the tenant will pitch in if the landlord's operating costs rise above a certain level. In real estate lingo, the point when the tenant starts to contribute is called the "stop level," because that's where the landlord's share of the costs stops.

guarantor

A person or entity that makes a legally binding promise to be responsible for another's debt or performance under a contract if the other defaults or fails to perform. The guarantor gives a "guaranty," which is an assurance that the debt or other obligation will be fulfilled.

guaranty

When used as a verb, to agree to pay another person's debt or perform another person's duty, if that person fails to come through. As a noun, the written document in which this assurance is made. For example, if you cosign a loan, you have made a guaranty and will be legally responsible for the debt if the borrower fails to repay the money as promised. The person who makes a guaranty is called the "guarantor." Also known as a "guarantee" or "warranty."

guardian

An adult appointed by a court to control and care for a minor or the minor's property. Someone who looks after a child's property is usually called a "guardian of the estate." An adult who has legal authority to make personal decisions for the child, including responsibility for his physical, medical, and educational needs, is often called a "guardian of the person." Sometimes just one person will be named to take care of all these tasks. An individual appointed by a court to look after an incapacitated adult may also be known as a "guardian" but is more frequently called a "conservator."

guardian *ad litem*

A person, not necessarily a lawyer, who is appointed by a court to represent and protect the interests of a child or an incapacitated adult during a lawsuit. For example, a minor party to a civil lawsuit must have a guardian *ad litem*—often a parent—to act on the minor's behalf regarding decisions like whether or not to accept a settlement offer. A nonparental guardian *ad litem* might be appointed to represent a child whose parents are locked in a contentious custody battle.

guardianship

A legal relationship created by a court between a guardian and a
ward—either a minor child or an incapacitated adult (also known as
a "conservatorship"). The guardian has a legal right and duty to care
for the ward. This responsibility typically involves making personal
decisions on the ward's behalf and managing property.

habeas corpus

Latin for "You have the body." A prisoner files a petition for writ of
habeas corpus to challenge the authority of the prison or jail warden
to keep the prisoner in custody. If the judge orders a hearing after
reading the writ, the prisoner can argue that the confinement is
illegal. *Habeas corpus* is an important protection against illegal
confinement, once called "the great writ." For example, it can be
used in cases where a person is being held without charges, or when
due process obviously has been denied, bail is excessive, parole has
been granted, an accused has been improperly surrendered by the
bail bondsman, or probation has been summarily terminated without
cause. A particularly frequent use of *habeas* writs is by convicted
prisoners arguing that the trial attorney failed to prepare the defense
and was incompetent. Prisoners sentenced to death also file *habeas*
petitions challenging the constitutionality of the state death penalty
law. Note that *habeas* writs are different from and don't replace
appeals, which are arguments for reversal of a conviction based
on claims that the judge conducted the trial improperly. Often,
convicted prisoners file both.

hearing

Any proceeding before a judge or other qualified hearing officer
without a jury in which evidence and argument is presented to
determine some issue of fact or both issues of fact and law. The term
usually refers to a brief court session that resolves a specific question
before a full trial takes place or to such specialized proceedings as
administrative hearings. In criminal law, a "preliminary hearing"
is held before a judge to determine whether the prosecutor has

presented sufficient evidence that a crime has occurred to hold the accused for trial.

hearsay rule

A rule of evidence that prohibits the use of out-of-court statements offered as proof of the subject of the statement. These statements aren't admitted as evidence because the person who made the statement isn't in court for the other party to cross-examine. For example, if Cathy, an eyewitness to an accident, later tells Betsy that the pickup ran the light, Betsy wouldn't be allowed to recount Cathy's remarks. However, out-of-court statements that aren't offered to prove the truth of the statement are admissible. Suppose Tom is called to testify, "On January 1, Bob said the Steelers stink." If the party calling Tom wants to prove that Bob was alive on January 1, Tom's testimony would be admitted because the other side could question Tom about whether the conversation took place on that date. Whether the Steelers are a poor team is beside the point. Even statements that are hearsay can be admitted if they fall within one of the many exceptions to the rule. In general, hearsay will be admitted if the circumstances of the statement indicate a high probability that the statement is true. For example, a statement uttered spontaneously and under duress—such as a victim's remarks immediately following an accident—could be admitted because the judge might find that the person had little time to plan to say anything other than the truth.

heir

Someone who has a right, under state law, to inherit a deceased person's property (which means the closest family members). The term is often used in a broader sense to include anyone who receives property from the estate of a deceased person.

heir apparent

A person expected to inherit property from the estate of a family member.

heir at law

A person entitled to inherit property under intestate succession laws.

hold harmless

In a contract, a promise by one party not to hold the other party responsible if the other party carries out the contract in a way that causes damage to the first party. For example, many leases include a hold harmless clause in which the tenant agrees not to sue the landlord if the tenant is injured due to the landlord's failure to maintain the premises. In most states, these clauses are illegal in residential tenancies but might be upheld in commercial settings.

holographic will

A will that is completely handwritten, dated, and signed by the person making it. Holographic wills are generally not witnessed and can be in the form of a letter. Although legal in many states, making a holographic will is never advised except as a last resort.

homestead

1. The house in which a family lives, plus any adjoining land and other buildings on that land.
2. Real estate not subject to the claims of creditors as long as it is occupied as a home by the head of the household. After the head of the family dies, homestead laws often allow the surviving spouse or minor children to live on the property for as long as they choose.
3. Land acquired out of the public lands of the United States. The term "homesteaders" refers to people who got their land by settling it and making it productive, rather than purchasing it outright.

homestead declaration

A form filed with the county recorder's office to put on record your right to a homestead exemption. In most states, the homestead exemption is automatic and the owner isn't required to record a homestead declaration to claim the homestead exemption. However, a few states require recorded homestead declarations.

homicide

The killing of one human being by the act or omission of another. The term applies to all such killings, whether criminal or not. Homicide is noncriminal in some situations, including deaths as the result of war and putting someone to death by the valid sentence of a court. Killing can also be legally justified or excused, as it is in cases of self-defense or when someone is killed by another person who is attempting to prevent a violent felony. Criminal homicide occurs when a person purposely, knowingly, recklessly, or negligently causes the death of another. Murder and manslaughter are both examples of criminal homicide.

hung jury

A jury unable to come to a final decision, resulting in a mistrial. Judges do their best to avoid hung juries, typically sending juries back into deliberations with an assurance (sometimes known as a "dynamite charge") that they will be able to reach a decision if they try harder. If a mistrial is declared, the case is tried again unless the parties settle the case (in a civil case) or the prosecution dismisses the charges or offers a plea bargain (in a criminal case).

illusory promise

A promise that pledges nothing because it is vague or because the promisor can choose whether or not to honor it. Such promises aren't legally binding.

impeach

1. To discredit; for example, to show that a witness isn't believable—perhaps because the witness made statements that are inconsistent with their present testimony, or has a reputation for not being a truthful person.
2. The process of charging a public official, such as the U.S. president or a federal judge, with a crime or misconduct, which results in a trial to determine whether the official should be sanctioned or removed from office. Under the U.S. Constitution, impeachment is

a political, not a criminal, proceeding. Officials are impeached—charged with misconduct—by the House of Representatives (U.S. Const. art. I, § 2, cl. 5) and are tried by the Senate. (U.S. Const. art. I, § 3, cl. 6.)

implied warranty

A guarantee about the quality of goods or services purchased that isn't written down or explicitly spoken. Virtually everything you buy comes with two implied warranties, one for "merchantability" and one for "fitness." The implied warranty of merchantability is an assurance that a new item will work for its specified purpose. The item doesn't have to work wonderfully, and if you use it for something it wasn't designed for, say trimming shrubs with an electric carving knife, the warranty doesn't apply. The implied warranty of fitness applies when you buy an item for a specific purpose. If you notified the seller of your specific needs, the item is guaranteed to meet them. For example, if you buy new tires for your bicycle after telling the store clerk that you plan to use them for mountain cycling and the tires puncture when you pass over a small rock, the tires don't conform to the warranty of fitness.

implied warranty of habitability

A legal doctrine that requires landlords to offer and maintain livable premises for their tenants. If a landlord fails to provide habitable housing, tenants in most states can legally withhold rent or take other measures, including hiring someone to fix the problem or moving out. See *constructive eviction.*

in camera

Latin for "in chambers." A legal proceeding is *in camera* when a hearing is held before the judge in their private chambers or when the public is excluded from the courtroom. Proceedings are often held *in camera* to protect victims and witnesses from public exposure, especially if the victim or witness is a child. There is still, however, a record made of the proceeding, typically by a court stenographer. The judge will seal this record if the material is extremely sensitive or likely to prejudice one side.

in terrorem clause

Latin meaning "in fear." This phrase is used to describe provisions in contracts or wills meant to scare a person into complying with the terms of the agreement. For example, a will might state that an heir who challenges the will's validity forfeits inheritance. If the will is challenged and found invalid, the clause itself will also be invalid, and the heir will take whatever they would have inherited if there had been no will.

in toto

Latin for "in its entirety" or "completely." For example, a judge who accepts a lawyer's argument *in toto* agrees with it entirely.

inadmissible evidence

Testimony or other evidence that fails to meet state or federal court rules governing the types of evidence that can be presented to a judge or jury. The main reason that evidence is ruled inadmissible is that it falls into a category considered so unreliable that a court shouldn't consider it as part of deciding a case—for example, hearsay evidence or an expert's opinion that isn't based on facts generally accepted in the field. Evidence will also be declared inadmissible if it suffers from some other defect—for example, as compared to its value, it will take too long to present or risks inflaming the jury, as might be the case with graphic pictures of a homicide victim. In criminal cases, evidence gathered using illegal methods is commonly ruled inadmissible. See *evidence, admissible evidence.*

incapacity

1. A lack of physical or mental abilities that results in a person's inability to manage personal care, property, or finances.
2. A lack of ability to understand one's actions when making a will or another legal document.

3. The inability of an injured worker to perform a job. This might qualify the worker for disability benefits or workers' compensation.
4. Under the Family Medical Leave Act (FMLA), the inability to work, attend school, or perform other regular daily activities due to a serious health condition, or because of treatment for or recovery from the condition.

indispensable party

A person or an entity (such as a corporation) that must be included in a lawsuit for the court to render a final judgment. For example, if a person sues his neighbors to force them to prune a tree that poses a danger to his house, the lawsuit must name all owners of the relevant property.

information

The name of the document, sometimes called a "criminal complaint" or "petition," in which a prosecutor charges a criminal defendant with a crime, either a felony or a misdemeanor. The information tells the defendant the crime charged, against whom, and when the offense allegedly occurred. The prosecutor isn't obliged to go into great detail. A defendant who wants more specifics must ask for it through a discovery request.

informed consent

An agreement to do something or to allow something to happen, made with complete knowledge of all relevant facts, such as the risks involved or any available alternatives. For example, a patient can give informed consent to medical treatment only after the health care professional has disclosed all possible risks involved in accepting or rejecting the treatment. A health care provider or facility can be held responsible for an injury caused by an undisclosed risk. In another context, a person accused of committing a crime can't give up constitutional rights—for example, to remain silent or to talk with an attorney—unless and until being informed of those rights, usually via the well-known *Miranda* warnings.

infraction

A minor violation of the law that is punishable by a fine—for example, a traffic or parking ticket.

injunction

A court decision commanding or preventing a specific act, such as an order that an abusive spouse stay away from the other spouse or that a logging company not cut down first-growth trees. Courts grant injunctions to prevent harm, often irreparable harm, as distinguished from most court decisions, which are designed to provide a remedy for harm that has already occurred. Injunctions can be temporary, pending a consideration of the issue later at trial (these are called "interlocutory decrees" or "preliminary injunctions"). Judges can also issue permanent injunctions at the end of trials.

injunctive relief

A court-ordered act or prohibition against an act that has been requested in a petition to the court for an injunction. Usually, injunctive relief is granted only after a hearing at which both sides can present testimony and legal arguments.

intangible property

Personal property without physical existence, such as stocks, bonds, bank notes, trade secrets, patents, copyrights, and trademarks. Such "untouchable" items can be represented by a certificate or license that fixes or approximates the value, but others (such as the goodwill or reputation of a business) aren't easily valued or embodied in any instrument. Compare *tangible personal property*.

intellectual property law

The area of law that regulates the ownership and use of property, such as books, inventions, business secrets, and trademarks, that, unlike real or personal property, are created by the human mind. Patent, copyright, trademark, and trade secret laws (jointly called "intellectual property laws") typically protect intellectual property.

intentional tort

A deliberate act that causes harm to another, for which the victim can sue the wrongdoer for damages. The term "tort" means a wrongful act that causes injury. While most "tort" (or personal injury) cases are based on one person's careless or negligent conduct (such as cases arising from a car accident), intentional torts stem from purposeful action. Acts of domestic violence, such as assault, are intentional torts (as well as crimes). Other common intentional torts include battery, false imprisonment, and intentional infliction of emotional distress.

inter vivos trust

The Latin name, favored by some lawyers, for a living trust. *Inter vivos* is Latin for "between the living."

interlocutory decree

A court judgment that isn't final until the judge decides other matters or until enough time has passed to determine if an interim decision is working. In the past, interlocutory decrees were often used in divorce. The divorce terms were included in an interlocutory decree, which would become final only after a waiting period to allow the couple time to reconcile. Most states no longer use interlocutory decrees of divorce.

interrogatory

Written questions about the facts of a case that an opposing party must answer under penalty of perjury. Lawyers can write "special" interrogatory questions or use pre-prepared form interrogatories that cover issues common in lawsuits. Each side can send a limited number of interrogatories to other parties (but not nonparty witnesses) during a lawsuit's discovery phase.

intestate

The condition of dying without a valid will. The probate court appoints an administrator to distribute the deceased person's property according to state law.

intestate succession

The method by which property is distributed when a person dies
without a valid will. Each state's law provides that the property
be distributed to the closest surviving relatives. In most states, the
surviving spouse, children, parents, siblings, nieces and nephews,
and next of kin inherit, in that order.

inure

To take effect, or to benefit someone. In property law, the term means
"to vest." For example, Jim buys a beach house that includes the right
to travel across the neighbor's property to get to the water. That right
of way is said, cryptically, "to inure to the benefit of Jim."

invitee

A business guest or someone who enters property held open to
members of the public, such as a visitor to a museum. Property
owners must protect invitees from dangers on the property. Social
guests that you invite into your home are called "licensees."

ipse dixit

Latin for "he himself said it." A statement that, while unsupported
and unproven, might carry some weight based solely on the authority
or standing of the person or court that issued it.

ipso facto

Latin for "by the fact itself." This term is used by Latin-addicted
lawyers when something is so obvious that it needs no elaboration
or further explanation. A simple example: A blind person, *ipso facto*,
can't obtain a driver's license.

irrevocable trust

A permanent trust. Once it is created, it can't be revoked, amended,
or changed unless a court finds that a change is necessary for the
trust to serve the purpose for which it was created.

issue

A term generally for all your children and their children down through the generations, including grandchildren, great-grandchildren, and so on. Also called "lineal descendants."

JNOV

See *judgment notwithstanding the verdict.*

joint tenancy

A way for two or more people to share ownership of real estate or other property. In almost all states, the co-owners (called "joint tenants") must own equal shares of the property. When one joint tenant dies, the other owners automatically own the deceased owner's share. For example, if spouses own a house as joint tenants and one dies, the survivor automatically becomes full owner. Because of this right of survivorship, the property goes directly to the surviving joint tenants without the delay and costs of probate.

judgment

A final court ruling resolving the key questions in a lawsuit and determining the rights and obligations of the parties. For example, after a trial involving a vehicle accident, a court will issue a judgment determining the fault of the parties and how much money must be paid.

judgment notwithstanding the verdict (JNOV)

Reversal of a jury's verdict by a judge when the judge believes that there were insufficient facts on which to base the jury's verdict or that the verdict didn't correctly apply the law. This procedure is similar to a situation in which a judge arrives at a particular verdict, called a "directed verdict."

jurisdiction

The authority of a court to hear and decide a case. To make a legally valid decision in a case, a court must have both "subject matter jurisdiction," or the power to hear the type of case in question, and "personal jurisdiction," or the power to make a decision affecting the parties involved in the lawsuit. Jurisdiction is also commonly used to define the amount a court can award. For example, small claims courts have jurisdiction only to hear cases up to a relatively low monetary amount. A court that "lacks jurisdiction" in a required area doesn't have the power to render a decision.

jury nullification

A jury's decision to acquit a defendant who has violated a law the jury believes is unjust or wrong. Jury nullification most commonly occurs in criminal cases when the jury disagrees with the punishment. Nullification was evident during the Vietnam War when juries acquitted Selective Service protesters opposed to the war. More recently, jury nullification occurred in California "three strikes" cases when the jury realized the conviction of a relatively minor offense would result in lifetime imprisonment.

jus naturale

Latin for "natural law." A system of legal principles ostensibly derived from universal divine truths.

kindred

Under some states' probate codes, all relatives of a deceased person.

larceny

Another term for theft. Although the definition of this term differs between states, it typically means taking property belonging to another with the intent to permanently deprive the owner of it. If the taking is nonforceful, it is larceny; if it is accompanied by force or fear directed against a person, it is robbery, a more serious offense.

lawful issue

Formerly, statutes governing wills used this phrase to specify children born to married parents and to exclude those born out of wedlock. Now, the phrase means the same as issue and "lineal descendant."

lease

An oral or written agreement (a contract) between two people concerning the use by one of the property of the other. A person can lease real estate (such as an apartment or business property) or personal property (such as a car or a boat). A lease should cover basic issues such as when the lease will begin and end, the rent or other costs, how to make payments, and any restrictions on the use of the property. The property owner is often called the "lessor," and the person using the property is called the "lessee."

legacy

An outdated legal word meaning personal property left by a will. The more common term for this type of property is "bequest." Compare *devise*.

legislative immunity

A legal doctrine that prevents legislators from being sued for actions performed and decisions made while serving in government. This doctrine doesn't protect legislators from criminal prosecution, nor does it relieve them from responsibility for actions outside the scope of their office, such as the nefarious activities of former Senator Bob Packwood back in the 1990s.

letters testamentary

The document given to an executor by the probate court authorizing the executor to settle the estate according to a will or the state's intestate succession laws.

lex loci

Latin for the "law of the place." It means local law.

liability

The state of being legally responsible for something. For instance, something a person or company owes, such as money, payroll taxes, a court judgment, an account payable, or a loan debt.

libel

An untruthful statement about a person, published in writing or through broadcast media that injures the person's reputation or standing in the community. Libel is a "tort" or civil wrong, and the injured person can file a lawsuit against the person who made the false statement. Slander is an spoken untruthful statement that isn't published in writing or broadcast through the media. Libel and slander are considered forms of defamation.

lien

A creditor's legal claim against particular property owned by a debtor as security for a debt. Liens the debtor agrees to, called "security interests," include mortgages, home equity loans, car loans, and personal loans for which the debtor pledges property as collateral. Nonconsensual liens are liens placed on property without the debtor's consent and include tax liens, judgment liens (liens a creditor obtains by suing and getting a court judgment against the debtor), and mechanics' liens (liens filed by a contractor who worked on the debtor's house but didn't get paid).

life beneficiary

A person who receives benefits, under a trust or by will, for their lifetime.

limited liability

The maximum amount a business owner can lose if the business is subject to debts, claims, or other liabilities. An owner of a limited liability company or a person who invests in a corporation (a shareholder) generally stands to lose only the amount of money invested in the business. If the limited liability company or corporation folds, creditors can't seize or sell an owner's home, car, or other personal assets. (This is known as "limited personal liability.") By contrast, owners of a sole proprietorship or general partnership have unlimited liability for business debts, as do the general partners in a limited partnership and limited partners who manage the business.

limited liability company (LLC)

A relatively new and flexible business ownership structure. Particularly popular with small businesses, the LLC offers its owners the advantage of limited personal liability (like a corporation) and a choice of how the business will be taxed. Partners can choose for the LLC to be taxed as a separate entity (again, like a corporation) or as a partnership-like entity in which profits are passed through to partners and taxed on their personal income tax returns. Although state laws governing the creation of LLCs and IRS regulations controlling their federal tax status are still evolving, LLCs are increasingly regarded as the small business legal entity of choice because of their flexibility.

limited liability partnership (LLP)

A type of partnership recognized in most states that protects a partner from personal liability for negligent acts committed by other partners or by employees not under their direct control. Many states restrict this partnership to professionals, such as lawyers, accountants, architects, and health care providers.

limited partnership

A business structure that allows one or more partners (called "limited partners") to enjoy limited personal liability for partnership debts while another partner or partners (called "general partners") have unlimited personal liability. The key difference between a general and limited partner concerns management decision making: General partners run the business. Limited partners, usually passive investors, can't make day-to-day business decisions. They risk being treated as general partners with unlimited personal liability if they do.

lis pendens

Latin for "a suit pending." The term refers to a written notice of a real estate lawsuit involving the property title or encumbrances. The plaintiff usually files the notice in the county land records office. Recording a *lis pendens* alerts a potential purchaser or lender that the property's title is in question.

living trust

A trust you can set up during your life. Living trusts are an excellent way to avoid the cost and hassle of probate because, after the death of the trust's founder, the property you transfer into the trust during your life passes directly to the trust beneficiaries after you die, without court involvement. The successor trustee—the person you appoint to handle the trust after your death—simply transfers ownership to the beneficiaries you named in the trust. Living trusts are also called "*inter vivos* trusts."

living will

A legal document in which you state your wishes about certain kinds of medical treatments and life-prolonging procedures. The document takes effect if you can't communicate your health care decisions when they must be made. A living will can also be called a "health care directive," "advance directive," or "directive to physicians."

malfeasance

Doing something illegal. This term is often used when a professional or public official commits an illegal act that interferes with the performance of duties. For example, an elected official who accepts a bribe in exchange for political favors has committed malfeasance. Compare *misfeasance*.

malpractice

The delivery of substandard care or services by a lawyer, doctor, dentist, accountant, or other professional. Generally, malpractice occurs when a professional fails to provide the quality of care that should reasonably be expected, resulting in patient or client harm. In a legal malpractice case, you must prove harm and that if the lawyer had handled the work properly, you would have won the case.

mandamus

Latin for "we command." A writ of *mandamus* is a court order that requires another court, government official, public body, corporation, or individual to perform a certain act. For example, after a hearing,

a court might issue a writ of *mandamus* forcing a public school
to admit certain students on the grounds that the school illegally
discriminated against them when it denied them admission. A writ
of *mandamus* is the opposite of an order to cease and desist, or stop
doing something. Also called a "writ of mandate."

marital property

Most of the property that spouses accumulate during a marriage
is called "community property" in some states. States differ as to
precisely what is included in marital property. Some states include
all property and earnings during the marriage, while others exclude
gifts and inheritances.

mechanic's lien

A legal claim placed on real estate by someone who is owed money
for labor, services, or supplies contributed to the property for the purpose of improving it. Typical lien claimants are general contractors,
subcontractors, and suppliers of building materials. A mechanic's lien
claimant can sue to have the real estate sold at auction and recover
the debt from the proceeds. Property with a lien on it can't be easily
sold until the lien is paid.

mediation

A conflict resolution method designed to help parties resolve disputes
without going to court. In mediation, a neutral third party (the mediator)
meets with the opposing sides to help them find a mutually satisfactory
solution. Unlike a judge in a courtroom or an arbitrator conducting
a binding arbitration, the mediator can't impose a solution. No formal
rules of evidence or procedure control mediation. The mediator and
the parties usually agree on an informal way to proceed.

mens rea

The mental component of criminal liability. To be guilty of most
crimes, a defendant must have committed the criminal act (the *actus
reus*) in a certain mental state (the *mens rea*). For example, the *mens rea*
of robbery is the intent to permanently deprive the owner of property.

minimum contacts

A requirement that must be satisfied before suing a defendant in a particular state. For the suit to go forward in the chosen state, the defendant must have some connections with that state. For example, advertising or having business offices within a state can provide minimum contacts between a company and the state.

minor

In most states, any person under 18 years of age. All minors must be under the care of a competent adult (parent or guardian) unless they are "emancipated"—in the military, married, or living independently with court permission. An adult must handle property left to a minor until the minor becomes an adult.

***Miranda* warning**

The warnings that law enforcement must give to a criminal suspect under arrest or in custody and about to be questioned. If the prosecution wants to use the suspect's statements in court, the prosecutor must prove that the suspect understood and knowingly "waived" or gave up certain rights. "*Miranda* rights" include the right to remain silent, the right to have a lawyer present during questioning, and the right to a court-appointed attorney if they can't afford one. In addition, the suspect must be told that anything they say can be used in court. To prove that a suspect understood and knowingly gave up these rights, police routinely give a *Miranda* warning before the suspect is arrested or questioned. Giving the *Miranda* warning is also known as "reading a suspect their rights."

misdemeanor

A crime less serious than a felony and punishable by no more than one year in jail. Petty theft (of articles worth less than a certain amount), first-time drunk driving, and leaving the scene of an accident are all common misdemeanors.

misfeasance

Performing a legal action improperly. This term is frequently used when a professional or public official does his job in a way that is not technically illegal, but is nevertheless mistaken or wrong.

Here are some examples of misfeasance in a professional context: a lawyer who is mistaken about a deadline and files an important legal document too late, an accountant who makes unintentional errors on a client's tax return, or a doctor who writes a prescription and accidentally includes the wrong dosage. Compare *malfeasance*.

mistrial

A trial that ends prematurely and without a judgment, due either to a mistake that jeopardizes a party's right to a fair trial or to a jury that can't agree on a verdict (a hung jury). A judge who declares a mistrial in a civil case will direct the case to be set for a new trial at a future date. Mistrials in criminal cases can result in a retrial, a plea bargain, or a dismissal of the charges.

motion

During a lawsuit, a request to the judge for a decision—called an "order" or "ruling"—to resolve procedural or other issues that come up during litigation. For example, after receiving hundreds of irrelevant interrogatories, a party might file a motion asking that the other side be ordered to stop engaging in unduly burdensome discovery. A motion can be made before, during, or after trial. Typically, one party submits a written motion to the court, at which point the other party can file a written response. The court then often schedules a hearing at which each side delivers a short oral argument. The court then approves or denies the motion.

motion *in limine*

A request was submitted to the court before trial to exclude evidence from the proceedings. A motion *in limine* is usually made by a party when simply mentioning the evidence would prejudice the jury against that party, even if the judge later instructed the jury to disregard the evidence. For example, if a defendant in a criminal trial were questioned and confessed to the crime without having been read his *Miranda* rights, his lawyer would file a motion *in limine* to keep evidence of the confession out of the trial.

natural person

A living, breathing human being, as opposed to a legal entity such as a corporation. Different rules and protections apply to natural persons and corporations, such as the Fifth Amendment right against self-incrimination, which applies only to natural persons.

naturalization

The process by which a foreign person becomes a U.S. citizen. Almost everyone who goes through naturalization must first have held a green card for several years. A naturalized U.S. citizen has the same rights as a native-born American citizen.

negotiable instrument

A written document that represents an unconditional promise to pay a specified amount of money upon the demand of its owner. Examples include checks and promissory notes. Negotiable instruments can be transferred from one person to another, as when you write "pay to the order of" on the back of a check and turn it over to someone else.

net lease

A commercial real estate lease in which the tenant regularly pays not only for the space (as in a gross lease) but also for a portion of the landlord's operating costs. When all three of the usual costs—taxes, maintenance, and insurance—are passed on, the arrangement is known as a "triple net lease." A net lease favors the landlord because these costs are variable and almost never decrease. Accordingly, it might be possible for a tenant to bargain for a net lease with caps or ceilings, limiting the rent the tenant must pay. For example, a net lease with caps can specify that the landlord will pay an increase in taxes beyond a certain point (or any new taxes). The same protection can be designed to cover increased insurance premiums and maintenance expenses.

no-fault divorce

Any divorce in which one spouse doesn't have to accuse the other of wrongdoing and can simply state that the couple no longer gets along. Until no-fault divorce arrived in the 1970s, the only way a person could get a divorce was to prove that the other spouse was at fault for the marriage not working. No-fault divorces are usually granted for incompatibility, irreconcilable differences, or irretrievable or irremediable breakdown of the marriage. Also, some states allow incurable insanity as a basis for a no-fault divorce. Compare *fault divorce*.

nolle prosequi

Latin for "we shall no longer prosecute." At trial, this is an entry made on the record by a prosecutor in a criminal case stating that they will no longer pursue the matter. An entry of *nolle prosequi* can be made at any time after charges are brought and before a verdict is returned or a plea entered. Essentially, it is an admission on the part of the prosecution that some aspect of its case against the defendant has fallen apart. Abbreviated "*nol. pros.*" or "*nol—pros.*" Prosecutors often need a judge's permission to "*nol—pros.*" a case.

nolo contendere

Latin for "I will not defend it." A plea entered by the defendant in response to being charged with a crime. When defendants plead *nolo contendere*, they neither admit nor deny that they committed the crime but agree to a punishment (usually a fine or jail time) as if guilty. Usually, this type of plea is entered because it can't be used as an admission of guilt in a civil suit against the defendant. By not admitting guilt during the criminal trial, the defendant can defend the civil case without explaining such an admission.

nondischargeable debts

Debts that can't be erased by filing for bankruptcy. If you file for Chapter 7 bankruptcy, these debts will remain when your case is over. If you file for Chapter 13 bankruptcy, the nondischargeable debts will have to be paid in full during your plan, or you will have a balance at the end of your case. Examples of nondischargeable debts include alimony and child support, most income tax debts, many student loans, and debts for personal injury or death caused by drunk driving. Compare *dischargeable debts*.

nondisclosure agreement

A legally binding contract in which a person or business promises to treat specific information as a trade secret and not disclose it to others without proper authorization. Nondisclosure agreements are often used when a business discloses a trade secret to a person or another business for such purposes as development, marketing, evaluation, or securing financial backing. Although nondisclosure agreements are usually in the form of written contracts, they can also be implied if the context of a business relationship suggests that the parties intended to make an agreement. For example, a business that conducts patent searches for inventors is expected to keep information about the invention secret, even if no written agreement is signed, because the nature of the business is to deal in confidential information.

nonprofit corporation

A legal structure authorized by state law allowing people to come together to benefit members of an organization (a club or mutual benefit society) or for some public purpose (such as supporting a hospital, an environmental organization, or a literary society). Nonprofit corporations, despite the name, can make a profit. Still, the business can't be designed primarily for profit-making purposes. The profits must be used for the benefit of the organization or purpose the corporation was created to help. When a nonprofit corporation dissolves, any remaining assets must be distributed to another nonprofit, not to board members. As with for-profit corporations, directors of nonprofit corporations are typically shielded from personal liability for the organization's debts. Some nonprofit corporations qualify for a federal tax exemption under Section 501(c)(3) of the Internal Revenue Code, with the result that contributions to the nonprofit are tax deductible by their donors.

novation

The substitution of a new contract for an old one. A novation might change one of the parties to the contract or the duties that must be performed by the original parties.

nuisance

Something that interferes with the use of property by being irritating, offensive, obstructive, or dangerous. Nuisances include various conditions, from a chemical plant's noxious odors to a neighbor's dog barking. The former would be a "public nuisance" affecting many people. The other would be a "private nuisance" bothering an individual or small group. Lawsuits can be brought to abate (remove or reduce) a nuisance. See *quiet enjoyment, attractive nuisance.*

nulla bona

Latin for "no goods." The sheriff writes this after finding no property that can be seized and sold to pay off a court judgment.

oath

An attestation that one will tell the truth, or a promise to fulfill a pledge, often calling upon God as a witness. The best-known oath is probably the witness's pledge "to tell the truth, the whole truth, and nothing but the truth" during a legal proceeding. In another context, a public official, for example, usually takes an "oath of office" before assuming the position and declaring to perform the required duties faithfully.

offer of proof

At trial, a party explains to a judge how a proposed line of questioning, or a particular item of physical evidence, would be relevant to its case and admissible under the rules of evidence. Offers of proof arise when a party begins a line of questioning that the other side objects to as calling for irrelevant or inadmissible information. If the judge thinks that the questions might lead to proper evidence, the judge will stop the trial, ask the parties to "approach the bench," and give the questioner a chance to show how, if allowed, the expected answers will be both relevant and admissible. This explanation is usually presented outside the jury's hearing but becomes part of the trial record. If later appealed, the appellate court will use the record to decide whether the judge's ruling was correct.

opening statement

A statement made by an attorney or self-represented party at the beginning of a trial before introducing evidence. The opening statement outlines the party's legal position and previews evidence to be presented later. The purpose of an opening statement is to familiarize the jury with what it will hear and why, not to present an argument as to why the speaker's side should win (persuasion is allowed as part of the closing argument).

order

A decision issued by a court. It can be a simple command—for example, ordering a witness to answer a proper question—or a complicated and reasoned hearing decision directing a party to do or refrain from some act. An order usually occurs before a case's "judgment" or final decision. For example, during the proceedings, the court might order that evidence gathered by the police not be introduced at trial.

order to show cause

An order from a judge that directs a party to come to court and convince the judge why they shouldn't grant an action proposed by the other side or by the judge on their own (*sua sponte*). For example, in a divorce, at the request of one parent, a judge might issue an order directing the other parent to appear in court on a particular date and time to show cause why the first parent shouldn't be given sole physical custody of the children. Although it would seem that the person receiving an order to show cause is at a procedural disadvantage— being, after all, the one who is told to come up with a convincing reason why the judge shouldn't order something—both sides typically have an equal chance to convince the judge to rule in their favor.

ordinance

A law adopted by a town or city council, a county board of supervisors, or another municipal governing board. Typically, local governments issue ordinances establishing zoning and parking rules and regulating noise, garbage removal, and the operation of parks and other areas that affect people who live or do business within the locality's borders.

own recognizance (OR)

In some cases, the judge lets a defendant out of jail without paying bail if the defendant promises to appear in court when next required to be there. Sometimes called "personal recognizance." Only those with strong ties to the community—such as a steady job, local family, and no history of failing to appear in court—are good candidates for "OR" release. If the charge is serious, OR might not be an option.

palimony

A nonlegal term coined by journalists to describe the division of property or alimony-like support given by one member of an unmarried couple to the other after they break up.

par value

The face value of a stock assigned by a corporation at the time the stock is issued. The par value is often printed on the stock certificate, but the market value of the stock might be much more or much less than par.

partnership

When used without a qualifier such as "limited" or "limited liability," usually refers to a legal structure called a "general partnership." This is a business owned by two or more people (called "partners" or "general partners") who are personally liable for all business debts. To form a partnership, each partner normally contributes money, valuable property, or labor in exchange for a partnership share, which reflects the amount contributed. Partnerships are easy to form since no registration is required with any governmental agency (although tax registration and other requirements to conduct business might still apply). Although not required, it is an excellent idea to prepare a written partnership agreement between the partners to define items such as ownership percentages, how profits and losses will be divided, and what happens if a partner dies or becomes disabled. Partnerships themselves don't pay federal or state income taxes; rather, profits are passed through to partners who report and pay income taxes on their personal returns. See also *limited partnership, limited liability partnership.*

party

A person, a corporation, or another legal entity that files a lawsuit (the plaintiff or petitioner) or defends against one (the defendant or respondent).

pendente lite

Latin for "while the action is pending." This phrase is used to describe matters that are contingent upon the outcome of a lawsuit. For example, money could be deposited by the defendant with the court pendente lite in order to compensate the plaintiff if the defendant loses the case. A defendant who wins gets the money back.

per stirpes

Latin for "by right of representation." Under a will, a method of determining who inherits property when a joint beneficiary has died before the will maker, leaving living children of their own. For example, Fred leaves his house jointly to his son Alan and his daughter Julie. But Alan dies before Fred, leaving two young children. If Fred's will states that heirs of a deceased beneficiary are to receive the property "per stirpes," Julie will receive one-half of the property, and Alan's two children will share his half in equal shares (through Alan by right of representation). If, on the other hand, Fred's will states that the property is to be divided per capita, Julie and the two grandchildren will each take a third.

peremptory challenge

During jury selection, an opportunity for a party to a lawsuit to dismiss or excuse a potential juror without having to give a valid reason, as would be the case when a juror is challenged for cause. Depending on court rules, each party typically gets to make from 5 to 15 peremptory challenges. Although parties can generally use their peremptory challenges as they see fit, the U.S. Constitution has been interpreted to prohibit their use to eliminate all jurors of a particular race or gender from a jury.

personal injury

An injury not to property, but to your body, mind, or emotions. For example, if you slip and fall on a banana peel in the grocery store, personal injury covers any actual physical harm (broken leg and bruises) you suffered in the fall as well as the humiliation of falling in public, but not the harm of shattering your watch.

petition

A formal written request made to a court, asking for an order or ruling on a particular matter. For example, if you want to be appointed conservator for an elderly relative, you must file a petition with a court. See also *complaint*.

piercing the veil

A judicial doctrine that allows a plaintiff to hold otherwise immune corporate officers and directors personally liable for damages caused by a corporation under their control. The veil is pierced when officers have acted intentionally and illegally or when their actions exceeded the power given them by the company's articles of incorporation.

plaintiff

The person, corporation, or other legal entity that initiates a lawsuit. In certain states and for some types of lawsuits, the term petitioner is used instead of plaintiff. Compare *defendant, respondent*.

plea

The defendant's formal answer to criminal charges. Typically, defendants enter one of the following pleas: guilty, not guilty, or *nolo contendere*. A plea is usually entered when charges are formally brought (at arraignment).

plea bargain

A negotiation between the defense and prosecution (and sometimes the judge) that settles a criminal case. The defendant typically pleads guilty to a lesser crime (or fewer charges) than originally charged, in exchange for a guaranteed sentence that is shorter than what the defendant could face if convicted at trial. The prosecution gets the certainty of a conviction and a known sentence, the defendant avoids the risk of a higher sentence, and the judge gets to move on to other cases.

pleading

A statement of the plaintiff's case or the defendant's defense, set out in generally accepted legal language and format. Today, in many states, the need to plead a case by drafting legal jargon—or borrowing from a legal form book—and printing it on numbered legal paper has been replaced by the use of preprinted forms. In this case, creating a proper pleading consists principally of checking the correct boxes and filling in the requested information.

post hoc

Part of the Latin phrase *post hoc, ergo propter hoc*, which means "after this, therefore because of this." The phrase represents the faulty logic of assuming that one thing was caused by another merely because it followed that event in time.

pot trust

A trust for children is one in which the trustee decides how to spend money on each child, taking money out of the trust to meet each child's specific needs. One important advantage of a pot trust over separate trusts is that it allows the trustee to provide for one child's unforeseen need, such as a medical emergency. However, a pot trust can also make the trustee's life difficult by requiring choices about disbursing funds to the various children. A pot trust ends when the youngest child reaches a certain age, usually 18 or 21.

pour-over will

A will that "pours over" property into a trust when the will maker dies. Property left through the will must go through probate before being placed into the trust.

power of appointment

The legal authority to decide who will receive someone else's property, usually property held in a trust. Most trustees can distribute the income from a trust only according to the terms of the trust, but a trustee with a power of appointment can choose the beneficiaries, sometimes from a list of candidates specified by the grantor. For example, Karin creates a trust with power of appointment to benefit the local art museum, symphony, library, or park, depending on the trustee's assessment of need.

power of attorney

A document that gives another person legal authority to act on your behalf. If you create such a document, you are called the "principal" and the person to whom you give this authority is called your "attorney-in-fact." A power of attorney can be "general," which gives your attorney-in-fact extensive powers over your affairs. Or it can be "limited" or "special," giving your attorney-in-fact permission to handle a specifically defined task. If you make a durable power of attorney, the document will continue in effect even if you become incapacitated. For examples, see *durable power of attorney for finances, durable power of attorney for health care.*

prayer for relief

What the plaintiff asks of the court—for example, the plaintiff can ask for an award of monetary damages, an injunction to make the defendant stop a certain activity, or both.

precedent

A legal principle or rule created by one or more decisions of a state or federal appellate court. These rules provide a reference point or authority for judges deciding similar issues in later cases. Lower courts must apply these rules when faced with similar legal issues. For example, if the Montana Supreme Court decides that a certain type of employment contract overly restricts the right of the employee to quit and get another job, all other Montana courts must apply this same rule.

presumption of innocence

One of the most sacred principles in the American criminal justice system, holding that a defendant is innocent until proven guilty. In other words, the prosecution must prove, beyond a reasonable doubt, each element of the crime charged.

pretermitted heir

A child or spouse who isn't mentioned in a will and whom the court believes was accidentally overlooked by the person who made the will. For example, a child born or adopted after the will is made might be deemed a pretermitted heir. If the court determines that an heir was accidentally omitted, that heir is entitled to receive the same share of the estate as they would have if the deceased had died without a will. A pretermitted heir is sometimes called an "omitted heir."

prima facie

Latin for "on its face." A *prima facie* case is one that, at first glance, presents sufficient evidence for the plaintiff to win. Such a case must be refuted in some way by the defendant for them to have a chance of prevailing at trial. For example, if you can show that someone intentionally touched you in a harmful or offensive way and caused some injury to you, you have established a *prima facie* case of battery. However, this doesn't mean that you automatically win your case. The defendant would win if he could show that you consented to the harmful or offensive touching.

principal

1. When creating a power of attorney or another legal document, the person who appoints an attorney-in-fact or agent to act on their behalf.
2. In criminal law, the main perpetrator of a crime.
3. In commercial law, the total amount of a loan, not including any capitalized fees or interest.
4. In the law of trusts, the property of the trust, as opposed to the income generated by that property. The principal is also known as the trust *"corpus"* (Latin for "body"). For example, Arthur establishes a new trust with $100,000, with interest and other income payable to Merlin; the $100,000 is the trust principal or *corpus*.

pro hac vice

Latin meaning "for this one particular occasion." The phrase usually refers to an out-of-state lawyer who has been granted special permission to participate in a particular case, even though the lawyer isn't licensed to practice in the state where the case is being tried.

pro per

A term derived from the Latin *in propria persona*, meaning "for one's self," used in some states to describe people who handle their own cases without a lawyer. In other states, the term *pro se* is used. A nonlawyer who files legal papers is expected to write "*in pro per*" at the bottom of the heading on the first page.

pro se

A Latin phrase meaning "for himself" or "in one's own behalf." This term denotes a person who represents themselves in court. It is used in some states in place of "*in pro per*" and has the same meaning.

probable cause

The amount and quality of information a judge must have before signing a search warrant allowing the police to conduct a search or arrest a suspect. If the police have presented reliable information that convinces the judge that it's more likely than not that a crime has occurred and the suspect is involved, the judge will conclude that there is "probable cause" and will issue the warrant. Police also need probable cause to conduct a warrantless search or seizure. When the police don't have time to go to a judge for a warrant (such as when they are in hot pursuit of a suspect), they still must have probable cause before arresting or searching.

probate

The court process following a person's death that includes:

- proving the authenticity of the deceased person's will
- appointing someone to handle the deceased person's affairs
- identifying and inventorying the deceased person's property
- paying debts and taxes
- identifying heirs, and
- distributing the deceased person's property according to the will or, if there is no will, according to state law.

Formal court-supervised probate is a costly, time-consuming process—a windfall for lawyers—which is best avoided if possible.

probate court

A specialized court or division of a state trial court that considers only cases concerning the distribution of deceased persons' estates. Called "surrogate court" in New York and several other states, this court typically examines the authenticity of a will—or, if a person dies intestate, figures out who receives their property under state law. It then oversees a procedure to pay the deceased person's debts and distribute assets to the proper inheritors. See *probate*.

prosecute

When a local district attorney, state attorney general, or federal U.S. attorney files a criminal case against a defendant.

prosecutor

A lawyer who works for the local, state, or federal government to file and litigate criminal cases.

public defender

A lawyer appointed by the court and paid by the county, state, or federal government to represent clients who are charged with violations of criminal law and are unable to pay for their own defense.

pur autre vie

Legal French meaning "for another's life." It is a phrase used to describe the duration of a property interest. For example, if Bob is given use of the family house for as long as his mother lives, he has possession of the house *pur autre vie*.

quantum meruit

Latin for "as much as is deserved." The reasonable value of services provided, which a winning party can recover from an opponent who broke a contract.

quasi-community property

A form of property owned by a married couple. If a couple moves to a community property state from a non-community-property state, property they acquired together in the non-community-property state may be considered quasi-community property. Quasi-community property is treated just like community property when one spouse dies or if the couple divorces.

quiet enjoyment

The right of a property owner or tenant to enjoy property without interference. Disruption of quiet enjoyment can constitute a nuisance. Leases and rental agreements often contain a "covenant of quiet enjoyment," expressly obligating the landlord to see that tenants have the opportunity to live undisturbed.

quitclaim deed

A deed that transfers whatever ownership interest the transferor has in a particular property. For example, a divorcing husband can quitclaim his interest in certain real estate to his ex-wife, officially giving up any legal interest in the property. However, the deed doesn't guarantee anything about what is being transferred. Compare *grant deed*.

real property

Another term for real estate. It includes land and things permanently attached to the land, such as trees, buildings, and stationary mobile homes. Anything that isn't real property is termed "personal property."

recording

The process of filing a copy of a deed or another document concerning real estate with the land records office for the county in which the land is located. Recording creates a public record of changes in ownership of all property in the state.

recusal

A situation in which a judge or prosecutor is removed or steps down from a case. This often happens when the judge or prosecutor has a conflict of interest—for example, a prior relationship with one of the parties.

red herring

A legal or factual issue that is irrelevant to the case at hand.

reformation

The act of changing a written contract when one of the parties can prove that the actual agreement was different than what's written down. The changes are usually made by a court when both parties overlooked a mistake in the document, or when one party has deceived the other.

remainderman

Someone who will inherit property in the future. For instance, if someone dies and leaves a home "to Alma for life, and then to Barry," Barry is a remainderman because he will inherit the house in the future after Alma dies.

replevin

A type of legal action where the owner of movable goods is given the right to recover them from someone who shouldn't have them. Replevin is often used in disputes between buyers and sellers—for example, a seller might bring a replevin action to reclaim goods from a buyer who failed to pay for them.

request for admission

A discovery procedure authorized by the Federal Rules of Civil Procedure and the court rules of many states, in which one party asks an opposing party to admit that certain facts are true. If the opponent admits the facts or fails to respond in a timely manner, the facts will be deemed true for purposes of trial. A request for admission is called a "request to admit" in many states.

res ipsa loquitur

A Latin term meaning "the thing speaks for itself." *Res ipsa loquitur* is a legal doctrine or rule of evidence that creates a presumption that a defendant acted negligently simply because a harmful accident occurred. The presumption arises only if:

1. the thing that caused the accident was under the defendant's control
2. the accident could happen only as a result of a careless act, and
3. the plaintiff's behavior didn't contribute to the accident.

Lawyers often refer to this doctrine as "*res ips*" or "*res ipsa*."

res nova

Latin for "a new thing," used by courts to describe an issue of law or case that hasn't previously been decided.

residuary beneficiary

A person who receives any property by a will or trust that isn't specifically left to another designated beneficiary. For example, suppose Antonio makes a will leaving his home to Edwina and the remainder of his property to Elmo. In that case, Elmo is the residuary beneficiary.

residuary estate

The property that remains in a deceased person's estate after all specific gifts are made, and all debts, taxes, administrative fees, probate costs, and court costs are paid. The residuary estate also includes any gifts under a will that fail or lapse. For example, Connie's will leaves her house and all its furnishings to Andrew, her VW bug to her friend Carl, and the remainder of her property (the residuary estate) to her sister, Sara. She doesn't name any alternate beneficiaries. Carl dies before Connie. The VW bug becomes part of the residuary estate and passes to Sara, along with all of Connie's property other than the house and furnishings. Also called the "residual estate" or "residue."

respondent

A term used instead of "defendant" or "appellee" in some states—especially for divorce and other family law cases—to identify the party who is sued and must respond to the petitioner's complaint.

restraining order

An order from a court directing someone not to do something, such as make contact with another person, enter the family home, or remove a child from the state. Restraining orders are typically issued in cases involving spousal abuse or stalking in an attempt to ensure the victim's safety. Restraining orders are also commonly issued to cool down ugly disputes between neighbors.

restraint on alienation

A provision in a deed or will that attempts to restrict ownership of the property—for example, selling your house to your daughter with the provision that it never be sold to anyone outside the family. These provisions are generally unenforceable.

right of survivorship

The right of a surviving joint tenant to take ownership of a deceased joint tenant's share of the property. See *joint tenancy*.

rule against perpetuities

An exceedingly complex legal doctrine that limits the time that property can be controlled after death by a person's instructions in a will. For example, a person wouldn't be allowed to leave property to her husband for his life, then to her children for their lives, then to her grandchildren. The gift would potentially go to the grandchildren at a point too remote in time.

ruling

Any decision a judge makes during the course of a lawsuit.

running with the land

A phrase used in property law to describe a right or duty that remains with a piece of property no matter who owns it. For example, the duty to allow a public beach access path across waterfront property would most likely pass from one property owner to the next.

S corporation

A term that describes a profit-making corporation organized under state law whose shareholders have applied for and received subchapter S corporation status from the Internal Revenue Service. Electing to do business as an S corporation lets shareholders enjoy limited liability status, as would be true of any corporation, but be taxed like a partnership or sole proprietor. Instead of being taxed as a separate entity (as would be the case with a regular or C corporation), an S corporation is a pass-through tax entity: Income taxes are reported and paid by the shareholders, not the S corporation. The IRS imposes qualification rules, such as shareholders are limited to 75, and citizenship requirements must be met.

search warrant

An order signed by a judge directing owners of private property to allow the police to enter and search for items named in the warrant. The judge won't issue the warrant unless convinced probable cause for the search exists—that reliable evidence shows that it's more likely than not that a crime has occurred and that the items sought by the police are connected with it and are at the location named in the warrant. In limited situations, the police can search without a warrant. Still, they can't use what they find at trial if the defense can show that there was no legal justification for the search.

secured debt

A debt on which a creditor has a lien. The creditor can institute a foreclosure or repossession to take the property identified by the lien, called the "collateral," to satisfy the debt if you default. Compare *unsecured debt*.

self-incrimination

A statement that might expose someone to criminal prosecution now or in the future. The Fifth Amendment of the U.S. Constitution prohibits the government from forcing people to provide evidence by answering questions that might lead to criminal prosecution.

self-proving will

A will that is created in a way that allows a probate court to easily accept it as the true will of the person who has died. In most states, a will is self-proving when two witnesses sign under penalty of perjury that they observed the will maker sign it, he or she told them it was his or her will, and that the will maker appeared to be of sound mind and proper age to make a will. If no one contests the will's validity, the probate court will accept the will without hearing the testimony of the witnesses or other evidence. To make a self-proving will in other states, the will maker and one or more witnesses must sign an affidavit (sworn statement) before a notary public certifying that the will is genuine and that all will-making formalities have been observed.

sentence

Punishment in a criminal case. A sentence can range from a fine and community service to life imprisonment or death. For most crimes, the sentence is chosen by the trial judge. The jury decides the sentence only in a capital case when it must choose between life in prison without parole and death.

separate property

In community property states, property owned and controlled entirely by one spouse in a marriage. In community property states, property acquired by a spouse before the marriage or after separation is typically that spouse's separate property, as is a gift or inheritance received solely by that spouse. In other states, a spouse's separate property is property owned or acquired before the marriage or after separation, and all property to which title is held in that spouse's name. At divorce, separate property isn't divided under the state's property division laws but is kept by the spouse who owns it. Separate property includes all property that a spouse obtained before marriage, through inheritance, or as a gift. It also includes property traceable to separate property—for example, cash from the sale of a vintage car owned by one spouse before marriage and any property that the spouses agree is separate property. Compare *community property* and *equitable distribution.*

servient tenement

Property that is subject to use by another for a specific purpose. For example, a beachfront house with a public walkway to the beach on its premises would be a servient tenement.

setback

The distance between a property boundary and a building. A minimum setback is usually required by law.

setoff

A claim made by someone that an amount owed should be reduced because the other person owes them money. This is often raised in a counterclaim filed by a defendant in a lawsuit. Banks can try to exercise a setoff by taking money out of a deposit account to satisfy past-due payments on a loan or credit card bill. Banks often take this action after receiving notice of a bankruptcy filing.

severability clause

A provision in a contract that preserves the rest of the contract if a court invalidates a portion of it. Without a severability clause, a decision by the court finding one part of the contract unenforceable would invalidate the entire document.

shareholder

An owner of a corporation whose ownership interest is represented by shares of stock in the corporation. A shareholder—also called a "stockholder"—has rights conferred by state law, by the corporation's bylaws, and, if one has been adopted, by a shareholder's agreement (often called a "buy-sell agreement"). These include the right to be notified of annual shareholders' meetings, elect directors, and receive an appropriate share of any dividends. In large corporations, shareholders are usually investors whose shares are held in the name of their broker. On the other hand, in incorporated small businesses, owners often wear many hats—shareholder, director, officer, and employee—so the distinctions between these legal categories can become fuzzy.

slander

A type of defamation. Slander is an untruthful oral (spoken) statement about a person that harms the person's reputation or standing in the community. Because slander is a tort (a civil wrong), the injured person can bring a lawsuit against the person who made the false statement. If the statement is made via broadcast media—for example, over the radio or on TV—or online or via social media, it is considered libel rather than slander because the statement has the potential to reach a wide audience.

small claims court

A state court that resolves disputes involving relatively small amounts of money—usually between $2,000 and $10,000, depending on the state. Adversaries usually appear without lawyers—some states forbid lawyers in small claims court—and recount their side of the dispute in plain English. Evidence, including the testimony of eyewitnesses and expert witnesses, is relatively easy to present because small claims courts don't follow the formal rules of evidence that govern regular trial cases. A small claims judgment has the same force as the judgment of any other state court. If the loser—now called the "judgment debtor"—fails to pay the judgment voluntarily, it can be collected using typical collection techniques, such as property liens and wage garnishments.

sole proprietorship

A business owned and managed by one person (or, for tax purposes, a husband and wife). For IRS purposes, a sole proprietor and the business are one tax entity, meaning business profits are reported and taxed on the owner's personal tax return. Setting up a sole proprietorship is cheap and easy since no legal formation documents must be filed with any governmental agency (although tax registration and other permit and license requirements might still apply). The main downside of a sole proprietorship is that its owner is personally liable for all business debts.

specific bequest

A specific item of property left to a named beneficiary under a will. For instance, a 1954 Mercedes-Benz.

specific intent

An intent to produce the precise consequences of the crime, including the intent to do the physical act that causes the consequences. For example, the crime of larceny is the taking of another person's personal property with the intent to deprive the other person of the property permanently. A person isn't guilty of larceny just because he took someone else's property; the prosecutor must prove the person took it with the purpose of keeping it permanently.

specific performance

A remedy provided by a court that orders the losing side to perform its part of a contract rather than, or possibly in addition to, paying money damages to the winner.

spendthrift trust

A trust created for a beneficiary the grantor considers irresponsible about money. The trustee keeps control of the trust income, either paying trust funds to the beneficiary or third parties (creditors, for example) on the beneficiary's behalf, bypassing the beneficiary completely. Spendthrift trusts typically contain a provision prohibiting creditors from seizing the trust fund to satisfy the beneficiary's debts. These trusts are legal in most states.

stare decisis

Latin for "let the decision stand," a doctrine requiring that judges apply the same reasoning to lawsuits as has been used in prior similar cases.

state court

A court that decides cases involving state law or the state constitution. State courts have jurisdiction over disputes involving defendants who reside in that state or have minimum contacts with the state, such as highway use, real property ownership, or business dealings. State courts can hear cases involving all subjects except those involving federal issues within the federal courts' exclusive jurisdiction. State courts are often divided according to the dollar amount of the claims they can hear, with small claims, justice, municipal, or city courts handling the most minor matters. In contrast, district, circuit, superior, or county courts (or, in New York, supreme courts) have jurisdiction over more complicated cases involving higher dollar amounts. State courts are also commonly divided according to subject matter, such as criminal court, family court, and probate court.

statute of limitations

The legally prescribed time limit in which a litigant must file a lawsuit. Statutes of limitation differ depending on the type of legal claim and often the state. For example, many states require that a personal injury lawsuit be filed within one or two years from the date of injury or, in some instances, from the date when it should reasonably have been discovered. Similarly, claims based on a written contract must be filed in court within four years from the date the contract was broken in some states and five years in others. Statute of limitations rules apply to cases filed in all courts, including federal court.

sua sponte

Latin for "of one's own accord." This term is commonly used to describe a decision or an act taken by a judge that a party didn't request.

subpoena

A subpoena requires a witness to appear in court.

subpoena duces tecum

A type of subpoena issued by a judge or licensed attorney compelling a witness to testify at a deposition or trial and to produce documents or things.

subrogation

A taking on of the legal rights of someone whose debts or expenses have been paid. For example, subrogation occurs when an insurance company that has paid off its injured claimant asserts the claimant's legal rights against a third party that caused the injury by suing the third party.

substituted service

A method for the formal delivery of court papers that takes the place of personal service. Personal service means that the papers are placed directly into the hands of the person to be served. Substituted service, on the other hand, can be accomplished by leaving the documents with a designated agent, with another adult in the recipient's home, with the recipient's manager at work, or by posting a notice in a prominent place and then using certified mail to send copies of the documents to the recipient.

substitution of parties

A replacement of one of the sides in a lawsuit because of events that prevent the party from continuing with the trial. For example, substitution of parties can occur when one party dies or, in the case of a public official, when that public official is removed from office.

sui generis

Latin for "of its own kind," used to describe something unique or different.

summary adjudication of issues

A partial summary judgment motion, in which the judge is asked to decide only one or some of the legal issues in the case. For example, in a car accident case, there might be overwhelming and uncontradicted evidence of the defendant's carelessness, but conflicting evidence as to the extent of the plaintiff's injuries. The plaintiff might ask for summary adjudication on the issue of carelessness, but go to trial on the question of injuries.

summary judgment

A final decision by a judge that resolves a lawsuit in favor of one of the parties. A motion for summary judgment is made after discovery is completed but before the case goes to trial. The party making the motion marshals all the evidence in its favor, compares it to the other side's evidence, and argues that a reasonable jury looking at the same evidence could only decide the case one way—for the moving party. If the judge agrees, a trial would be unnecessary, and the judge would enter judgment for the moving party.

summons

A paper prepared by the plaintiff and issued by a court that informs the defendant of a lawsuit. The summons requires that the defendant file a response with the court—or, in many small claims courts, simply appear in person on an appointed day—within a given time or risk losing the case under the terms of a default judgment.

sunset law

A law that automatically terminates the agency or program it establishes unless it is expressly renewed. For example, a state law establishing and funding a new drug rehabilitation program within state prisons might provide that the program will shut down in two years unless it is reviewed and approved by the state legislature.

sunshine laws

Statutes that provide public access to governmental agency meetings and records.

superior court

The main county trial court in many states, mainly in the West. See *state court*.

Supremacy Clause

Provision under Article IV, Section 2, of the U.S. Constitution, providing that federal law is superior to and overrides state law when they conflict.

Supreme Court

America's highest court with the final power to decide cases involving the interpretation of the U.S. Constitution, certain legal areas set forth in the Constitution (called "federal questions"), and federal laws. It can also make final decisions in certain lawsuits between parties in different states. The U.S. Supreme Court has nine justices—one of whom is the chief justice—appointed for life by the president and must be confirmed by the U.S. Senate.

Most states also have a supreme court, which is the final arbiter of the state's constitution and state laws. However, in several states, the highest state court uses a different name—most notably New York and Maryland, where it's called the "Court of Appeals," and Massachusetts, where it's called the "Supreme Judicial Court."

tangible personal property

Personal property that can be felt or touched. Examples include furniture, cars, jewelry, and artwork. However, cash and checking accounts aren't tangible personal property. The law is unsettled as to whether computer data is tangible personal property. Compare *intangible property*.

temporary restraining order (TRO)

An order that tells one person to stop harassing or harming another that is issued after the aggrieved party appears before a judge. Once the TRO is issued, the court holds a second hearing where the other side can tell their story, and the court can decide whether to make the TRO permanent by issuing an injunction. Although a TRO will often not stop an enraged spouse from acting violently, the police are more willing to intervene if the abused spouse has a TRO.

tenancy by the entirety

A special kind of property ownership available in about half the states that's reserved for married couples (or sometimes domestic partnerships). Both spouses or partners have the right to enjoy the entire property. Neither one can unilaterally end the tenancy, and creditors of one spouse can't force a sale of the property to collect on a debt. When one spouse or partner dies, the survivor automatically gets title to the entire property without a probate court proceeding. Also called "tenancy by the entireties."

tenancy in common

A way two or more people can own property together in equal or unequal shares. Each has an undivided interest in the property, an equal right to use the property, and the right to leave their interest upon death to chosen beneficiaries instead of to the other owners (as is required with joint tenancy). In some states, two people are presumed to own property as tenants in common unless they agree otherwise in writing.

testate

The circumstance of dying after making a valid will. A person who dies with a will is said to have died "testate." Compare *intestate*.

testify

To provide oral evidence under oath, at trial, or in a deposition.

tort

A wrongful act that causes injury. A tort can be an intentional act like a punch to the face or sexual assault. But more often, torts result from negligence (carelessness), like distracted driving, slip and fall accidents, and medical malpractice. A tort can cause physical injuries, psychological injuries, financial losses, or property damage. Every personal injury lawsuit involves a tort.

tortious interference

The causing of harm by disrupting something that belongs to someone else—for example, interfering with a contractual relationship so that one party fails to deliver goods on time.

trust *corpus*

Latin for "the body" of the trust. This term refers to all the property transferred to a trust. For example, if a trust is funded or "established" with $250,000, that money is the *corpus*. Sometimes the trust *corpus* is known as the "*res*," a Latin word meaning "thing."

trustee

The person who manages assets owned by a trust under the terms of the trust document. A trustee's purpose is to safeguard the trust and distribute trust income or principal as directed in the trust document.

ultra vires

Latin for "beyond powers." It refers to conduct by a corporation or its officers that exceeds the powers granted by law.

unclean hands

A legal doctrine that prevents a plaintiff from benefiting from fraud, deceit, or other inequitable behavior when related to the subject matter of the lawsuit. Some jurisdictions apply the doctrine to equitable relief claims (injunctive relief or specific performance), while others allow its use as an affirmative defense.

unconscionable

When one party to a contract takes advantage of the other due to unequal bargaining positions, perhaps because of the disadvantaged party's recent trauma, physical infirmity, ignorance, inability to read, or inability to understand the language. It usually includes the absence of any meaningful choice on the part of the buyer and contract terms so one-sided that they unreasonably favor the seller. A contract will be terminated as unconscionable if the unfairness is so severe that it is shocking to the average person.

unjust enrichment

A legal principle that if a person receives money or other property unfairly and at the expense of another—that is, by chance, mistake, or without any personal effort—the recipient should return the property to the rightful owner. In lawsuits based on unjust enrichment, courts can order that the property be returned (referred to as "making restitution").

unsecured debt

A debt that doesn't give the creditor the right to take a particular item of property if the debtor doesn't pay. Examples include credit card debts and medical bills. Compare *secured debt*.

variance

An exception to a zoning ordinance, usually granted by a local government. For example, if you own an oddly shaped lot that couldn't accommodate a home due to your city's setback requirement, you could apply at the appropriate office for a variance allowing you to build closer to a boundary line.

venue

State laws or court rules that establish the proper court to hear a case, often based on the defendant's convenience. Because state courts have jurisdiction to hear cases from a wide geographical area (for example, California courts have jurisdiction involving most disputes arising between California residents), additional rules, called "rules of venue," have been developed to ensure that the defendant isn't needlessly inconvenienced. For example, the correct venue for one Californian to sue another is usually limited to the court in the judicial district where the defendant lives, an accident occurred, or a contract was signed or to be carried out. Practically, venue rules mean that defendants can't usually be sued far from where they live or do business, if no key events happened at that location. Venue for a criminal case is typically the judicial district where the crime was committed.

vested remainder

An unconditional right to receive real property at some point in the future. A vested interest can be created by a deed or a will. For example, if Julie's will leaves her house to her daughter, but the daughter will gain possession only after Julie's husband dies (a life estate), the daughter has a vested remainder in the house.

volenti non fit injuria

Latin for "to a willing person, no injury is done." This doctrine holds that a person who knowingly and willingly puts themselves in a dangerous situation can't sue for any resulting injuries.

with prejudice

A final and binding decision by a judge about a legal matter that prevents further pursuit of the same matter in any court. A judge who makes such a decision dismisses the matter "with prejudice." The parties can also agree to dismiss a claim with prejudice.

witness

A person who testifies under oath at a deposition or trial, providing firsthand or expert evidence. The term also refers to someone who watches another person sign a document before adding their name to confirm or "attest" that the signature is genuine.

wrongful death

A death caused by the wrongful act of another, either accidentally or intentionally. Every state has a wrongful death law that lets the decedent's estate or surviving relatives sue to recover compensation for the damages caused by having to live without the decedent. This compensation can include, among other things, the decedent's lost earnings and the emotional comfort and support the decedent would have provided. Examples of wrongful conduct that can lead to death include drinking and driving, manufacturing a deficient product, building an unstable structure, or failing to diagnose a fatal disease.

zoning

The local laws dividing cities or counties into different zones according to allowed uses, from single-family residential to commercial to industrial. Zoning ordinances control the size, location, and use of buildings within these various areas and profoundly affect traffic, health, and livability.

Topic-Specific Research Sites

Bankruptcy

- **Administrative Office of the United States Courts: Bankruptcy Basics (www.uscourts.gov/services-forms/bankruptcy/bankruptcy-basics).** This consumer-friendly site includes information about laws, news, a glossary, and links to forms, fees, and court websites.
- **U.S. Department of Justice U.S. Trustee Program (www.justice.gov/ust).** This site includes credit counseling and debtor education course resources, current means testing figures, and information about the 341 meeting of creditors.
- **Nolo's Bankruptcy Page (www.nolo.com/legal-encyclopedia/bankruptcy).** Includes easy-to-understand articles written in plain English on all aspects of bankruptcy.

Copyright

- **The U.S. Copyright Office (www.copyright.gov).** This site offers regulations, guidelines, forms, and links to other helpful copyright sites.
- **Stanford University's Copyright and Fair Use site (https://fairuse.stanford.edu).** This site links to relevant primary sources, such as statutes, regulations, and court cases, and secondary sources, such as blogs and charts.
- **Intellectual Property Mall at the University of New Hampshire's Franklin Pierce School of Law (www.ipmall.info).** An excellent general intellectual property site.
- **Nolo's Copyright Law Page (www.nolo.com/legal-encyclopedia/ copyright-law).** Easy-to-understand articles explain copyright basics, including registration, fair use, stopping infringers, and more.

Corporate Law

- **The Securities and Exchange Commission (www.sec.gov).** It has investment statutes and regulations, current litigation, opinions, and staff legal bulletins.

Criminal Law and Criminal Justice

- **Nolo's Criminal Law Center ((www.nolo.com/legal-encyclopedia/criminal-law).** This is a great place to start for questions about criminal procedure.
- **CriminalDefenseLawyer.com (www.criminaldefenselawyer.com).** You'll find articles and resources on every aspect of a criminal case.
- **The Collateral Consequences Resource Center (www.ccresourcecenter.org).** CCRC offers extensive information and tracks legal developments on criminal record sealing and expungement, restoration of rights, and laws on criminal records and employment.

Divorce and Family Law

- **DivorceNet (www.divorcenet.com)** A site with excellent state-specific legal resources on divorce, separation, mediation, and child custody and support.
- **Adoption.com: Where Families Come Together (https://adoption.com).** This site provides information about adoption agencies, international adoption, and other issues.
- **WomensLaw.org (www.womenslaw.org)** provides state-by-state legal information about domestic violence and how to obtain a restraining order, with downloadable forms and links to local resources.
- **Nolo's Divorce and Family Law Page (www.nolo.com/legal-encyclopedia/family-law-divorce).** Rules for prenuptial agreements, marriage, and divorce, along with the laws on child support, child custody, adoption, same-sex issues, and elder care.

Elder Law

- **The SeniorLaw website (www.seniorlaw.com/elder-law-legal-resources-on-the-web).** SeniorLaw links to sites about guardianships, conservatorships, Medicare and Medicaid, living wills, health care directives, durable powers of attorney, senior abuse, and other issues commonly affecting seniors.
- **The National Academy of Elder Law Attorneys (www.naela.org).** NAELA provides information and links to elder law resources.

Environmental Law

- **The Environmental Law Institute (www.eli.org/buildings).** ELI's website hosts a wealth of information on indoor air quality and green buildings. The website includes reports and surveys of state-specific laws on mold, radon, and air quality requirements for schools and childcare centers.

First Amendment/Free Speech

- **Electronic Frontier Foundation (www.eff.org).** This site focuses on free speech law and policy issues in the online environment.

Health Care

- **Kaiser Family Foundation (www.kff.org).** KFF is a nonprofit that focuses on health law and policy. Its website includes poll results, research reports, and news on many health-related topics.

Landlord-Tenant Law

- **U.S. Department of Housing and Urban Development Tenant Rights (www.hud.gov/topics/rental_assistance/tenantrights).** This HUD page provides useful links to a variety of legal resources for tenants in each state and U.S. territories.
- **National Apartment Association (www.naahq.org).** The NAA website is directed chiefly toward landlords, but the organization tracks legislation and provides information on issues that interest tenants, too.

- **Nolo's Legal Resources for Tenants (www.nolo.com/legal-encyclopedia/legal-resources-for-tenants.html).** Websites and articles for renters seeking help related to landlord-tenant issues and eviction.

LGBTQ Law

- **GLBTQ Legal Advocates and Defenders (www.glad.org).** GLAD is a legal rights organization dedicated to ending all forms of discrimination against gays and lesbians.
- **The Movement Advancement Project (www.lgbtmap.org).** MAP is a nonprofit think tank that tracks more than 50 LGBTQ-related legal topics nationwide. You can search for laws and policies by issue or by state.
- **American Civil Liberties Union's LGBTQ Rights Page (www.aclu.org/issues/lgbtq-rights).** The ACLU tracks bills and court cases related to LGBTQ issues nationwide.

Patents

- **The U.S. Patent and Trademark Office (www.uspto.gov).** This is the place for recent policy and statutory changes and hearing transcripts on patent law issues.
- **Google Patents (https://patents.google.com).** Another powerful tool from Google that allows you to search the full text of millions of patents from the United States and around the world.

Small Business

- **Small Business Development Center National Information Clearinghouse (www.sbdcnet.org).** Provides a broad range of industry-specific market research reports and small business information on topics such as business plans, website design, finances, government contracts, franchising, and more.
- **The Small Business Administration (www.sba.gov).** This free site provides information about starting, financing, and expanding your small business.

- **Nolo's Small Business Page (www.nolo.com/legal-encyclopedia/ small-business).** Articles on starting and running a successful small business. Topics include bookkeeping, hiring independent contractors, sales and marketing strategies, and more.

Tax Law

- **The Internal Revenue Service (www.irs.gov).** This site has tax information, publications, and downloadable forms.
- **Federation of Tax Administrators (www.taxadmin.org).** A complete, reliable site for state tax information.

Trademarks. U.S. Patent and Trademark Office (www.uspto.gov)

The website of choice for trademark searching, trademark registration, papers issued by the USPTO on various trademark and domain name issues, and general information about trademark laws. Also available through this site are the rules used by the trademark examiners and descriptions of goods and services deemed acceptable for trademark registration applications.

- **ICANN (www.icann.org).** This website is the starting place for researching domain name disputes and the rules that apply to them.

Wills and Estate Planning

- **National Academy of Elder Law Attorneys (www.naela.org).** A site dedicated to improving the quality of legal services provided to older adults and people with disabilities.
- **Nolo's Wills, Trusts, and Probate Page (www.nolo.com/legal-encyclopedia/ wills-trusts-estates).** Everything you need to know about estate planning and creating a will, living trust, power of attorney, or living will. Also provides information about avoiding probate and estate tax and acting as an executor.

Workplace Rights

- **Equal Employment Opportunity Commission (www.eeoc.gov).** The EEOC has resources both for employers and employees. Everything you need to know for compliance is here.
- **U.S. Department of Labor, State Labor Laws (www.dol.gov/agencies/whd/state).** The DOL maintains pages with state-specific information on minimum wage laws, child labor laws, paid rest break laws, and more.
- **National Labor Relations Board (www.nlrb.gov).** The NLRB publishes decisions here.
- **Workplace Fairness (www.workplacefairness.org).** This nonprofit provides lots of free information on employment law issues.

Your Money

- **National Consumer Law Center (www.nclc.org).** This site offers information and advice on low-income consumer issues.
- **National Consumer Financial Protection Bureau (www.consumerfinance.gov).** This government agency provides information for consumers on issues related to banks, credit, mortgages, and debt collection.
- **USA.gov Consumer Protection (www.usa.gov).** The government offers consumer advice on money issues.
- **The Better Business Bureau (www.bbb.org/en/us).** This site allows you to file consumer complaints online.

Index

A

Administrative agency websites, researching on, 29

Administrative law, 47

Administrative regulations
    federal, 5, 10
    state, 6, 10

Admissions of fact, 209

Advance sheets, 160–162
    citations to, 127

Algorithms, and search engine results, 64

ALI. *See* American Law Institute (ALI)

A.L.R. See American Law Reports (A.L.R.)

A.L.R. Fed. See American Law Reports, Federal (A.L.R. Fed)

Alternative dispute resolution, 210–211

Ambiguities in statutes, interpretation of, 103–104

American Jurisprudence (Am. Jur.), 26, 69–71

American Jurisprudence Legal Forms (Am. Jur. Legal Forms), 73–76

American Law Institute (ALI), 83

American Law Reports (A.L.R.), 26, 72–73

American Law Reports, Federal (A.L.R. Fed), 72–73

Am. Jur. See American Jurisprudence (Am. Jur.)

Analysis section, of legal memorandum, 199

Answers, 206–207

Appeals, 215–216
    briefs, 215
    court where normally filed, 150
    decisions, 215
    filing cases directly in appellate and supreme courts, 216
    from final decisions, 215
    how case is decided, 154
    interlocutory appeals, 215
    opinions, 148–154
    oral arguments, 215
    Petition for Hearing, filing of, 216
    Petition for Writ of Certiorari, filing of, 216
    trial court record, 215

Appeals process, 144

Appellants, 147

Appellate courts, 13–14
    state intermediate courts, 168
    state supreme courts, 14, 167
    See also U.S. Courts of Appeal; U.S. Supreme Court

Appellees, 147

Artificial intelligence
    generative artificial intelligence tools, 23, 27, 67, 128

Atlantic Regional Digest, 135

Attorney General opinions, and interpretation of statutes, 106

Attorneys, finding and working with, 218–219

B

C

 **More from Nolo**

Nolo.com offers a large library of legal solutions and forms, created by Nolo's in-house legal editors. These reliable documents can be prepared in minutes.

Create a Document Online

Incorporation. Incorporate your business in any state.

LLC Formation. Gain asset protection and pass-through tax status in any state.

Will. Nolo has helped people make over 2 million wills. Is it time to make or revise yours?

Living Trust (avoid probate). Plan now to save your family the cost, delays, and hassle of probate.

Download Useful Legal Forms

Nolo.com has hundreds of top quality legal forms available for download:

- bill of sale
- promissory note
- nondisclosure agreement
- LLC operating agreement
- corporate minutes
- commercial lease and sublease
- motor vehicle bill of sale
- consignment agreement
- and many more.

More Bestselling Books

Represent Yourself in Court
How to Prepare & Try a Winning Case

Nolo's Encyclopedia of Everyday Law

The Criminal Law Handbook
Know Your Rights, Survive the System

Everybody's Guide to Small Claims Court

Law Forms for Personal Use

Every Nolo title is available in print and for download at Nolo.com.

www.nolo.com

 **Save 15%** *off your next order*

Register your Nolo purchase, and we'll send you a
coupon for 15% off your next Nolo.com order!

Nolo.com/customer-support/productregistration

On Nolo.com you'll also find:

Books & Software
Nolo publishes hundreds of great books and software programs for consumers and
business owners. Order a copy, or download an ebook version instantly, at Nolo.com.

Online Forms
You can quickly and easily make a will or living trust, form an LLC or corporation,
or make hundreds of other forms—online.

Free Legal Information
Thousands of articles answer common questions about everyday legal issues,
including wills, bankruptcy, small business formation, divorce, patents,
employment, and much more.

Plain-English Legal Dictionary
Stumped by jargon? Look it up in America's most up-to-date source for definitions
of legal terms, free at Nolo.com.

Lawyer Directory
Nolo's consumer-friendly lawyer directory provides in-depth profiles of lawyers all
over America. You'll find information you need to choose the right lawyer.